Literary Lives

General Editor: **Richard Dutton**

This series offers stimulating acc...
and influential English-languag...
writers' working lives, not in th...
trace the professional, publishing ...

...ired
the
; to
ng.

Published titles include:

Cedric C. Brown
JOHN MILTON

Peter Davison
GEORGE ORWELL

Richard Dutton
WILLIAM SHAKESPEARE

Jan Fergus
JANE AUSTEN

Caroline Franklin
BYRON

James Gibson
THOMAS HARDY

Kenneth Graham
HENRY JAMES

Paul Hammond
JOHN DRYDEN

Lisa Hopkins
CHRISTOPHER MARLOWE

W. David Kaye
BEN JONSON

Mary Lago
E. M. FORSTER

Clinton Machann
MATTHEW ARNOLD

Alasdair D. F. Macrae
W. B. YEATS

Joseph McMinn
JONATHAN SWIFT

Kerry McSweeney
GEORGE ELIOT

John Mepham
VIRGINIA WOOLF

Michael O'Neill
PERCY BYSSHE SHELLEY

Leonée Ormond
ALFRED TENNYSON

Harold Pagliaro
HENRY FIELDING

George Parfitt
JOHN DONNE

Gerald Roberts
GERARD MANLEY HOPKINS

Felicity Rosslyn
ALEXANDER POPE

Tony Sharpe
T. S. ELIOT
WALLACE STEVENS

Peter Shillingsburg
WILLIAM MAKEPEACE THACKERAY

Angela Smith
KATHERINE MANSFIELD

Grahame Smith
CHARLES DICKENS

Janice Farrar Thaddeus
FRANCES BURNEY

Linda Wagner-Martin
SYLVIA PLATH

Nancy A. Walker
KATE CHOPIN

Gary Waller
EDMUND SPENSER

Cedric Watts
JOSEPH CONRAD

John Williams
MARY SHELLEY
WILLIAM WORDSWORTH

Tom Winnifrith and Edward Chitham
CHARLOTTE AND EMILY BRONTË

Sarah Wood
ROBERT BROWNING

John Worthen
D. H. LAWRENCE

David Wykes
EVELYN WAUGH

Literary Lives
Series Standing Order ISBN 0–333–71486–5 hardcover
Series Standing Order ISBN 0–333–80334–5 paperback
(outside North America only)

You can receive future titles in this series as they are published by placing a standing order. Please contact your bookseller or, in case of difficulty, write to us at the address below with your name and address, the title of the series and one of the ISBNs quoted above.

Customer Services Department, Macmillan Distribution Ltd, Houndmills, Basingstoke, Hampshire RG21 6XS, England

Robert Browning

A Literary Life

Sarah Wood

First published 2001 by
PALGRAVE
Houndmills, Basingstoke, Hampshire RG21 6XS and
175 Fifth Avenue, New York, N.Y. 10010
Companies and representatives throughout the world

PALGRAVE is the new global academic imprint of
St. Martin's Press LLC Scholarly and Reference Division and
Palgrave Publishers Ltd (formerly Macmillan Press Ltd).

ISBN 0–333–64337–2 hardback
ISBN 0–333–64338–0 paperback

This book is printed on paper suitable for recycling and
made from fully managed and sustained forest sources.

A catalogue record for this book is available
from the British Library.

Library of Congress Cataloging-in-Publication Data
Wood, Sarah, 1963–
    Robert Browning : a literary life / Sarah Wood.
        p. cm. — (Literary lives)
    Includes bibliographical references (p.) and index.
    ISBN 0–333–64337–2
    1. Browning, Robert, 1812–1889. 2. Poets, English—19th
    century—Biography. I. Title. II. Literary lives (Palgrave (Firm))

    PR4231 .W657 2001
    821'.8—dc21
    [B]
                                                        2001021888

10   9   8   7   6   5   4   3   2   1
10   09 08 07 06 05 04 03 02 01

Printed and bound in Great Britain by
Antony Rowe Ltd, Chippenham, Wiltshire

For Rose and Miranda

Contents

Preface

All readers of Robert Browning sooner or later find Elizabeth Barrett ahead of them.[1] The courtship correspondence that passed between the poets in 1845–6 testifies to the power of reading and writing to seduce and enthral, but it does more. The letters make that rather indeterminate experience of reading into the motivating force in an unforgettable *story*, its uncertain sensations and intensities secured as a kind of historical drama. Elizabeth Barrett's critical reputation is currently re-ascending partly as a result of deliberate decisions to look at her work *apart* from her marriage and her popularly mythologized biography. Margaret Reynolds's 1992 Ohio edition of *Aurora Leigh* has been a landmark in this process, as has Marjorie Stone's 1995 critical study, *Elizabeth Barrett Browning*.[2] New thinking about sexual difference and closer reading of the poems themselves suggest that Elizabeth Barrett's poetry cannot be exclusively claimed by either a female or a male 'line' of poets.[3] When a John Woolford or a Catherine Maxwell argue that the male Romantic poets who influence both Browning and Elizabeth Barrett themselves undergo feminization in their writing, the discussion has come a long way from its initial biographical frame. Yet the rhetorical link between reading and seduction, manifested so powerfully in the collected and preserved love letters, always makes a short-circuit possible.

It was the poets' son Pen who chose to publish the little archive of letters which told the story of his own origins. Reading them puts every reader both within and outside a family romance in which the two authors always will have been *parents*. And if reading poetry can feel like reading a letter, addressed to us alone, then Elizabeth Barrett, Browning's most beloved correspondent, remains in the offing for any subsequent lover of his work. Elizabeth Barrett, and no other, won Browning by reading and responding to what she read.[4] She may not ever have been his ideal reader but she is his most exactly imagined and demonstrably transformed one.[5] How could any latecomer rival what these two managed to effect between them?

And so the celebrations continue, starting with Joseph Arnould's breathless letter to Alfred Domett in 1846:

> This lady so gifted, so secluded, so tyrannised over, fell in love with Browning in the spirit, before she ever saw him in the flesh – in

plain English loved the writer before she saw the man. Imagine ... the effect which his graceful bearing, high demeanour, and noble speech must have had on such a mind when she first saw the man of her visions in the twilight of her darkened room. She was at once in love as a poet-soul only can be: and Browning, as if by contagion or electricity, was no less from the first interview wholly in love with her.[6]

Imagine. Elizabeth Barrett touchingly identified the genre of her relationship with Browning as the fairy tale. Gossip reverberated among friends on either side: Arnould's letter suggests that Barrett had responded to poetic gifts plus his old pal's evident manly charms whereas Browning fell in love because of his poet's capacity to catch her passion by contagion. On the other side, Elizabeth Barrett's old friend Miss Mitford was really unable to see that Elizabeth Barrett had done at all well for herself. Acquaintances and visitors to the poets' homes in Italy and France continued to peer at the couple and their household and write up their impressions, until Pen published the love letters in 1899. This elicited some bad-tempered justification of the fairy tale's ogre – Elizabeth Barrett's father – by his family. Charles J. Moulton Barrett huffed in a letter to the *Standard* that 'few sons, either for gain or for love of notoriety would make public the confidential letters of their mother'.[7] In the twentieth century there were popular biographies that drew on the confidences: Dorothy Baynes's *Andromeda in Wimpole Street: the Romance of Elizabeth Barrett Browning* (1929), Dallas Kenmare's *The Browning Love-Story* (1957) and Julia Markus's *Dared and Done: the Marriage of Elizabeth Barrett Browning and Robert Browning* (1993). The story has also inspired fiction – the incomparable laughter of Virginia Woolf's *Flush: a Biography* (1933) and Margaret Forster's gripping slantwise presentation via Elizabeth Barrett's servant Wilson, *Lady's Maid* (1990). Still the great example, the most widely disseminated, is Sydney Franklin's 1934 film of Rudolf Besier's 1930 play *The Barretts of Wimpole Street*.

Franklin remade the film in 1957; both versions are available on video and regularly appear on television. 'The famed romance between nineteenth-century poets Elizabeth Barrett and Robert Browning is recounted in this historical drama. Barrett, an invalid confined to her bed, is wooed into happiness and recovery by a fellow poet Robert Browning.'[8] This book does not reproduce that narrative. The film is a wonderfully camp, richly costumed Hollywood psychodrama, with star casting for Elizabeth Barrett's weirdly possessive father.

Browning's poetry is played for laughs (it's incomprehensible but Elizabeth spends ages reading it anyway), while the poets are figures of supremely straight-faced ardour and susceptibility. Besier's script gives a good impression of the heated atmosphere as Browning grabs Elizabeth Barrett's hands in Act II:

> *Browning*: ... I've more life than is good for one man – it seethes and races in me. [...] Mayn't I give it to you? Don't you feel new life tingling and prickling up your fingers and arms right into your heart and brain?
> *Elizabeth (rather frightened and shaken)*: Oh please ... Mr Browning, please let go my hands ....
> [*He opens his hands; but she still leaves hers lying on his palms for a moment. Then she withdraws them, and clasping her cheeks, looks at him with wide, disturbed eyes.*][9]

The male Victorian readers who fill my pages are by no means 'wooed into happiness and recovery' by reading Browning: they are far more likely to complain of feeling irritated, led on and confused. *But they can't stop.* And this is what they have in common with Elizabeth Barrett. She wrote to Browning:

> You *influenced* me, in a way in which no one else did. For instance, by two or three half-words you made me see you, & other people had delivered orations on the same subject quite without effect. I surprised everyone in this house by consenting to see you – Then, when you came, . . you never went away – I mean, I had a sense of your presence constantly.[10]

Fifteen years after marrying Browning she wrote to his sister Sarianna that 'women adore him everywhere far too much for decency'[11] and this raw impression of Browning's personal impact and power also speaks to those – men and women, then and now – who cannot have done with reading him. He's not the kind of poet that it's easy to resist.

In actuality, happiness and recovery were not the end of the Barrett-Browning story. Like other literary marriage plots, *The Barretts of Wimpole Street* breaks off before the length of Pen's hair, Louis Napoleon and spiritualism began to play their slightly divisive parts in the home epic that followed the poets' great beginning.[12] The romance has its fabulous obelisk: many who have never knowingly read a word of Browning know about the letters, the visits, the secret love and the sudden departure thanks to Rudolf Besier and Sydney Franklin. Robert Browning's name does not appear in the film's title and Wimpole Street was never his address. He was a visitor to the Barrett house and what mark does a visit leave?

S. W.

Acknowledgements

At moments like this authors know they are at their least original. Where do they begin? Danny Karlin read the penultimate draft in a deeply learned, characteristically generous way. He also taught me how to read *Sordello*. Tim Clark's supportive reading was a great help with the critical framing of the book; he also invited me to give Chapter 5 as a paper to his colleagues at Durham, where his and their comments were invaluable. Thanks also to Andy Thompson at Cherwell College for the lucky chance to discuss Ruskin and Browning with 'A' level students and colleagues. Catherine Maxwell, Forbes Morlock and Marcus Wood responded creatively to draft chapters at various stages. Without Ann Wordsworth's unforgettable teaching I might not have been unable to stop reading Browning in the first place. Ken Newton kindly asked me to give an early version of Chapter 3 as a paper at Dundee where the subsequent discussion introduced several new ideas. Part of Chapter 7 appeared in *Browning Society Notes* 24 (May 1997). Jane Moody gave useful initial advice on early Victorian drama. I also wish to thank the Armstrong Baylor Library for permission to reproduce the cover photograph. Emma Smith and Linda Squire gave me a computer to finish writing the book on and made work possible in a hundred other ways. Thanks also to F. E. Brown, Delia da Sousa Correa, Doris Cossette, Charlotte Hoare, Kate Macfarlane, Nicholas Royle, Roy Sellars, Lottie Stephenson and Beatrice Wood for their incalculable contributions.

Abbreviations

Arnold	*The Complete Prose Works of Matthew Arnold*, 11 vols, ed. R. H. Super (Ann Arbor, MI, 1960–77).
Arnold, Letters	*The Letters of Matthew Arnold*, ed. Cecil Y. Lang, (Charlottesville, VA, 1996–).
Arnold, Poems	*The Poems of Matthew Arnold*, ed. Kenneth Allott (London, 1965).
Bloom and Munich	*Robert Browning: A Collection of Critical Essays* (Englewood Cliffs, NJ, 1979).
DLB	*The Dictionary of Literary Biography*
DNB	*The Dictionary of National Biography*
Carlyle	*The Works of Thomas Carlyle*, 30 vols (London, 1896–9).
Kelley	*The Browning's Correspondence*, eds Philip Kelley et al. (Winfield, KS, 1984–).
Litzinger and Smalley	*Browning: The Critical Heritage*, eds Boyd Litzinger and Donald Smalley (London, 1970)
Longman	*The Poems of Browning*, eds John Woolford and Daniel Karlin (London, 1991–).
Mill	*The Collected Works of John Stuart Mill*, 33 vols, gen. ed. John M. Robson (Toronto, 1981–91).
Ohio	*The Complete Works of Robert Browning*, 14 vols, gen. eds Roma A. King et al. (Athens, OH, 1969–).
Orr, *Life*	Alexandra Sutherland Orr, *The Life and Letters of Robert Browning* (1891).
Penguin	*Robert Browning: The Poems*, 2 vols, eds John Pettigrew and Thomas J. Collins (Harmondsworth, 1981).
Ruskin	*The Complete Works of John Ruskin*, 39 vols, eds E. T. Cook and Alexander Wedderburn (1903–12).
Woolford and Karlin	John Woolford and Daniel Karlin, *Robert Browning* (London, 1996).

Note on texts

For general purposes I refer to the two-volume Penguin edition, which takes the 1888 *Poetical Works* as its copy text, and therefore includes all the authorial revisions Browning busied himself with throughout his career. Penguin is complete but for the plays and *The Ring and the Book* and has the advantage of being widely available in libraries. Unfortunately, the second volume of poems and *The Ring and the Book* are currently out of print. As this is a study of Browning's creative development it is essential to cite the earliest published versions of his work. Therefore, in my discussion of *Pauline* (1833), *Sordello* (1840) and 'The Laboratory' I refer to the Longman edition, which takes its copy texts from the first editions. I also refer to Longman for the 'Essay on Chatterton' (1842) which reprints the first edition in II, pp. 478–503. I cite the first edition of the 'Essay on Shelley' (1852), reprinted in *Peacock's Four Ages of Poetry, Shelley's Defence of Poetry, Browning's Essay on Shelley*, ed. H. F. B. Brett-Smith (Oxford, 1921) and in Penguin I, pp. 1001–13. I cite *Strafford* and *The Return of the Druses* from *The Complete Works of Robert Browning*, ed. Roma A. King et al. (Athens, OH, 1969–). In quoting from Browning correspondence I retain Browning's and Elizabeth Barrett's use of the two-point ellipsis (..), which carries the force of a dash.

Introduction: 'Browning in Westminster Abbey'

In 1891 Henry James found it impossible to leave the site of Browning's ashes in Poets' Corner without a sense that the poet should have been there to give his own thoughts on the deposition of his remains. It was 'exactly one of those occasions in which his own analytic spirit would have rejoiced and his irrepressible faculty for looking at the human condition in all sorts of slanting coloured lights have found a signal opportunity.'[1] The entombment was a historic moment in Browning's long-delayed entry into the canon of English poets. He has always been a debatable figure since the mixed reception of *Pauline* in 1833, which included William Johnson Fox's '*Eureka!*' at the discovery of an authentic new poet and *The Literary Gazette*'s summary verdict 'this is a dreamy volume, without an object, and unfit for publication'.[2] It took thirty years before Browning became popular with the 1863 *Poetical Works* and *Dramatis Personae* in 1864. Academic honours were awarded in the late 1860s and 1870s but it was still possible to claim in print that he was no poet, as Alfred Austin's 'The Poetry of the Period' did in 1869. Indeed, Matthew Arnold commended the article for its independence of thought and clear critical criteria. In 1881 the Browning Society was founded, an event which delighted the poet but, as he put it, undoubtedly had 'a grotesque side'. By that time there was a consensus that Browning was highly fit for publication: the debate had shifted to defining where exactly his strength lay. He was received as a philosopher, but found wanting in consistency of thought.[3] He was admired as a creator of characters, but found deficient in verbal poetry.[4] He was entombed in Westminster Abbey, but there was no lasting agreement about why.

James was the most acute contemporary observer of the Browning phenomenon. (Browning haunted James, the writer of ghost stories,

even while he was still alive. The novelist wondered ceaselessly how
the Browning who appeared so ordinary and predictable in London
society of the 1880s could write such rare strange poetry. He wrote a
story about it, but 'The Private Life' (1893) was less an answer than
another rehearsal of the question.) According to James's 'Browning in
Westminster Abbey' part of the poet's audience, at its most modern,
was canonized with him. With his passing into Poets' Corner 'some-
thing of our latest sympathies, our latest and most restless selves,
passed the other day into the high part – the show-part, to speak
vulgarly – of our literature' (p. 533). The poet was a socially active
contemporary, a 'figure of London', but James also suggests that
through that context he both haunts and anticipates his readers.
Browning even, at the end of James's short tribute, becomes the
legatee of his age, as if those left behind would predecease him: 'we
leave our sophisticated modern conscience, and perhaps even our
sophisticated modern vocabulary, in his charge among the illustrious'
(p. 534). He has already outlived those who survive him and by his
death we are in a sense bereft of ourselves.

I include us, now, in the age of Browning. He is still a contempo-
rary in publishing terms, widely available in a range of printed selec-
tions, academic editions and recorded readings. Some
half-remembered lines – 'God's in his heaven, all's right with the
world!' (*Pippa Passes*, 1841), 'Oh, to be in England' ('Home Thoughts
from Abroad', 1845), 'It was roses, roses, all the way' ('The Patriot',
1855) – have passed into the language. And in terms of reading,
Browning poems can still seem to anticipate our intense private expe-
riences: 'Never the time and the place / And the loved one all
together!' (1883) or, more compellingly, make experiences we will
never have stay unforgettably with us: 'My first thought was, he lied
in every word, / That hoary cripple, with malicious eye ...' ('Childe
Roland to the Dark Tower Came', 1855) or 'It happened thus: my slab,
though new / Was getting weather-stained' ('Bad Dreams IV', 1889).
The poetry is Browning's monument, regardless of the demotion of
Westminster Abbey and England from their former identification with
the culture of the whole English-speaking world.

What does it mean to call poetry a monument? The question seems
to me to lie at the heart of the project of a literary life. In the English
poetic tradition reading literature has been associated with bereave-
ment at least since Milton's 'Epitaph on the Admirable Dramatic Poet
W. Shakespeare' (1632). The 'Epitaph' is a powerful shaper of
Romantic and Victorian conceptions of imaginative experience.

According to Milton, Shakespeare's words are inscribed on readers' hearts: 'each heart / Hath, from the leaves of thy unvalued book, / Those Delphic lines with deep impression took.' The book is not the monument, but a medium through which the strange force of literature can pass. The reader is, up to a point, figuratively, the monument: 'Then thou, our fancy of itself bereaving, / Dost make us marble with too much conceiving.'

Yet the force of literature is not itself stony. Readers are not, or not entirely, the petrified victims of genius. James speaks of posterity as a movement, a passing. A few Browning lines have, as I mentioned, dissolved into our common language, and some fragments have lodged there independently of the poet's name and reputation. Even marble can crumble or dissolve, even the 'monument more enduring than bronze' built by Horace, can melt.[5] Who, since Ezra Pound, remembers even the first phrase of 'exegi monumentum aere perennius'? Browning often described the creation of a distinctive language as forging: the melting, welding and hammering of malleable metal. He also writes about posterity in terms of an 'oozing' that escapes through the tomb ('The Bishop Orders His Tomb', 1845), or fluid properties of liquid dye ('Popularity', 1855).

Ruskin takes up the idea of reading as a dissolution of the poet's idiom during a discussion of 'The Bishop Orders His Tomb' in *Modern Painters* V (1860). Poetry should be 'soluble', fit for translation and assimilation into a 'current of common thought' (Ruskin VI, 449). Browning's dense language is slow to dissolve, it needs unusual patience and Ruskin hopes that it will be recognized as a 'talisman'. The talisman has an effect on the water in which it is immersed but it does not altogether disappear into the general flow. It should resist complete translation into everybody's language. Ruskin says the

> worst of it is that this kind of concentrated writing needs so much *solution* before the reader can fairly get the good of it, that people's patience fails them, and they give the thing up as insoluble; though, truly, it ought to be to the current of common thought like Saladin's talisman, dipped in clear water, not soluble altogether, but making the element medicinal.

Browning never took the understanding of his readers for granted, and his writing foresees the patterns of its own reception by critics and the broader public. From the early narratives *Pauline* (1833) and *Sordello* (1840) to the shorter dramatic poems that currently typify Browning

as he appears on school and college syllabuses, and on to the complex
and prolonged argument of *Pacchiarotto* (1876) or the *Parleyings* (1887)
Browning's works show a restless concern with reading, its conditions,
its *impasses* and its possibilities. Swinburne called Browning's poetry a
'glittering and quivering web of living thought.' For him, reading
Browning is participation in a movement of superhuman rapidity:

> He never thinks but at full speed: and the rate of his thought is to
> that of another man's as the speed of a railway to that of a wagon
> or the speed of a telegraph to that of a railway. It is hopeless to
> enjoy the charm or apprehend the gist of his writings except with a
> mind thoroughly alert, an attention awake at all points, a spirit
> open and ready to be kindled by the contact of the writer's.[6]

The difficulties to be overcome operate at the level of syntax, vocabulary,
narrative structure and especially figurative stability – should the reader
pursue a literal or a figurative interpretation of a particular passage or
poem? To what reality does a Browning poem refer and where can an
interpretation settle? Swinburne's description suggests the exceptional
mobility of Browning's poetic language. In mid-career Browning defined
poetry as 'putting the infinite within the finite', an impossible feat which
demands exhilarating efforts from the reader.[7] The relation between
reader and text is built on breaks, fragments, 'touches and bits and out-
lines which *succeed* if they bear the conception from me to you.'
Language is not a tool for explaining ideas. Yet if original work is to exist,
it is necessary that some sort of teaching take place.

More recently Hillis Miller has argued that Browning 'wants his
words to be thick and substantial, and to carry the solid stuff of
reality'.[8] Miller convincingly develops this idea of 'reality' in terms of
bodily experiences and physical forms, which Browning wants his
poetic language to convey and imitate. The reader in turn is urged to
participate in the mimetic movement: 'the words invite us to imitate
with our bodies what they describe, or to react to the poem as if it were
a physical stimulus.' Miller makes it possible to imagine poetic
language traversing the reader's body in a linguistically induced shiver
of aesthetic experience. In 'Childe Roland to the Dark Tower Came',
for example, 'the reader is continually coaxed by the language to expe-
rience [the] ghastly scene as if it were his own body which had got into
this sad state'. This sympathetic suffering is the opposite of the expe-
rience of becoming marble that Milton describes in the 'Epitaph on
Shakespeare'. A reader of Browning would memorialize the poet by

being enticed into the animation of his writing. And yet reading Browning, as his contemporaries recognized, is not just a matter of being swept along on a tide of words.

According to Ruskin, Browning's poetry exemplifies the fact that the more patience a work needs, the more concentrated it is, the more slowly it will return to the watery anonymity of a common language. I link the concentration of Browning's language, its thick ooziness through the reader's mind, to its enduring power to memorialize names, not by setting them in stone, but by setting them in motion. In Browning's case the names take various forms, not often the stable proper name 'Robert Browning', as on the title page or memorial plaque (though that does occur here and there). With literary monuments, the name disappears into the work. Derrida describes this disappearing mark as 'not necessarily a *name*, for it can take a quite different form: a phrase (abbreviated or not), a sound, a motif, an emblem, etc.'.[9] Moving beyond the notion of the proper name and its various forms as conventionally recognized, Derrida puts forward the notion of a '*grande signature*': 'not only the corpus but also the life ... a writing not limited to the works' (p. 197). This extension of the notion of name and signature overlaps interestingly with the reading methods Browning recommends for the study of what he calls a subjective poet: 'Both for love's and for understanding's sake we desire to know him, and as readers of his poetry must be readers of his biography also.' I have tried to combine a chronological account of Browning's literary career with an attempt to clarify the peculiar power of his language through the responses of his contemporaries. Browning's many poems about tombs, monuments and posterity could be read in terms of the inscription and dissolution of signatures, movements of writing that play across his corpus with tremendous vitality. This idea is most fully discussed in Chapter 5, on Browning and Ruskin.

Where an identifying mark partly dissolves into, or crystallizes out of, the lines of a poem, it leaves enough of its untranslatable singularity to make those lines stick in your mind, or as Browning more corporeally puts it in the 'Epilogue' to *Pacchiarotto and How He Worked in Distemper* (1876), catch in your throat. Paradoxically it is the indeterminate, apparition-like status of signatures that makes them a haunting and powerful literary phenomenon. Patience sometimes fails people, as Ruskin points out, but an insoluble line or passage can be powerful enough to call a reader back and make him or her keep wondering. One wonders more, reading Browning, because Shelley's mark so often appears there, especially in passages about creativity, originality or posterity. Browning features Shelley as a pure face, a lyric light, close to 'what God sees', and dangerously close to a pure language unmarked by any idiom whatsoever. Part of the force of Browning's work lies in a capacity to show and hide what he called the 'self-sufficing central light' of his main precursor's poetic faculty, breaking that dazzling white light into prismatic colours. Through the figure of Shelley and the associated imagery surrounding Elizabeth Barrett, Browning gives form to a struggle with writing itself as an inappropriable primary power. Browning's 'Essay on Shelley' suggests that we need the biography of a subjective poet like Shelley because he figures so clearly what in poetry is neither biographical nor subjective: 'we must look deep into his human eyes' to see the 'pictures' he 'carries' there. The inward humanity of the subjective poet, Browning argues, is a surface that bears marks.

For Browning understanding is not simply a problem for the intelligence, it also entails a love which would be prepared to meet the poetry half-way, so to speak. Love should not be doglike: his poetry requires the recognition that poetic strength must be met with strength. This literary life of Browning highlights the gaps in understanding that arose when Browning was read by contemporaries. He required a certain 'licence' from his imaginary audience before his poems could come onto the page but readers who don't give him complete licence often produce the most interesting commentaries on his work. Ruskin is the chief example, the most sensitively literary in his irritation, but Mill, Macready, Carlyle and Arnold also misunderstood Browning in curiously revealing ways.

'How difficult to banish the idea that Robert Browning would have enjoyed prefiguring and disintegrating the mystifications, the reservations, even perhaps the slight buzz of scandal in the Poets' Corner, to which his own obsequies might give rise!' comments James (p. 531). The journey to Poets' Corner through an Abbey 'so thick, under its high arches, its dim transepts and chapels [with] the population of its historic names and figures' sounds comfortable enough. In 'Childe Roland to the Dark Tower Came' Browning thought of poetic endeavour in terms of a squat doorless tower amid a desolate landscape where Roland and his precursors would gather to die. The companionship of 'all the lost adventurers my peers' is a recurrent theme in his poetry, and the personally optimistic Browning took an austere view of the ironies of literary fame. Chapter 1 opens with an account of Browning's first poem, and of his initial conception of his relation to writing. John Stuart Mill's powerfully unsympathetic reading of *Pauline* (1833) provoked Browning to some responses that reveal his preoccupations. Chapter 2 takes up *Sordello*'s account of creativity and suffering. Browning's contemporaries often found his work outrageously difficult, and reviews of *Sordello* (1840) emphasize this problem. The poem baffled critical expectations: why should Browning's account of 'incidents in the development of a soul' have proved so hard to follow? The biography of a poet provided Browning with a chance for extensive research into how life and poetry can possibly coexist. The poem may not succeed in familiar terms, but it is a mine for Browning's later poetry, which returns to it again and again as his literary life goes forward.

The notion of dramatic poetry was crucial for Browning's use of the materials of experience. He did not imitate experience in his poetry, but used lived experience as a means of representation for what it is impossible to apprehend anywhere else but literature. Chapter 3 relates Browning's work as a playwright to his exploration of the rhetorical possibilities of dramatic poetry. Drama, acting and the theatre were more than metaphors for Browning's deskbound poetic activity. He undertook practical involvement with the theatre, despite his suspicion of the popular stage. The series *Bells and Pomegranates* (1841–6) contains both plays and poems, and the poet's disputes with the actor-manager William Macready over the presentation of his work took the conflict characteristic of his poetry beyond the more abstract debates over Browning's early long poems. The shift to shorter dramatic poetry was followed by Browning's courtship correspondence with Elizabeth Barrett. At the chapter's close I link their letters to Browning's mould-breaking poetic advance.

The historian Thomas Carlyle recognized a heroic quality in Browning and became his beloved friend in the early 1840s. The friendship persisted warmly despite political and aesthetic differences until Carlyle died in 1881. Carlyle saw great promise in the poet's early work, admired the 'Essay on Shelley' (1852) and *Men and Women* (1855) but was constantly disappointed by Browning's obscurity. Chapter 4 shows how Browning responded to, and resisted, Carlyle from their first exchanges in the 1840s to Browning's *Parleying* 'With Bernard de Mandeville' (1887). Browning has his own notions of time and history, very different from Carlyle's.

Elizabeth Barrett's *Aurora Leigh* (1856) outshone Browning's bid for a wider audience, *Men and Women* (1855). The licence Browning demanded from his readers still outraged the critical beliefs of his baffled admirer John Ruskin. This relation is the core of Chapter 5. The aesthetic stance set forth in Ruskin's *Modern Painters* (1842–60) owes, like Browning's poetry and criticism, a considerable debt to vvordsworth and an English romantic tradition stemming from Milton. Ruskin's close readings of 'Popularity' and his account of the earlier monologue 'The Bishop Orders His Tomb at St Praxed's Church' (1845) introduce the themes of fame, posterity and monumentalization in Browning's poetry.

In 1860 Browning discovered at Florence the collection of late seventeenth-century legal documents relating to the murder of Pompilia and her parents by her husband Guido Franchescini; the bound collection of trial documents, legal arguments, affadavits and letters is now known as Old Yellow Book. *The Ring and The Book* (1868–9) describes how the Book is used as a source, and thus raises the issue of translation. *The Ring and the Book* 'translates' earlier Browning poems, especially *Sordello*. Chapter 6 relates *The Ring and The Book* to Browning's classical 'transcriptions' of the 1870s and especially to his version of the *Agamemnon of Aeschylus* (1877). Browning's preface to that work contains an implicit attack on the vision of translation set forth in Matthew Arnold's lectures on Homer. Arnold feared confusion while Browning embraced the opportunities of writing in a world of warring idioms and irreducible differences between languages. The year 1861 was that of Elizabeth Barrett-Browning's death: in the course of this chapter I continue to examine Browning's conception of her as an idealized fusion of being and poetic language. The ideal of a 'lyric Love' is the polar opposite of the sense of catastrophic conflict between lived existence and poetry that fuels much of Browning's work.

Chapter 7 approaches Browning through his relation to literature as an institution. He was not a bard like Sordello, but an author. Like Milton and Wordsworth before him he was conscious that his productions formed part of a literary archive. He was also interested in the network of laws that controlled author's rights: he admired the Puritan John Lilburne who defied state restrictions on publication in the mid-1600s, he wrote a defence of the eighteenth-century poet and forger Chatterton and he supported the reform of copyright in his own day. *Paracelsus*, a work of the 1830s, explores Browning's thinking about authorship as a dangerous kind of revelation, and literature as the summons that brings together a community chosen from among the living and the dead.

Browning cultivated a generous imaginary reader who helped the release of inhibitions in composition, and he presented his work with prefaces, advertisements and dedications that tried to determine how his poems should be read. Still, he also conceived of his readership as an undifferentiated and sometimes hostile 'public'. As an old man he turned on his critics savagely in *Pacchiarotto and How He Worked in Distemper*. In *Sordello*, nearly forty years before, he had written of the inevitable indifference of poetry's audience towards the author's intentions. Sordello gave up poetry and died young. But Browning, in James's words, 'played with the curious and the special, they never submerged him, and it was a sign of his robustness that he could play to the end' (p. 533).

1
Pauline and Mill

Browning was 14 when his friend Sarah Flower sent copies of two of his poems to her guardian, the Unitarian minister William Johnstone Fox. She added at the end of the letter: 'I must just say a little word about that boy's poems. he [sic] is mad to publish them – you know there is a whole book full from which these two are extracted. What ought he to do?'[1] Fox did not yet know 'that boy': Sarah Flower probably hoped that her guardian, something of a public figure in London's religious, political and intellectual life, might be able to place the poems somewhere. Like Browning and his family Fox was 'a schismatic and frequenter of Independent Dissenting Chapels'.[2] He was also known as an orator for the cause of Parliamentary reform. As editor of a journal, *The Monthly Repository*, he was in a position to be of practical use to Browning by publicly noticing his poetry. Fox ran *The Monthly Repository* as a Unitarian periodical until 1831 when he bought the copyright and shifted his attention to social and political reform and literary criticism. His career shows a steady movement from religious concerns to broader issues of radical mass politics. He was friendly with the actor-manager William Macready, the eminent dramatist and lawyer Thomas Noon Talfourd and the literary and dramatic critic John Forster, all of whom later knew Browning well. Through Fox, Browning began the transition from writing verse admired by his family and friends, to publishing his work to be read by strangers.

Browning recalled that Fox in 1827 'praised some [poems], prophesied great things of the future, and advised me to consign the present work to the fire'.[3] From this volume, called *Incondita*, only 'The Dance of Death' and 'The First Born of Egypt' survive the author's rigorous censorship.[4] Browning throughout his career insisted on suppressing work he did not like, often before anyone else had read it. There were periods in his life when he wrote little, notably in the late 1850s, but the ruthlessness about destroying his poetry did not fade with the passage of time. Later, Browning went to some lengths to retrieve the *Incondita* poems from the papers of the Flower sisters. When Eliza died in 1846 Browning wrote to Sarah, and then on Sarah's death in 1848 wrote again to Richard Hengist Horne to ask him to help dispose of any 'boyish rubbish'[5] kept by Eliza. That approach was unsuccessful so Browning tenaciously waited until 1871 when Fox's daughter finally gave him Eliza Flower's album with some of the *Incondita* poems in it and he was able to burn it, fifty-odd years after Fox's advice to consign his juvenilia to the fire.

At about the time of Sarah Flower's letter, Browning was for the first time reading Shelley. His cousin James Silverthorne gave him *Miscellaneous Poems* (1826), an unauthorized Shelley collection published by William Benbow. Browning quickly got hold of more: *History of a Six Weeks' Tour* (written with Mary Shelley, 1817), *The Revolt of Islam* (1818), *Rosalind and Helen* (1819), *The Cenci* (1820), *Prometheus Unbound* (1820), *Epipsychidion* (1821), *Adonais* (1821) and *Posthumous Poems* (1824). Fox was the first of many critics to allude to Shelley's influence on Browning in his warm review of the poet's first publication, *Pauline; a Fragment of a Confession* (1833), for *The Monthly Repository*.

Pauline

This first poem is remarkable for its combination of gripping urgency and disconcerting fragmentation. *Pauline*, a first-person account of the moods and impulses of a young would-be poet, takes its first bearings from an eroticized relation to its reader's imagined body:

> Pauline, mine own, bend o'er me – thy soft breast
> Shall pant to mine – bend o'er me – thy sweet eyes,
> And loosened hair, and breathing lips, and arms
> Drawing me to thee – these build up a screen
> To shut me in with thee, and from all fear ...
>
> (ll. 1–5)

'Pauline' is not, as the poem's title might suggest, a character from the speaker's sexual past. She doesn't figure much in the poem's narrative, but shares the position of addressee with its readers. Who is confessing

to her? Someone very close, who wants to be closer still, the first lines
suggest. The repeated 'bend o'er me' seems to call the reader to closer
study of the poem itself. Breast, eyes, hair, lips and arms, 'Pauline' is
open and yielding. It is as if the 'me' that is speaking wants to be safely
enclosed inside her body. There is a strong flavour of the relation
between mother and child in the opening address, but the poem
reaches back beyond oedipal desire into a buried past. It has secrets
and ghosts: 'Thou lovest me – the past is in its grave, / Tho' its ghost
haunts us' (ll. 39–40). The poem unfolds a narrative of loss not clearly
specified to Pauline or to the reader. The trauma that the narrator
refers to, and which may be taken to have caused the brokenness of his
narrative, cannot – is not intended to be – mourned or forgotten. As
often in Browning, the past is still surprising.

Nevertheless, *Pauline* uses the connectives of conventional narra-
tive: 'Thou wilt remember ...,' 'Then came a pause ...,' 'I paused again
...,' 'Souls alter not, and mine must progress still' (ll. 55, 344, 394,
588). These are interspersed with numerous reconfigurations of the
narrator's self, some of which are literal and some metaphorical: 'I am
ruined ...,' 'I was a fiend ...,' 'then I was a young witch,' 'A mind like
this must dissipate itself' and 'as some temple seemed / My soul' (ll.
89, 99, 112, 291, 469–70). The poem also includes moments when
recollection seems to meet with some unspecified resistance: 'O let me
look back ...,' 'I will tell / My state as though 'twere none of mine –
despair / Cannot come near me,' 'There's some vile juggle with my
reason here – / I feel I but explain to my own loss / These impulses ...'
(ll. 430, 586–7, 681–3). Even the familiar poetic bearings of the
seasons are complicated by returns from the past: 'Autumn has
come – like Spring returned to us' and 'spring comes, / And sunshine
comes again like an old smile' (ll. 230, 971–2). The future in the
poem, its project of transformation first suggested in the epigraph
from Marot which translates as 'I am no longer what I was, and I
never will be that again', never does come free from its past.

The 'me', the Poet who wants to tell his life story before undertaking
a 'task', cannot separate his identity from states of dream, thought and
hauntedness which resist being rendered as confessional narrative (l.
53). When narrative emerges, it soon disappears. The narrator-poet
chooses a poetic model 'Sun-treader', undertakes to read his work and
study philosophy and then to examine experience. Then in a
surprising representation of loss as gain, he tells how he 'suddenly,
without heart-wreck ... awoke / As from a dream' and abandons the
project (ll. 447–8). He claims, by reading and uncanny powers of

sympathy, to 'have gone in thought / Thro' all conjuncture' (ll. 702–3). After 800 lines, the narrative is abandoned also: the narrator asks 'where does this tend – these struggling aims!' and questions the possibility of a '"waking" point' of consciousness untouched by dream or imagining (l. 813).

At this point in the poem a note in French, signed PAULINE, suggests that the poem's fragmentariness and lack of clarity are essential to it. The poem's closing 200 lines look forward to death, 'Yet while [my spirit's] last light waits, I would say much': he claims Pauline's devotion, resolves 'No more of the past – I'll look within no more', imagines a life of song, reading and inspecting the contents of his mind, going with Pauline like twin gods 'over the dead – to call and to awake – / Over the unshaped images which lie / Within my mind's cave' (ll. 863, 937, 968–70). This morbidly hopeful mood is not, however the poem's last: the narrator continues uncertainly, 'whate'er come of it', to relate that the present poem 'shall remain to tell for ever / That when I lost all hope . . . / Suddenly beauty rose on me again' (ll. 986, 1004–6). Repetition, not resolution, will save him: 'For having thus again been visited, / Shall doubt not many another bliss awaits' (ll. 1008–9). The final verse-paragraph invokes the Sun-treader and makes more general address to 'All in whom this wakes pleasant thoughts of me' (l. 1029). Any reader thus moved by the poem shall 'Know my last state is happy – free from doubt, / Or touch of fear. Love me and wish me well!' (ll. 1030–1).

It seems that the confession was a last testament before death, or a future as open and unknown as death. The reader, who began the poem leaning over it and was represented as its female lover, ends in company with the fictive poet's bereaved friends. This ungraspable 'me' has the forwardness to imagine what his loss might mean to the poem's readers. The poem has projected the greatest possible intimacy with this 'me' who never settles into a human or linguistic identity: who is neither psyche nor text. Did Browning seek to conjure an audience of lovers for his fragment, their love constituted privately by reading? We might feel that the ambition of a poem that claims us as its own and asks us to physically protect it in line 1 uses us, treats readers as objects in the quest for fame. However, the idea of use presupposes a manipulative consciousness on the poem's side which never manages to come together. Read me, love me, says the poem: I am not sure that I exist.

Fame is not a goal in *Pauline*. Renown is conceived negatively, as the loss of the narrator's power to contain 'all the world' in his solitary praise of the little known Sun-treader, or as a dream to be sacrificed for the chance to pin the Sun-treader down: 'E'en in my wildest dreams, / I proudly feel I would have thrown to dust / The wreaths of fame which seemed o'erhanging me, / To see thee for a moment as thou art' (ll. 199, 202–5). The wreaths of fame continued to hang out of Browning's reach in 1833. *Pauline* survived a critical trampling from *The Literary Gazette*, *The Athenaeum*, *The Atlas*, *Tait's Edinburgh Magazine* and *Fraser's Magazine*. John Stuart Mill, an important contributor to *The Monthly Repository*, was to have reviewed the poem also but a dismissive line about '*Paulina*' [sic] appeared in *Tait's*, so he returned his annotated copy to Fox, who gave it back to Browning. The poet added indignant defensive marginalia to the poem's existing textual apparatus of motto, preface and a footnote in French from the fictional Pauline herself. Browning's pencilled notes explain that the poem's celebrated but popularly neglected 'Sun-treader' was Shelley.

Pauline emphasizes and reflects on the protagonist's relationship to an earlier poet, and Shelley poems such as *Alastor* and *Epipsychidion* are clearly relevant references for *Pauline*. But Browning gives influence a twist. The poem brings together multiple sources as its editors have noted: the genre of confession suggests debts to Rousseau and de Quincey, that of the fragment indicates Shelley, yes, but also Keats, Wordsworth, Coleridge and Byron and beyond that, classical authors, particularly Sappho.[6] Browning always read widely and in other languages than English: his father's library was large and intriguing and the older Browning encouraged his son to read 'Bunyan, *Robinson Crusoe*, Raleigh's *History of the World*, Milton, Shakespeare, Camoens, Tasso, ... Mandeville, Pliny, Theophrastus and on and on'.[7] The biographer of Browning's youth, John Maynard, also records reading in history, the *Biographie Universelle* (1822, a valuable reference work later) and such curiosities as Nathaniel Wanley's *Wonders of the Little World: or, a General History of Man* (1678) and a life of *Paracelsus* in three volumes. As a poet he is an extraordinary combination of learned breadth and thematic repetitiveness.

Browning's poetry constantly returns both explicitly and allegorically to the theme of influence. The abortive beginnings of literary life engross the three early narratives, *Pauline*, *Paracelsus* (1835) and *Sordello* (1840) in particular. But Browning's is not a work of synthesis between literature and life. His poems and letters firmly distinguish between literary production and the life he was born into. If life was a poem, it was not his poem but God's. In one letter to Elizabeth Barrett he refers to the idea of 'R. B. a poem', denying that his work can be a source of knowledge about him:

What I have printed gives *no* knowledge of me – it evidences abilities of various kinds, if you will, – and a dramatic sympathy with certain modifications of passion . . *that* I think: but I never have begun, even, what I hope I was born to begin and end, – "R.B. a poem."[8]

Browning's review essay on Tasso and Chatterton argues 'that the very notion of obtaining a free way for impulses that can find vent in no other channel . . . is implied in all literary production'.[9]

Early Browning poems repeat the solipsistic quest of a would-be creative hero, ending in death: his models are *Alastor* and *Hyperion*. Yet something distinctive is already happening at this stage of Browning's career. The hero of *Pauline*'s strange combination of shifting mood and blocked obsession introduces a specific dilemma for Browning readers. We also, like Browning, experience dramatic sympathy with the heroes' modifications of passion; we are at the same time faced with difficult interpretive questions. In Harold Bloom's words we are at once 'incapable of knowing what is literal and what figurative where all, in a sense, is figurative' and wondering whether the psychology of the hero exists as such: 'is there a self that is not trope or an effect of verbal persuasion?'[10] This modern view finds no counterpart in the understanding of Browning's poetry by his contemporaries, whose notions of poetic language and of identity were elaborated in different terms. John Stuart Mill's notes on the poem follow *Pauline* in a concern with 'self-consciousness' and subjectivity, but Mill's sense of the relation of poetry to the self had been forged in a particular way. His thought in this respect is quite alien from Browning's, as I show later in this chapter.

Pauline indicates that Shelley resembles Browning because Shelley's was, as 'Mont Blanc' (1817) puts it, 'a voice . . . not understood / By all'. Critical recognition did not come in his lifetime and in Browning's writing literary ambition works on a scale that is bigger than a poet's life. Ambition is not an impulse that precedes and is satisfied by the composition, publication and reception of poetry, it extends into the lives of readers and beyond the death of poets. This kind of ambition is directed at literature, and succeeds or fails as literature. Browning sometimes describes literary power in terms of power struggles between poets. Some poets are clearly of secondary importance, like Aprile in *Paracelsus* or Eglamor in *Sordello*. These are easily assimilated into the narrative of the central character's development. One also comes across presences that are more difficult to dismiss or more profoundly threatening, the ideal reader 'Pauline' and the poet

'Sun-treader', for instance, or the unnamed poet (clearly Shelley) who silently joins the audience at the opening of *Sordello* and who must be displaced before the poem can proceed. These resistant presences are haunting, not quite of the narrative, not simply internal to the psychic landscape of the protagonist.

Later poems describe literature's power to disturb in a more playful way. In the dramatic lyric 'Sibrandus Schafnaburgensis', the second of a pair of 'Garden Fancies' (1844), the reader dutifully finishes Sibrandus's pedantic book then as revenge stuffs it into a crack in a tree where it gets ruined. He wonders 'How did he like it when the live creatures/Tickled and toused and browsed him all over …?' and contemplates 'All that life and fun and romping,/All that twisting and frisking and coupling,/While slowly our poor friend's leaves were swamping/And clasps were cracking and covers suppling!' Here, as in the opening of *Pauline*, the book has feelings and is treated as a subject capable of physical response; but now the reader is not swamped by a claustrophobia-inducing embrace. The long-suffering book is no longer identified with the poem that is describing it: 'Come, old martyr! What, torment enough is it?' the reader asks as he returns the battered book to his shelf. It becomes difficult to decide whether the book has determined its own fate by its particular pedantry, demanding it be outraged as a proper revenge for the life that it lacks, or whether the time it spends imprisoned in a tree like Shakespeare's Ariel is a mere accident, the result of the way that on this occasion the reader decided to construct it: initially with reverence, 'as a curious traveller counts Stonehenge', then with a mixture of violent disrespect and attempted seduction: 'As if you had carried sour John Knox/To the play-house at Paris, Vienna or Munich,/Fastened him into a front-row box,/And danced off the ballet in trousers and tunic.' Which has the power? the book finally rescued and left to 'rot at ease till the Judgement-day' or the reader, a creature of a particular spring morning, his life limited like the beetles and efts in his garden, who puts it back on his shelf? Later works, 'Popularity', 'How It Strikes a Contemporary' (1855), parts of *The Ring and the Book* (1868–9) and the 'Epilogue' to *Pacchiarotto and How He Worked in Distemper* (1876), think about reading as the reception of poetry by various imagined and actual publics. In these poems some readers are friends, others are, through ignorance or malice, enemies: *Pauline* and 'Sibrandus Schafnaburgensis' suggest that the question of reception in Browning's work lies within his poems as well as outside them in the critical writing of his day. Browning's literary life shows that his worldly decisions and dealings with theatres and publishers, critics and audiences, were often affected by too powerful a propensity to imagine and invent the genesis and reception of his poetry. For example, Browning's identification of Shelley as the great influence on the hero of *Pauline* reads his own work too narrowly. *Pauline*'s 'Sun-treader' is a composite figure, a personification of literary power which is part of a more general strategy. The poem combines textual and psychological configurations, using a vocabulary of self-consciousness which doesn't exactly fit either textuality or psychic life. In the poem self-consciousness becomes phantomatic, anachronistic and generally abnormal.

Self-consciousness and poetic textuality

The literary apparatus surrounding the poem and its fragmented quality disrupt the notion that *Pauline* speaks with a human voice. Mill detects this ahumanity, but understands the cause in terms of his own theory of poetry and poetic subjectivity. He traces the textual effect to a psychological origin and criticizes the author of *Pauline* for insincerity and obscurity. He also finds the woman Pauline psychologically unconvincing:

> This writer seems to me possessed with a more intense and morbid self-consciousness than I ever knew in any sane human being – I should think it a *sincere confession*, though of a most unloveable state, if the 'Pauline' were not evidently a mere phantom.[11]

For Mill this was a morbidity of character, but the vagaries of *Pauline* are more productively understood in terms of the effects of using 'self-consciousness' (Browning's and Mill's word) as a trope for the effects and workings of poetic language. Browning had turned up Keats's *Endymion* (1818) and *Lamia ... and other poems* (1820) with the Shelley books he bought from Hunt and Clarke's shop in 1827, and one can hear Keats, Wordsworth and Milton as well as Shelley in *Pauline*'s multiple voice. Influence does not follow the customary cultural patterns of inheritance from a single father, or of love for a single wife. The influence of Shelley is of interest to Browning students because it provides a way of decompressing without imaginative reduction the compact and even cryptic energies of Browning's poetry.[12]

Pauline reflects on literary fame in terms of the exaggerated love of an idealist for his remote ideal. The loving reader's happiness comes from 'HIS award, ... / ... HIM whom all honor – whose renown springs up / Like sunlight which will visit all the world' (ll. 142, 144–5).

However, alongside admirers are sneerers, who spiderlike spin 'still new films' to veil themselves (l. 149). With actual fame came personal exposure and biographism, which the later Browning loathed. Published Browning would have to acknowledge unsympathetic readers, like Mill, or non-readers like the reviewer in *Tait's* who passingly referred to *Pauline* as 'a piece of pure bewilderment' but this was not the worst aspect of the business of literary reproduction and reception: Browning tried to cultivate a robust attitude to reviews.[13] The destination of the Sun-treader's poetry, nothing less than 'the world', is for Browning the reflected image of poetry's dispersed origins. Poetry comes from all over the place, its origins include language prior to appropriation by authors or readers, as well as anonymous works, forgotten authors and the great names of the canon.

Browning's awkward engagements with his literary public reminded him that beyond the enclosing fiction of Pauline's readerly embrace, or of literary influence as worship at a 'sacred spring / Scarce worth a moth's flitting' (ll. 172–3), lay an open sea of unenclosed writing. The sacred spring known only to 'me' becomes an uncontrollable flow, a massive pulsion:

> – Then girt with rocks which seek to turn or stay
> Its course in vain, for it does ever spread
> Like a sea's arm as it goes rolling on,
> Being the pulse of some great country – so
> Wert thou to me – and art thou to the world.
>
> (ll. 186–90)

Part of Shelley's initial attraction for Browning was perhaps the virtual suppression of his works by his disapproving father Sir Timothy Shelley. The model of a cultish, little-known Sun-treader would counter Browning's potentially overwhelming sense that literature tends to resist appropriation. *Pauline* was anonymous, and the handful of shorter poems that appeared after it in *The Monthly Repository* and *Hood's Magazine* were signed only 'Z'. Browning destroyed a second part of *Pauline* and 'other works, written in pursuance of it', before beginning to write what he called 'a genuine work of my own'.[14] Not until *Paracelsus* came out in 1835 did Browning attach his own name to a poem. Young Browning may have been 'mad to publish' but he was also reticent about openly claiming authorship. This reticence allowed him more readily to superimpose his own plans on the risky business of publication. Fox was an important ally, not only the editor of an appropriate journal, but the right kind of reader. As it happened, Browning found and wooed in letters and conversation an actual audience of lovers. His mother, father and younger sister Sarianna were enlisted from the start.

Browning's education

Browning's Congregationalist family background debarred admission to Oxford or Cambridge where entry was restricted to Anglicans. Robert Browning Senior, clerk at the Bank of England, would not have been rich enough to send his son to Oxford or Cambridge: the costs were upwards of two hundred pounds a year, twice the price of a place at the new London University. Browning attended classes at London for less than a year in 1828–9 but university was not for him the kind of stimulus that it was for Tennyson or Arnold. Browning travelled from home to study Latin, Greek and German. At Cambridge in the 1820s Tennyson joined the Apostles (the Cambridge Conversazione Society) where he began important intellectual friendships with Arthur Hallam, whose death occasioned *In Memoriam*, Richard Chenevix Trench and Richard Monckton Milnes, later a friend of Browning's. Arnold met Clough in a debating group called the Decade at Oxford in the 1840s. London University did not offer a ready-made milieu for young poets. It had a Literary and Philosophical Society, but that was more of a forum for rhetorical display by would-be lawyers and parliamentarians than a chance to form a phalanx. Browning's 'set' of friends in the 1830s and 1840s, like his father's library, was of varied and non-academic composition, initially an informal discussion group centring on Christopher Dowson (who ran a shipping business), Alfred Domett (a traveller, poet, lawyer and later colonizer in New Zealand), Joseph Arnould (who combined being a successful lawyer with artistic and literary interests and ended up as a judge in Bombay) and an older sea captain, James Pritchard. In 1834 they started a journal, *The Trifler*, to which Browning contributed a stylish defence of debt.

The poetry prizes at Oxford and Cambridge might have provided the first chance to publish away from the 'sympathy of dear friends' that Browning dreaded should *Pauline* fail. Alfred Tennyson's 'Timbuctoo' won the Chancellor's Medal at Cambridge in 1829. Matthew Arnold's 'Cromwell' took Oxford's Newdigate Prize in 1843. Browning used informal contacts, principally Fox and the poet and journalist Thomas Hood, to publish short poems in mixed-content periodicals. Anonymity was customary for early volumes. Alfred and Charles

Tennyson published *Poems by Two Brothers* anonymously in 1827. Arnold's *The Strayed Reveller, and Other Poems* (1849) came out under the name 'A'. Elizabeth Barrett's *Prometheus Bound ... and Miscellaneous Poems* came out in the same year as *Pauline* – anonymously like all her publications until *The Seraphim, and Other Poems* (1838). Considering the unbookish occupations of his father and his friends, Browning's choice of poethood as a career was unconventional. The decision to withdraw from university signalled a withdrawal from the kind of practical professional life lived by his father and by Domett, Dowson and Arnould. At about eighteen Browning chose a career most unlikely to make financial independence possible and remained at home until he eloped with Elizabeth Barrett at the age of 34. In some ways Browning's education at home resembled that of his wife-to-be, an unmarried daughter in her father's house. Elizabeth Barrett's invalid status delayed marriage and exempted her from household duties: the effect of her ill-health was to give her time to read and write, which she did even during periods of extreme sickness. Browning chose to remain with his family, devoting his time to literature.

Browning's family were supportive of his vocation. He had free access to a large and unusual domestic library from an early age, and his father paid for the printing of *Incondita* and everything else from *Paracelsus* to the end of *Bells and Pomegranates* in 1846. Yet the public of 'dear friends' was not enough: Browning found in Fox 'my literary father'.[15] In 1833, years after Sarah Flower's letter and the initial meeting about *Incondita*, Browning nervously contacted Fox again to bring *Pauline* before him. He hoped for a notice in Mill's *Westminster Review*. The young poet hesitated to call himself a poet or refer to poetry by name. He was 'a sayer of verse & a doer of it'; to him poetry was more than words, it was also a form of consequential action.[16] He emphasizes his youth and thereby his precocity when he tells Fox that he 'may recall an oddish sort of boy', echoing Sarah Flower's reference to '"the boy" Robert'.

The reception of *Pauline* and Browning's 'childish scheme'

The *Monthly Repository* carried Fox's enthusiastic review of *Pauline* in 1833, and published five short Browning poems anonymously between October 1834 and Fox's departure as editor in 1836. Other notable contributions to the periodical under Fox's editorship were Crabbe Robinson's papers on Goethe, Harriet Martineau's poems and essays, music by Eliza Flower and controversial essays on social issues by W. Bridges Adams ('Junius Redivivus'). Mill wrote philosophical pieces under the name 'Antiquus'. Browning put a lot of imagination into trying to connect his writing to his life. He kept his loophole of anonymity and cherished a private plan for *Pauline* by which it would contribute to a secret drama for him alone.

Fox came closest of all the poem's reviewers to collaborating with a project revealed by Browning in a note written opposite the title page in Mill's returned review copy of the poem. The 'childish scheme' combined anonymity and glory:

> The following Poem was written in pursuance of a foolish plan which occupied me mightily for a time, and which had for its object the enabling me to assume & realize I know not how many different characters; – meanwhile the world was never to guess that 'Brown, Smith, Jones, & Robinson' (as the Spelling-books have it), the respective Authors of this poem, the other novel, such an opera, such a speech &c &c were no other than one and the same individual. The present abortion was the work of the *Poet* of the batch, who would have been more legitimately *myself* than most of the others; but I surrounded him with all manner of (to my then notion) poetical accessories, and I had planned quite a delightful life for him.
>
> Only this crab remains of the shapely Tree of Life in this Fools paradise of mine.
>
> RB   (Longman I, p. 16n.)

This scheme did not dedicate the author to poetry; it boldly enlisted poetry in a theatrical venture to diversify the author's selves. The creative possibilities of language and music would secretly be used to fulfil an ambition to be 'I know not how many characters' while remaining 'one and the same'. The plan of anonymous publication required an intended 'world' to receive the poem, novel, opera, speech, while never knowing the author's identity.

There is no evidence that Fox knew about Browning's private scheme, although he knew that Browning was the author of *Pauline*, but his review acknowledges and legitimates the poem, and by extension recognizes the '*Poet*' who was according to the note 'more legitimately *myself*' than the rest of the batch. Through anonymity Browning attempted to draw ownership off the title page into the text where, his plan suggests, it may still be privately controlled by him, even after publication. (But not naming the author on the title page also worked against this plan, as it means that some readers may take the author to be omnipresent in the work, like God, and are more likely to assume that *Pauline* is the author's confession.) Fox's review connects the poem's anonymity with its depiction of an internal world: 'the hero is anonymous as the author, and this is no matter; for *poet* is the title both of the one and the other … We have never read anything more purely confessional.'[17] His review associates the author of *Pauline* with Tennyson and names him a 'poet', citing the 'thrill', the 'power' and the 'sensation' produced by the poem for its readers. All is done in terms of the poem: even when he qualifies his praise and calls *Pauline* 'a hasty and imperfect sketch', Fox borrows the terminology of the French footnote which his review describes as *Pauline*'s 'chief blemish'.

The French note signed 'PAULINE' describes the effect of the poem's originality on its readers. At line 811 'O God! where does this tend – these struggling aims!' when the main text seems to be losing direction, the note steps forward to insist that although the Poet 'will not always be perfectly understood in what remains to be read of this strange fragment' ('ne soit toujours parfaitement compris dans ce qui reste à lire de cet étrange fragment') yet *Pauline* has the merit of 'giving a fairly exact idea of the kind of work of which it is only a sketch' ('une idée assez précise du genre qu'elle n'a fait qu'ébaucher'). Browning's use of French distances Pauline as the poem's addressee from the English poetic tradition in which Browning was working. She reveals her affiliations when she laments that her friend the poet is a stranger to the 'grande principe de composition' that operates in the works of Shakespeare, Raphael and Beethoven, invoking a cosmopolitan tradition that crosses poetry, painting and music. Here is a reader whose head is not full of the words of English Romantic poets, and her defence of *Pauline*'s fragmentariness does not appeal, as Browning editors rightly do, to precedent fragment-poems by Wordsworth, Coleridge, Byron, Keats and Shelley. For her, *Pauline* is therefore all the more recognizable as singular. French also offers its own specific possibilities as a critical language; it has its own way of meaning. The French term 'genre' felicitously refers to literary type and to the personal style of an individual, linking literary language with the coming into being of strange selves. The note's insistence that the work belongs to a genre which has not yet fully emerged contradicts the dead end of Browning's verdict that *Pauline* was an 'abortion'. For its first defender the poem belongs to a 'genre' but is also 'une production si singulière'. '[U]ne idée assez précise' leaves room for a failure of communication in which the identifying marks by which readers could ascertain genre would go unremarked or would mark the 'étrange fragment' as a one-off that is formally unclassifiable. The note seems to claim that the poem is a kind of thinking which is exact and which puts across ideas in a way that leaves the reader feeling that 'This idea, which I do not altogether grasp, is perhaps equally unintelligible to him' ('Cette idée que je ne saisis pas parfaitement lui est peutêtre aussi inintelligible qu'à moi'). Pauline's doubt that the author of the confession understands his own text introduces irony into the conventional true-or-false polarity of confession. Fox's comments echo Pauline's qualified praise and her guidance to the reader. He sees that the poetry is in some ways without precedent and demands to be read on its own terms. Pauline warns – don't try to make the work cohere or you may violate its singularity.

A warm relationship developed between Browning and Fox. The poet wrote to tell him: 'not a particle of your article has been rejected or neglected by your observant humble servant, & very proud shall I be if my new work bear in it the marks of the influence under which it was undertaken.'[18] Despite the value of Fox's critical countersignature for Browning, it is debatable whether the *Monthly Repository*'s review is more help than *The Literary Gazette*'s dismissive 'unfit for publication' in actually understanding *Pauline*.[19] What Fox did was to emphasize the poem's seriousness, unfamiliarity and substance: Browning

> has not given himself the chance for popularity which Tennyson did [in *Poems, Chiefly Lyrical*]. His poem stands alone, with none of those slight but taking accompaniments, songs that sing themselves, sketches that everybody knows, light little lyrics, floating about like humming birds, around the trunk and foliage of the poem itself.[20]

The guarantee money for *Pauline*, thirty pounds, was put up by his aunt, as Browning had not told his parents of the scheme. Three pounds fifteen shillings went on advertising, the rest on printing and Aunt Alicia lost the lot. Browning later claimed that sales had been non-existent – and, as was the custom at this time in British publishing, the volume was withdrawn after a few months. Browning later recalled retrieving some unbound sheets from Saunders & Otley. *The Atlas*, a general news-oriented journal in the style of *The Spectator*, faulted the poet's 'adaptation of style to thought' or of language to image.[21] In a judgement echoed and amplified by Wilde nearly sixty years later the reviewer found the poem's 'poetical spirit' thwarted by 'prosaic' language. Wilde put it more remarkably: 'Meredith is a prose Browning and so is Browning. He used poetry as a medium for writing in prose.'[22] *The Atlas* appeals to notions of literary decorum and 'becoming dignity' that Wilde might have found old-fashioned. The anonymous reviewer described a mismatch between 'plain' language and 'mystical' image and homed in on the poem's status as a *'Fragment of a Confession'*: 'the author is in the confessional and acknowledges to his mistress the strange thoughts and fancies with which his past life has been crowded.' According to this assessment the poem's language became inauthentic in the process: 'He does not always speak of his agonies in language worthy of one who evidently understood them so well; he sometimes runs slip-shod through his afflictions.' Another crucial value was beauty: 'there are many passages in the piece of considerable beauty, and a few of such positive excellence that we augure very favourably of the genius that produced them.' The review quotes the passage about the 'Sun-treader' (ll. 151–90). Beauty was a striking and virtually self-evident feature of parts of *Pauline* for Mill, who marked a few passages 'beautiful' and 'most beautiful'.[23] *The Athenaeum*, the most widely read of the week-lies and carrying a broad range of literary, artistic and scientific material, found 'a grain of sand' in the otherwise palatable clarity of the poem conceived as 'a cup of pure water'.[24] The metaphor describes flaws in clarity ('a touch of the mysterious, which we cannot admire'), momentary failures in poetic melody and a quality of 'abruptness'. Rebellious, irreverent *Fraser's Magazine*, which carried much of Carlyle's early writing, wrote facetiously of the poem's madness. The reviewer translates the Latin preface as referring to a poet 'as mad as Cassandra, without any of the power to prophesy like her, or to construct a connected sentence like anybody else'.[25]

Browning's response to criticism is complex. He refers dismissively to an unappreciative and undifferentiated public, the Mantuans in *Sordello* or his London audience in a letter to Ruskin (1855) and in *The Ring and the Book* (1868–9), but when he undertakes dialogues with individual readers he shows a specifically *literary* awareness of the pressures at work upon reading and critical judgement. The 'Essay on Shelley' is particularly clear: 'the misapprehensiveness of his age is exactly what a poet is sent to remedy.' If Browning, unlike Tennyson, refused to take bad notices personally, it is perhaps because he believes that writing is not informed by personality. The early narratives tell of creative failure and difficulty, of losing one's way in a dramatic and disastrous fashion: 'O God, where do they tend – these struggling aims?/What would I have?' asks the narrator of *Pauline* (ll. 811–12); Paracelsus finally learns his 'own deep error' from the poet Aprile only just before his prayer to die is answered; Sordello receives a last chance to redeem himself and his heart breaks with the strain of the choice between political and poetic life. Yet the hot-blooded and intense Browning did not seem concerned about the mental agony of composition or the misery of getting uncomprehending reviews. He calmly reabsorbs *Fraser's* designation of him as 'Mad Poet of the batch' of works under review in his account of the plan for *Pauline*: 'The present abortion was the work of the *Poet* of the batch.'

Browning's belated note introducing the scheme that frames *Pauline* resembles the poem's reviews by its lament over the blemish that disfigures his creative performance. His writing had failed to act according to plan, system or law. Instead of a smooth movement from thought to word, from plan to publication, or from dream to acknowledged reality, Browning's 'Tree of Life' had produced strange fruit. The older Browning's embarrassed attitude to the publication of *Pauline* might be understood as a partial recognition of the strangely intractable and untimely nature of what he had written. *Pauline* itself is a far more fascinating and ambitious poem than a reading guided by its author's repudiations would suggest. It is not merely a means to the end of becoming a Poet, the sort of preliminary ritual described in the lines to Pauline: 'thou said'st a perfect bard was one/Who shadowed out the stages of all life, / And so thou badest me tell this my first stage; –/'Tis done' (ll. 883–6). According to this logic, the perfect poet merely shadows lived experience. But, as Pauline's own note in the text argues, poetic authenticity may lie in the very abruptness and peculiarity of language that the reviewers balk at, and which impedes or condenses *Pauline*'s narrative. Pauline, the author of the note, has a defensive function, but what she defends is not the poet but the poem itself. Browning's scheme is 'childish' because it does not face the paradox that the poet's ends depended on a poem that is endlessly re-readable and never done with.

When he wrote to Fox to seek a review for *Pauline*, he asked to be left the 'loophole' of anonymity to avoid the 'sympathy of dear friends'.[26] Anonymity would also let him slip away into his work. Later, he refers to the law of poetic metre, and that reference also gets drawn into literature and made ironic. Defending the metrics of *Men and Women* he cordially insists to Ruskin 'I stand here for law!'[27] The phrase is Shakespeare's, the 'I' is Shylock. Shakespeare's claim to authority in aesthetic matters is founded on his dramatic works: he made no critical laws elsewhere. Browning suggests in 'House' (1876) that this resistance to coming forward was crucial to Shakespeare's achievement.

'House' also argues that nosey, judgemental readers should be kept in their place. The Latin preface to *Pauline* defends the poem by sketching the stance of unprejudiced, prudent, discerning readers. *Pauline* will tell its tale and it should not be interrupted by judgements. Those who

> have so much discretion of prudence as bees have in gathering honey, read securely . . . you shall receive no little profit, and much pleasure; but if you shall find any things that may not please you, let them alone and make no use of them, for I do not approve of them, but declare them to you.
>
> (Longman I, p. 28n.)

The preface suggests that the poem should be taken or left, but the reader should not try to sift the material or intervene in it. Mill's reading disregards this disingenuous advice. Reading was too thoroughly knitted into him to be carried out as if he were a bee.

Mill's feelings about *Pauline*

The part of Mill's *Autobiography* that charts the emotional crisis of his early twenties also describes his developing awareness of 'the internal culture of the individual' as necessary for personal well-being (Mill I, p. 147). During a period of depression in 1828 Mill discovered through personal experience that poetry and art were crucial 'instruments of human culture' because they nourished and enriched the capacity to feel. Some poetry was unhelpful to Mill's inner state, for example Byron's 'lament of a man who had worn out all pleasures' resembled too closely his own dejected mood (Mill I, p. 151). However, Wordsworth suited him exactly:

> What made Wordsworth's poems a medicine for my state of mind, was that they expressed, not mere outward beauty, but states of feeling, and of thought coloured by feeling, under the excitement of beauty. They seemed to be the very culture of the feelings, which I was in quest of.

Universality was an important part of this culture of feelings: the Wordsworth poems were 'a source of inward joy, of sympathetic and imaginative pleasure, which could be shared in by all human beings'. They also seemed separate from the troubles of mankind, having 'no connexion with struggle or imperfection'. Struggle and imperfection are crucial to Browning's mature poetics, and *Pauline* in 1833 offered Mill a very different kind of experience from that formative reading of Wordsworth which had brought him closer to the 'common feelings and common destiny of human beings' (Mill I, p. 153). In *Pauline* Mill faced a fragmentary and openly difficult poem, surrounded by the foreign trappings of textual apparatus, and concerned with struggle that is never resolved at a psychological or aesthetic level by a hero who distances himself both from shared feelings and collective destiny.

Mill had also liked Wordsworth's landscapes, and his notice in *The London Review* (July 1835) praises Tennyson's *Poems, Chiefly Lyrical* (1833) for the poet's 'power of *creating* scenery, in keeping with some state of human feeling; so fitted to it as to be the embodied symbol of it, and to summon up the state of feeling itself, with a force not to be surpassed by anything but reality' (Mill I, p. 399). Unlike *Paracelsus* (1835) and *Sordello* (1840), which conjure up specific locations and historical settings, *Pauline*'s landscapes are marked by internalization in a way that defies the idea of a match between separate inner and outer worlds. The narrator's expansionist, incoherent self provides the terms to represent the poem's England and Switzerland, its rivers and hedgerows, its birds and insects. Scenery is more psychological than naturalistic. A similar distortion occurs in *Pauline*'s interpersonal relationships which dramatize a 'me' whose opacity comes from language rather than dense empirical being.

Mill's pencillings at the back of *Pauline* begin by associating poetic power with 'morbid self-consciousness' (Longman I, p. 17n.). His review of *Poems, Chiefly Lyrical* amplifies this criticism by explaining that the poetic temperament requires 'a philosophy' to accompany it or the poet risks becoming like Shelley. Feelings should be subordinated to systematic thought:

> Where the poetic temperament exists in its greatest degree, while the systematic culture of the intellect has been neglected, we may expect to find, what we do find in the best poems of Shelley – vivid representations of states of passive and dreamy emotion, fitted to give extreme pleasure to persons of similar organization to the poet, but not likely to be sympathized in, because not understood, by any other persons ... (Mill I, pp. 413–14)

It might be argued that literature can, precisely, produce sympathy with 'states of ... emotion ... not understood', which is why it is so advanced, so alluring and so risky in relation to other ways of knowing. However, Mill sets poetry in the context of human progress.

Organized understanding is crucial for Mill because 'the noblest end of poetry as a pursuit' consists of 'acting upon the desires and characters of mankind through their emotions, to raise them towards the perfection of their nature'. His psychological curiosity responds to the rhetorical uncertainty of the self in *Pauline*, hoping to find signs of progress. Browning never believed that poetry was improving to readers, nor did he idealize literary influence as a movement heading upward to perfection. The narrator of *Pauline* sets up a poetic exemplar, 'Sun-treader' (Shelley), but their relationship is complicated and ambivalent. Sun-treader enters the poem as an indicator of the later poet's own inner vitality. The self-scrutinizing (but not in Mill's sense self-analytic) narrator describes the clarity and significance he has begun to find in 'aught connected with my early life' (l. 137). The contemplation of his own juvenilia – 'rude songs or ... wild imaginings' – was instigated by 'the glow I felt at HIS award', a feeling which '[a]ssured me all was not extinct within' (ll. 138, 142–3). Beside this potentially confusing description of the admired earlier poet in terms of internal sensations and self-consciousness Mill asks 'what does this mean? His opinion of yourself? only at the fourth reading I found out what this meant' (Longman I, p. 35n.). Browning explains that the award was made by others to Shelley, writing in the margin: 'The award of fame to Him – The late acknowledgement of Shelley's genius.' In *Pauline* the public recognition of Sun-treader does not signify social progress, but a moment in the development of his disciple's sensibility.

Mill understands the poem's interest in the self merely as self-interest.

> He is evidently *dissatisfied*, and feels part of the badness of his state, but he does not write as if it were purged out of him – if he once could muster a hearty hatred of this selfishness, it would *go* – as it is, he feels only the *lack* of *good*, not the positive *evil*. He feels not remorse, but only disappointment.
>
> (Longman I, p. 17n.)

Mill makes no distinction between critical appraisal of Browning's poem and fault-finding in the character of its narrator. He and other reviewers certainly found things that did not please them. But despite the Preface's use of the same Latin verb ('securite legite'), to reassure the prudent reader that *Pauline* makes safe reading, as describes bees gathering honey from flowers ('melle legendo apes'), no one technique of extraction will work for this polyglot fragment. The linguistic work of translation out of Latin, medieval and modern French demands Swinburne's 'mind thoroughly alert, ... attention awake at all points, a spirit open and ready to be kindled by the contact of the writer's'.[28] And in such an open spirit the troubled progress of the narrative, its fragmentations and sudden shifts of mood and location produce such a variety of effects that the Latin preface's claim that the author was only telling these things to the reader seems disingenuous. Mill dismisses the preface: 'too much pretension in this motto.' The preface is about how to read and the effects of reading, suggesting that the pretensions of the self in the poem need not be taken literally. As the header to what Mill took for a 'psychological history', however, the preface overestimates the power of literature (Longman I, p. 17n.).

References to 'forbidden matters', 'the seeds of heresies' and the dangers of the book to biased, weak or hostile readers may have been appropriate for Cornelius Agrippa's treatise on magic, but where is the danger, Mill must have wondered, in reading a poem to find out about human nature? The preface insists that for some readers the poem is a threat: 'the gate of Acheron is in this book; it speaks stones – let them take heed that it beat not out their brains' (Longman I, p. 28n.). That is why 'some of a disordered judgement and some that are perverse ... may ... cry out ... that I teach forbidden [Arts], sow the seeds of heresies, offend the pious, and scandalize excellent wits'. The apparent paranoia of Browning's application of these terms to reading poetry draws attention to a dilemma for readers. Read the preface literally and it proposes an equation between the effects of poetic language and the unvarying outcome of magic spells; read it figuratively, in a spirit of dramatic sympathy, and the preface loses its framing status and gets drawn into the general aberration of the poem.

Expecting sincerity, Mill found parts of the poem lacking in genuine feeling. He was also left bewildered by the rapid transition from an outer landscape of hills, rocks, trees and hedges to the agonized questions 'Why have I girt myself with this hell-dress? / Why have I laboured to put out my life?' (ll. 831–2). 'Why should this follow the description of scenery?' Mill wrote in the margin, adding thirty lines later 'strange transition' beside the shift from a short verse-paragraph that vows allegiance to Shelley represented as Christ, and forswears 'all earth's reward' in exchange for the belief that the narrator is 'not unloved' to a section opening 'And now, my Pauline, I am thine forever' (l. 860).

Decentred consciousness

Mill does not recognize that the scenery and the flight through it with Pauline are also internal phenomena. The movement through time and space at will is the work of a consciousness that the poem has already explicitly described:

> I am made up of an intensest life,
> Of a most clear idea of consciousness
> Of a self – distinct from all its qualities
> From all affections, passions, feelings, powers;
> And thus far it exists, if tracked, in all . . .
>
> (ll. 268–72)

A creative and commanding 'centre' counters this tendency to be scattered and this need to be 'tracked'. The word describes the arduousness and uncertainty of following a Browning poem far better than the preface's classical comparison with a bee steadily gathering honey. Imagine pursuing something or someone only to discover that the distinction between one's quarry and its habitat has disappeared: one becomes the other. In *Pauline* the 'consciousness' Mill had hoped to find keeps merging with its settings (the times, the topography, the relationships, the reading: 'all'). Instead of a clear and familiar distinction between character and background, or in pictorial terms, figure and ground, the poem posits a sharp separation of the self from 'all its qualities, / From all affections, passions, feelings, powers'. The centre of self in this odd set-up is also the 'centre of all things' and has the absolute power to 'create and rule and call / Upon all things to minister to it': how, then, can the reader recognize this consciousness, except as a creative energy that ceaselessly invents itself in terms of – anything at all? There is no quest for stability in this chiasmus that links self-consciousness to consciousness of everything and existence to everything; it goes with 'a principle of restlessness / Which would be all, have, see, know, taste, feel, all – / This is myself' (ll. 277–9). *This is myself?*

Pauline is not one fragment, as the title suggests, but an ensemble of fragments. Imagination is what tries to hold it together. The poem claims that imagination can control the effects of time. There, according to the hero of *Pauline*, lies the power to protect his mind from surprise in the future, or to summon up the past and dismiss it at will. This single power is the poem's sole constancy, sometimes more palpable than the relationship with Pauline herself. It is

> the only [power]
> Which marks me – an imagination which
> Has been an angel to me – coming not
> In fitful visions, but beside me ever,
> And never failing me; so tho' my mind
> Forgets not – not a shred of life forgets –
> Yet I can take a secret pride in calling
> The dark past up – to quell it regally.
>
> (ll. 283–90)

From imagination comes an unrecognizable continuity, and from gazing on the mighty dead comes the narrator's conquest of death. Mill, longing for some conceptual stability, corrected the poem 'not imagination but *I*magination. The absence of the capital letter obscures the meaning' (Longman I, p. 43n.). Browning did not adopt the change; this imagination was singular. The relation to literary precursors is described in terms of a gaze which forms a kind of imma-terial connection between their works and the narrator's self.

> No fear was mine
> As I gazed on the works of mighty bards,
> In the first joy at finding my own thoughts
> Recorded, and my powers exemplified,
> And feeling their aspirings were my own.
>
> (ll. 384–8)

Mill found the poem's emphasis on 'me' repulsive because he read it as a psychic state of self-obsession. *Pauline* colonizes the self; there is no Imagination other than *my* imagination.

According to the restless principle of a self that exists in all, the survival of 'souls I'd keep for ever / In beauty' enables the triumph of the 'I' even as it withers unseen. For to 'feed their fame … from my heart's best blood' is to become them. What Browning calls love is a delight in exchange (withering for flourishing) that makes rivalry unnecessary:

Nought makes me trust in love so really,
As the delight of the contented lowness
With which I gaze on souls I'd keep for ever
In beauty – I'd be sad to equal them;
I'd feed their fame e'en from my heart's best blood,
Withering unseen, that they might flourish still.

(ll. 554–9)

Mill's remarks pursue the relation between author and work and his frustration reveals the severe limitations of readings of *Pauline* as autobiography. At the time when Fox sent him the poem to review Mill was much interested in the question 'What is Poetry?' – indeed he wrote an essay of that title for the *Monthly Repository* in January 1833 and another, called 'Two Kinds of Poetry', in October.[29] Fox must have hoped for a supportive notice. Mill ignores Browning's warning about the magical power of poetic language to transform the narrator's self and thereby to unsettle and fragment the reader who must track him. For Mill true poetry remains close to experience: poetic 'symbols' are 'the nearest possible representations of ... feeling' (Mill I, p. 348). Poetry articulates private emotion 'to oneself alone': but 'when the act of utterance is not itself an end, but a means to an end', that is merely eloquence (Mill, I, p. 349). The idea of poetry as an act of confession might be very attractive in this context, and Mill took *Pauline* to be a record of experience. Recording, even printing and publishing, do not betray the integrity of poetry as a non-public discourse: 'It may be said that poetry, which is printed on hot-pressed paper, and sold in a bookseller's shop, is soliloquy in full dress and upon the stage. But there is nothing absurd in the idea of such a mode of soliloquizing.'

Mill ignored those aspects of *Pauline* which insist that it is a textual '*Fragment*' with literary precedents. The character Pauline has no substance, his notes insist, and in the terms of 'What is Poetry?' the confession was merely an insincere rhetorical device. The address and date at the end of the poem 'Richmond./October 22, 1832' vex Mill: 'the transition from speaking to Pauline to writing a letter to the public with *place & date*, is quite horrible' (Longman I, p. 89n.). He was not to know that the place and date make a connection between the poem and its author's biography and are privately significant in terms of young Browning's plan to assume and realise a number of characters, all creative, by producing a variety of works. Richmond, 22 October, 1832 would mark the birth of the Poet character. In response to Mill Browning recounts the genesis of 'the childish scheme' to publish work in a variety of genres after he had seen the great actor Edmund Kean's inspiring performance as Richard III that October at Richmond. The reference to theatricals would hardly have dissipated Mill's antipathy to manipulative 'eloquence' where poetry had been expected.

Reading and knowledge

The poet's scheme demands readerly assent, and Mill's sometimes outraged and judgemental reading refuses to be persuaded into acceptance of the poem's strangeness. In *Pauline* itself an interesting passage describes the hero's early reading as a defence against shock. The passage claims that perception and feeling came to the poet-hero through reading and imagination rather than through experience. Sense and love

> came to me in my first dawn of life,
> Which passed alone with wisest ancient books,
> All halo-girt with fancies of my own,
> And I myself went with the tale – a god,
> Wandering after beauty, or a giant,
> Standing vast in the sunset – an old hunter,
> Talking with gods – or a high-crested chief
> Sailing with troops of friends to Tenedos; –
> I tell you, naught has ever been so clear
> As the place, the time, the fashion of those lives.
> I had not seen a work of lofty art,
> Nor woman's beauty, nor sweet nature's face,
> Yet, I say, never morn broke clear as those
> On the dim clustered isles in the blue sea,
> The deep groves, and white temples, and wet caves –
> And nothing ever will surprise me now –
> Who stood beside the naked Swift-footed,
> Who bound my forehead with Proserpine's hair.
>
> (ll. 318–35)

In *Pauline* Browning gives an account of initiation into a supernatural mode of knowledge which extends before and beyond ordinary time. This initiation could allow the novice, who had lived so little, to become a poet. For Mill such an account must be fallacious. The philosopher had firmly rejected Coleridge's claim that allegory and symbol could describe a truth independent of experience.

Mill's essay on Coleridge (1840) denies literature any such revelatory power:

> We see no ground for believing that anything can be the object of our knowledge except our experience, and what can be inferred from our experience by analogies of experience itself; nor that there is any idea, feeling, or power, in the human mind, which, in order to account for it, requires that its origin be referred to any other source.   (Mill X, pp. 128–9)

The passage on reading in *Pauline* does indeed idealize literature as a form of imaginative transcendence, in a move compatible with Browning's 'foolish plan' to win glory secretly by writing under pseudonyms. Mill's reading of the poem punctures the idealization for two reasons of different kinds. He declines to accept all the poem's 'wild thoughts' and adopts *Pauline*'s own strategy of fragmentation, claiming that a 'cento of most beautiful passages might be made from this poem'. Mill also read literally and the poem's content was often at odds with his own philosophical, aesthetic and ethical principles. The Poet in *Pauline* may have wanted to deny that reading was subject to time (to forgetting and surprise) but Mill refused to recognize the fictive temporality that allowed the Poet's 'sense that tho'' those shadowy times were past, / Their spirit dwelt in me' (ll. 342–3). Cleaving to an empirical and experiential notion of time Mill added in the margin 'What times? Your own imaginative times? Or the antique times themselves?'

The 'Essay on Shelley' (1852) returns to the rhetorical entanglement between imaginative times enclosed by the poet and the conflict-ridden time of reading. Browning uses the example of Homer and the Homerides to describe the broad influence of the imaginative moment of a seer-poet. Here he answers Mill's question about his own and antique times, indicating that the spirit of earlier work combines with later writing only to become prey again to time's revenges. There is no 'now' that allows the reader to enjoy the clarity of literature stretching into the future, guaranteeing no surprises:

> There is a time when the general eye ... desires rather to learn the exacter significance of what it possesses, than to receive any augmentation of what is possessed. Then is the opportunity for the

poet of loftier vision, to lift his fellows ... up to his own sphere, by intensifying the import of details and rounding the universal meaning. The influence of such an achievement will not soon die out. A tribe of successors (Homerides) working more or less in the same spirit, dwell on his discoveries and reinforce his doctrine; till, at unawares, the world is found to be subsisting wholly on the shadow of a reality, on sentiments diluted from passions, on the tradition of a fact, the convention of a moral, the straw of last year's harvest. Then is the imperative call for the appearance of another sort of poet ...

Intense vision easily becomes shadow, all it takes is time. It was to be one of Browning's fates that the audacity of his poetry was assimilated as 'doctrine'.

Mill's most frequent marginal comments were accusations of obscurity. The numerous minor revisions made by Browning for the 1888 edition of his works in an attempt to lay bare the poem's thought with dashes and exclamation marks or reordering of words do not make the poem much easier to read. The clarity and distinctness sorely missed by Mill and other readers do appear in *Pauline*, not as features of its style but as qualities of perception associated with the hero's lost youth. When the Poet longs to be young again, to retreat beyond the 'care and strife and toil' of later existence, he finds that only the trees and plants and birds by his former home 'seem *clear* and ... worth our thoughts' (Mill longingly underlined 'clear'). Whatever is 'connected with my early life' – poetry and 'imaginings' – becomes 'most distinct amid / The fever and the stir of after years!' (ll. 137–40). The illumination for this clarity comes from honouring Shelley; but the relations of influence are darker than this idealization by *Pauline*'s narrator suggests. There is no way back to youth or youth's home, lit by Shelley's renown spreading '[l]ike sunlight'. The hero retains only his nostalgia; he cannot return to the place that has become clear and distinct thanks to his precursor. The obscurity and confusion that tantalizes him and vexes Mill is part of the 'fever and stir' of poetic textuality which propels the poem towards its future. The phrase owes something to 'Tintern Abbey' (1798) where Wordsworth describes 'the fretful stir / Unprofitable, and the fever of the world'. The thought in this part of *Pauline* is Wordsworthian also, contrasting an absent landscape of youth with the current 'unintelligible world'. Yet Wordsworth does return to his 'dark sycamore', while Browning's beloved landscapes are almost always lost or phantasmic.

Peculiar property

In *Pauline* poetry is troped as 'song' and music has an exceptional power to counter the fixity of visual images. Its effect is supernatural, summoning 'dancing shapes' which can cross the boundaries between the world of the living and that of the dead. The references to a 'way' filled with 'shapes' and to 'life's path' are reminiscent of Shelley's *Triumph of Life* (1824). In one passage of that poem Rousseau's ghost describes a 'Shape all light' who scatters 'invisible rain' which 'did ever sing / A silver music on the mossy lawn' (ll. 352–5). For Browning also, music suggests an alien, ghostly authority:

> A low voice calling Fancy, as a friend,
> To the green woods in the gay summer time.
> And she fills all the way with dancing shapes,
> Which have made painters pale; and they go on
> While stars look at them, and winds call to them,
> As they leave life's path for the twilight world,
> Where the dead gather.
>
> (ll. 367–74)

Music in *Pauline* has a kind of autonomy, preceding the efforts of a musician: 'I in dream have seen / Music wait on a lyrist for some thought, / Yet singing to herself until it came' (ll. 377–9). This music without a lyrist, without thought, suggests the dream of an author-less, languageless and inarticulate poetry. Browning in his old age wrote to an aspiring untalented poet that his work lacked 'the little indefinable touch which makes each poem the peculiar property of the writer, – encloses, as it were, from the common utterance of youth and sensibility'.[30]

Enclosure is an important movement in *Pauline*, sought, promised but never quite achieved. The hero seeks shelter, from the first call to Pauline 'mine own, bend o'er me', to the flight ending in protective hedgerows, described late in the poem using terms that recall Wordsworth's 'Tintern Abbey'. The exhortation 'see how I could build / A home for us, out of the world, in thought!' asks us to see 'home' all over the place (ll. 729–30). Pauline is invited to fly with the narrator, not to settle with him. They move rapidly from night to morning to noon until they find not heights of exaltation but blind depth: 'Shut thy soft eyes – now look – still deeper in!' (l. 765). Is this 'in' inside or outside the eye? In the woods a small pool undoes the opposition between depth and surface, land and water: 'but one – / One thin clear sheet has over-leaped and wound / Into this silent depth, which gained, it lies / Still, as but let by sufferance' (ll. 769–72). The thin clear sheet suggests a blank sheet of paper which has ambitiously 'overleaped' and deviously 'wound' to reach a place where it does not belong. 'Wound' and 'sufferance' also hint at a traumatic penetration into the 'very heart of the woods' (l. 766). The sheet of water is alien to what surrounds it, and it 'lies / Still' like a beautiful blank scar, imitating the silence of the beautiful enclosed scene into which it has broken and tricked its way. For a moment before it 'rejoins its parent river with a shout' the thin clear sheet represents writing as peculiar property, alien to the natural world, alien to the heart, a haunting stillness (l. 780).

Pauline's hero rises 'a few miles above' the scenes he describes and emphasizes distance and space as the old woods 'part, like a ruined arch, – the sky! / Nothing but sky appears, so close the roots / And grass of the hill-top level with the air' (ll. 782–4). In this space floats an extraordinary far-fetched simile that brings to view something foreign and familiar, at once beautifully freighted with light and a huge rotting piece of carrion. The passage takes up a moment in *Hamlet* when Polonius tries to humour the prince by agreeing with his interpretation of the shape of a cloud. Hamlet has just accused Guildenstern of trying to manipulate him: 'You would play upon me; you would seem to know my stops; you would pluck out the heart of my mystery.' Hamlet then leads Polonius by the nose through versions of the cloud as a camel and a weasel, and finally Polonius assents that it looks 'very like a whale' (*Hamlet*, Act III, Scene II). The heart of Hamlet's mystery remains hidden from Guildenstern and Polonius. Their interpretations leave the core of the play untouched and Hamlet parodies their attempts to understand him. It is also thus with *Pauline*. The poem demands resistance rather than assent from its readers; it reads against the grain. Wordsworth's understated lonely cloud of imaginative vision in 'Daffodils' (1807) has become a great luminous deathly mass, hyperbolically satirizing Browning's great Romantic precursor and the lesser poetic talents that feed off his work: 'Blue sunny air, where a great cloud floats, laden / With light, like a dead whale that white birds pick, / Floating away in the sun in some north sea' (ll. 785–7).

In *Pauline* Browning uses the language of self-consciousness and the technique of fragmentation to float his literary career. The assistance of Fox and his aunt Silverthorne's loan were essential, but the poem also negotiates the question of its status as property. It is and remains in Pauline's phrase a 'singular production', yet it belongs to Browning: in 1847 Dante Gabriel Rossetti read the poem in the British Library, admired it greatly and used his knowledge of *Paracelsus* to work out who had written it. Mill's hostile reading of *Pauline*, his refusal to read it according to the peripheral instructions of preface, motto and French annotation by 'Pauline' herself was only the first of a series of critical misprisions visited upon Browning for good and ill throughout his career.

   Sordello, in which he explicitly addresses the causes and effects of misunderstanding on a poet's mind, was subject to the most persistent and crudely revealing incomprehension. Browning's *Prelude* defies simplification and takes the fragmentary arrangement of Pauline to a point where readers no longer found the poem's hero mad, but questioned their own sanity.

2
Sordello and the Reviewers

Taking pains

From 1834 until 1838 Browning repeatedly wrote to friends that the poem was nearly done: 'You will see Sordello in a trice, if the fagging-fit holds' he told Fanny Haworth, two years before publication.[1] The preface to *Paracelsus* (1835) had promised that the next poem would emerge in 'a more popular, and perhaps less difficult form'. Fifteen years after publication Browning still hoped that *Sordello*'s difficulty for readers could be got over by more hard work from him. The poem was 'my best performance hitherto: I am not without evidence that the good of it is to be got at even now by the pains-taking, – and I hope & believe that, by myself taking proper pains in turn, – I shall make the good obtainable at a much easier rate'.[2] The promised major revisions did not happen but this chapter will explore Browning's association of the poem with pain that is not incidental but 'proper' to a poet's work. *Sordello* is set in Lombardy in the late twelfth and early thirteenth centuries. Sordello grows up in seclusion at Goito, bereaved and disinherited, in a state violently at war with itself, Guelfs versus Ghibellins. He turns to poetry as a form of self-expression and happens to hear the bard Eglamor perform at a 'Court of Love'. Sordello delivers an inspired improvisation which gets him the job of minstrel to the lady Palma at Mantua. He suffers pain from poetry where he expected pleasure: his audience disregards his wish to reveal himself through his work. He spends a year in retirement at Goito and then Palma declares her love for him and her plan that he become the leader of the Ghibellin party in Lombardy. They go to Ferrara, where the horrors of a siege shock Sordello. He resolves to help the people, and realizes that he cannot provide any quick political solutions. He tries to persuade the Ghibellin leader, Taurello Salinguerra, to go over to the more progressive Guelfs. It is revealed that Sordello is in fact Taurello's son and Taurello offers him the leadership of the Ghibellins, but this would mean betrayal of the Multitude. Sordello dies trying to decide how best to exercise his responsibility towards them. Why so much pain in these 'incidents in the development of a soul' (Longman I, p. 353n.)?

Early critical responses to *Sordello* were not interested in taking pains. But they are vexed by the poem's unintelligibility, to which they refer in metaphors of baffled sensory perception and physical incoherence. The *Athenaeum* complains of: 'the impenetrable veil, both of manner and language, in which [Browning] has contrived to wrap up whatever truths or beauties this volume, may contain' and advises that if Browning's Muse 'would be appreciated by understandings of this earth, she must keep somewhere or other on this side of the clouds'.[3] *The Monthly Chronicle*'s hopes are dashed: 'We opened "Sordello" ... with the most pleasurable anticipations, and closed it with the most painful disappointment, after reading patiently through the six books, still hoping – still deceived.'[4] The reviewer finds the poem 'dull to sleepiness' and speculates 'Mr Browning seems to have forgotten that the medium of art must ever be the *beautiful*; he seems to be totally indifferent to pleasing our imaginations and fancy by the music of verse and thoughts, by the grace of his diction as well as his imagery'. He finds 'a positive want of dramatic or speculative interest in the story, and a by no means new or newly put moral'. One review in particular is interesting for its literal approach: it was also the most hostile. *The Spectator* says:

> Whatever may be the poetical spirit of Mr. Browning, it is so overlaid in Sordello by digression, affectation, obscurity, and all the faults that spring, it would seem, from crudity of plan and a self-opinion which will neither cull thoughts nor revise composition, that the reader – at least a reader of our stamp – turns away.[5]

Rather than agree or disagree with these responses, we might ask to what in the poem they are responding.

All but two 1840 reviews of *Sordello* lament its flawed narrative and careless composition. The majority of early critics expected Browning to make the poem's mixture of psychological development and historical drama appear more clearly to the reader. One reviewer took a different approach and tried to imagine how the reading mind should be in order to cope with *Sordello*. In 1842 Richard Hengist Horne's admiring review in *The Church of England Quarterly* compares it to *Julian and Maddalo, Endymion* and *Prometheus Unbound*. He also warns: 'It abounds in things addressed to a second sight, and we are often required to *see double* in order to apprehend its meaning. The poet may be considered the Columbus of an impossible discovery.'[6] Could the painfulness of reading *Sordello* be related to this doubleness of an impossible discovery? Is it this that makes readers turn away?

In 1845, five years after publication, Elizabeth Barrett wrote to Browning that *Sordello* was 'like a noble picture with its face turned to the wall just now – or at least, in the shadow'.[7] It wanted 'drawing together & fortifying in the connections and associations .. which hang as loosely every here and there, as those in a dream, & confound the reader who persists in thinking himself awake'. Her description sets the poem up as in need of additions to become a coherent story: 'such a work as it might become if you chose .. if you put your will to it –!' She may not have remembered that Sordello's 'Will' fails to communicate itself to his audience at Mantua: 'every time / He gained applause by any given rhyme / His auditory recognized no jot / As he intended . . . / His Will . . . conceive it caring for his Will!' (II, ll. 621–7). And later in the poem, when it appears to run out of steam, the narrator laments that he is less determined than Sordello and needs some inspiration:

> I sung this on an empty palace-step
> At Venice: why should I break off, nor sit
> Longer upon my step, exhaust the fit
> England gave birth to? Who's adorable
> Enough reclaim a – no Sordello's Will
> Alack! – be queen to me?
>
> (III, ll. 659–61)

He finds a ghost to be his queen, a 'care-bit erased / Broken up' beauty who, as Betty Miller notices, prefigures Elizabeth Barrett's worn physical charm. The 'sad disheveled ghost' typifies mankind in a form that takes the narrator's taste. *Sordello* continues thanks to the narrator's surrender to spectral inspiration. Elizabeth Barrett's advice to Browning to use his will to correct the poem's dreamlike quality misses the point that *Sordello*'s poetics don't attempt to establish continuous lines of communication between the poem and its audience. The poem is constantly aware that creativity comes fitfully and is marked by a step out of one reality into another. The poem's relation to its reader is founded on states of loss, suffering, ruin, breakdown, along the lines of Sordello's sympathy with the People: 'what else could knit/Him theirs but Sorrow?' (VI, ll. 249–50).

'The unwritten *every-other-line*'

In February 1856 Browning himself also told the American publisher James Fields that he would work on the poem for a projected American edition: 'I shall make it as easy as its nature admits, I believe – changing nothing and simply *writing in* the unwritten *every-other-line* which I stupidly left as an amusement for the reader to do.'[8] This is a departure from the poetics of *Paracelsus*, which depends on chasms in the poem which are to be supplied by the reader's cooperative imagination (see Chapter 7). It also contradicts the important argument about the ellipses in his poetry in a letter to Ruskin written just three months before Browning promised Fields to put in the 'unwritten every-other-line'. This exchange is discussed more fully in Chapter 5, but here it suffices to quote Browning's injunction to Ruskin: 'You ought, I think, to keep pace with the thought tripping from ledge to ledge of my "glaciers", as you call them; not stand poking your alpenstock into the holes, and demonstrating that no foot could have stood there; – suppose it sprang over there?'[9] It seems that Browning wavered between agreeing with his muse Elizabeth Barrett that *Sordello* could be made easier to read, and feeling that its nature was to be difficult and its relation to the reader must demand some crevasse-leaping and double vision.

During this period Browning annotated *Sordello*. His marginalia make repeated reference to 'mesmerism' which is a name for Sordello's (unsuccessful) occult method of achieving the kind of mental dominion which the Poet in *Pauline* wants at times. Sordello's story is not intended to exemplify the proper course of poetic development for the poem's audience. In fact in Book II Sordello's grand dreams and theories articulate the deluded imaginative condition of a young poet who confuses poetic achievement with the effortless transmission of his own inner states to others and their recognition of his power:

> Perceive
> What I could do, a mastery believe,
> Asserted and established to the throng
> By their selected evidence of Song

> Which now shall prove whate'er they are, or seek
> To be, I am – who take no pains to speak,
> Change no old standards of perfection, vex
> With no strange forms created to perplex,
> But mean perform their bidding and no more ...
>   (II, ll. 429–37)

Sordello subsequently experiences his poetry's refusal to be used in this facile way. The Mantuans make their own use of it. At the level of the reception of Browning's poem, reader after reader testified that to 'hear Sordello's story told' was no easier than Browning's long task of writing suggests. The poem was not a means of mesmeric emotional identification and did not adjust itself automatically to readers' limited capacities: 'At their own satiating-point give o'er' (II, l. 438). Reading *Sordello* remains exhausting work. No reader moving through the whole piece could miss the irony of the sentence that indicates Sordello's naively lazy preference for poetry over heroic feats: 'Song, not Deeds/(For we get tired) was chosen' (II, ll. 440–1). What remains afterwards, according to the last lines of the poem, is the strangest of memorials, the pungent animal smell left by a vanished ghost.

Apparitions of language

Sordello is sceptical about its hero's ambitions towards poetic mesmerism, but its narration is full of apparitions. Browning's phantoms and angels characterize powers of poetic textuality that cannot be understood in terms of perception. They may point to truth, but as figurations and inventions they are not self-evidently authentic. Apparitions produce strong effects on those who see them, but they need thinking about in the context of language, signs and names rather than in terms of their immediate impact – terrifying or delightful. Book One is narrated to a ghostly audience, interrupted by a frightening spirit until Verona 'appears' suddenly through the shattered crust of the Past, and later the narrator's rhymes themselves are compared to 'an escape of angels' (I, l. 883). In Book Two Sordello's characters are compared to angels that escape from his language. Book Three resumes thanks to a disheveled and ghostly muse. Book Four gives Sordello a phantom Rome to typify 'the scheme to put mankind/Once more in full possession of their rights' (IV, ll. 992–3). In Book Five Sordello ponders the 'apparition i' the midst' of the human crowd of a 'thousand phantasms' who would typify them all effectively for political purposes (V, ll. 119, 114). These apparitions defy the mode of perception that Victorian reviewers and Elizabeth Barrett use to describe and reduce the act of reading. They are there and not there, from the start blank, ruined, rejected or phantasmic.

When the poem represents interpretative activity as making something present and complete it is in the context of mystification and delusion. In the singing contest at the Court of Love Sordello supplies 'each foolish gap and chasm' left in a song by Eglamor, then, winning, falls into a trance (II, l. 73). He never understands what has happened, but afterwards weaves theories of telepathic communication and godlike poetic power to explain and assimilate the victory. Sordello finds in Book Two that 'Perceptions whole' may reject 'so pure a work of thought / As Language' (II, ll. 590–1). It is only in Book Five, when Sordello briefly abandons poetry for action so that 'within his soul / Perceptions brooded unexpressed and whole', that he can digest what he perceives: ''Tis Knowledge, whither such perceptions tend; / They lose themselves in that, means to an end' (V, ll. 435–6, 443–4).

Still, *Sordello* is a poem, and the lesson of Book Two prevails as Sordello addresses Salinguerra with fine words about Life and Men: poetic language is incompatible with knowledge, it is an apparition which defies absorption into the minds that entertain it. The castle-building becomes an increasingly grandiose frenzy; Sordello offers to

> ... unveil the last of mysteries
> I boast! Man's life shall have yet freer play:
> Once more I cast external things away
> And Natures, varied now, so decompose
> That ... but enough!
>
> (V, ll. 596–600)

Despite Sordello's plan to inspire mankind to advance by completing his 'half-words', poetry is not the 'dim vulgar vast unobvious work' that would assuage the 'dim vulgar vast unobvious grief' of the crowd (VI, ll. 153, 149). Like *Sordello*'s other apparitions, poetry brings surprise and resists assimilation into the perceptible world; more – it decomposes the nature of the reader. Sordello's 1863 dedicatee Joseph Milsand, author of an important article on Browning in the *Revue Contemporaine* (September 1856), used the term *étonnement*, 'un sentiment pénible pour les hommes', to describe the effect of Browning's work.[10]

Reading and love

The revised version of *Sordello* in the *Poetical Works* of 1863 was dedicated to Milsand, and the dedication insists on the vocabulary of feeling. It would falsify Browning's poetics to reduce them to rules when they are so frequently articulated in terms of hate and love, as well as being discussed in the context of impassioned human relationships. Reading is not merely a matter of the author's faultless expression:

> Dear Friend, – Let the next poem be introduced by your name, and so repay all trouble it ever cost me. I wrote it twenty-five years ago for only a few, counting even in these on somewhat more care for its subject than they really had. My own faults of expression were many; but with care for a man or a book such would be surmounted, and without it what avails the faultlessness of either?
>
> (Longman I, p. 353n.)

Love mattered to Browning the poet as a way of sustaining the seclusion of writing. An audience of lovers was his alternative to a judgemental public of strangers. A letter to his friend Domett who had surmised that in *Sordello* Browning was 'difficult on system' emphasizes the effects of the solitude of composition. A readership of lovers could be inscribed in the poem as part of its inspiration, but Browning acknowledged the limits of his control. When the poem ends it must face twice as many strangers as angelic friends. Publication 'is not confined' to the generous imaginary readers required for composition, and *Sordello* becomes, willy-nilly, part of a world outside its own dramatizations. Enter Stokes and Nokes, characters inspired by Sidney's *Apology for Poetry* (1595):[11]

> The fact is I live by myself, write with no better company, and forget that the 'lovers' you mention are part & parcel of that self, and their choosing to comprehend *my* comprehensions – but an indifferent testimony to their value: whence it happens, that precisely when 'lovers,' one and all, bow themselves out at the book's conclusion ... enter (according to an old stage-direction) two fishermen to the one angel, Stokes and Nokes to the Author of 'Venice' [Domett himself] (who *should* have been there, *comme de droit*, had I known him earlier), and ask, reasonably enough, why the publication is not confined to the aforesaid brilliant folks, and what do hard boards and soft paper solicit if not *their* intelligence, such as it may be?[12]

Browning is saying that what *Sordello* solicits is intelligent love which makes the reader 'part and parcel of' his writing self. No account of Browning's difficulty can be complete without the reminder that more than intelligence is being required. Browning wrote to an admirer in 1868 'I am heartily glad I have your sympathy for what I write. Intelligence, by itself, is scarcely the thing with respect to a new book – as Wordsworth says (a little altered), "you must like it before it be worthy of your liking."'[13]

The mutual solicitation of the solitary disheveled ghost and the solitary poet in Book Three of *Sordello* figures the anticipatory liking that reading requires. The poet must 'Slouch bonnet, unloop mantle, careless go, / Alone (that's saddest but it must be so) / Through Venice' to find her (III, ll. 733–5). Their solitude is opposed to the togetherness of the crowd or the indifferent reading public, and to the stance of the critic who stands in judgement over what he reads. Browning's comic sketch of Stokes watching one of his plays in the letter to Domett quoted above strongly contrasts with *Sordello*'s recommendation of loosened clothes. Stokes is wrapped up against the play:

> I see *him* – (first row of the pit, under the second Oboe, hat between legs, play-bill on a spike, and a 'comforter' round his throat 'because of the draught from the stage'–) and unless *he* leaves off sucking his orange at the pathetic morsels of my play – I hold them nought.

The critic's chilly indifference is a challenge to Browning. His plays 'shall be plain enough if my pains are not thrown away'.

Poetry and fear

In *Sordello* surprise can come as wonder as well as alarm. Palma's relation with Sordello is characterized by pleasurable shock and intensity: her first sight of him leaves her eyes 'bluer with surprise' (I, l. 756). The poem has passages of startling beauty. But uncomfortable strangeness occurs far more often in the poem and in its relation to the reader. In *Pauline* Browning produced an internally fragmented text. *Sordello* repeatedly dramatizes the break-up of one poetic world by another. Right from the start sudden fear surfaces to shock the narrator. He, '[m]otley on back and pointing-pole in hand', seems at first oriented exclusively to communicating with his audience of living admirers and dead poets reduced to the safe status of 'Friends' and brothers

(I, ll. 30–1, 54). But when he tries to conjure the apparition of Verona he loses control of the occasion. A spirit cuts in:

> Then, appear,
> Verona! stay – thou, spirit, come not near
> Now – nor this time desert thy cloudy place
> To scare me, thus employed, with that pure face!
> I need not fear this audience, I make free
> With them, but then this is no place for thee!
>
> (I, ll. 59–64)

Pauline bargained with such eruptions, using idolization to keep influence in its exalted place. *Sordello*'s project opposes idealization at every turn, and actually dares to dramatize the overthrow of the author's plans – in Sordello, in the fictional narrator with his pointing-pole, and even, during Book Three, in the author himself, suffering a touch of writer's block in Venice. We find each of them at moments unable to go on. Here at the beginning of the poem the spirit comes from an indistinct 'cloudy' place to disrupt the appearance of Verona and keep the narrative in its theatrical starting-place and explanatory mode. Unlike the orderly rows of living and dead poets ('they sit, each ghostly man / Striving to look as living as he can, / Brother by breathing brother;' I, ll. 49–51) the terrible apparition has a face unmarked by the effort to look lifelike. It is hard to recognize what is so terrifying about the purity of its face. It is associated with the pure white light of lyric poetry that Browning told Elizabeth Barrett he feared, and the 'great light, a whole one' of inspiration. There is also a flicker of Shelley's 'To a Skylark' (1820): 'Hail to thee, blithe Spirit! / Bird thou never wert' with its quietly disturbing assurance that if the poet learned from the skylark 'Such harmonious madness / From my lips would flow / The world should listen then – as I am listening now.' Even without the help of the headnotes added for the collected editions of 1863 and 1868, the pure face, radiance of lyric and poetic inspiration, all point to Shelley, who once told John Gisborne: 'you might as well go to a gin shop for a leg of mutton as expect anything human or earthly from me!'[14]

The narrator defends himself in the half-seduced inverted syntax that Faustus uses at the end of Marlowe's play: 'Ugly hell gape not, come not *Lucifer*, / Ile burne my bookes, ah Mephastophilis!' (*Dr Faustus* (1604), Scene XIII). Browning tells the apparition, who seems to be about to destroy this book, to 'stay,' 'come not near / Now', 'not this time desert thy cloudy place'. Verona appears, 'a darkness' to counter the Shelleyan luminosity, or keep it imprisoned 'at the core' of Browning's dramatic many-surfaced poem:

> Lo, the Past is hurled
> In twain: upthrust, out-staggering on the world,
> Subsiding into shape, a darkness rears
> Its outline, kindles at the core, appears
> Verona.

> (I, ll. 73–7)

In Book Three Sordello's thoughts return to the apparatus of core and surface that characterized the time-disfiguring appearance of Verona. He resolves to become sovereign but his thoughts emphasize not the concord and unity this might bring but the separateness of the reigning core from the crust, the people. He would bring life and unity despite the risk that 'he should live, a centre of disgust / Even, apart, core of the outward crust / He vivifies, assimilates' (III, ll. 543–5). Sordello is politically naive, of course, to think that he would give life to those he ruled. The poem teaches about the impossibility of assimilation, the necessity of apartness. This is not experiential wisdom but brought about by the poem's language.

'Break / O' the consciousness'

Sordello and Browning constantly diverge in the poem as the work reflects upon and reiterates the adventures of a developing soul. Therefore when a theory of continuity between poet and poem is prefaced: 'Sordello said once' (III, l. 599) or 'In just such songs as, Eglamor (say) wrote' there is no justification for reading what follows as Browning's own belief (III, l. 600). On the contrary, poetic theories are not to be taken literally in a poem that reveals in its central character the impossibility of joining literary creativity and non-literary experience in a transcendental theory of poetry and life. But what does this passage say about the man and work? Eglamor, the vanquished rival who did not survive defeat at the Court of Love, is the poet of complete song. There you 'judge the song and singer One / And either purpose answered, his in it / Or its in him' (III, ll. 604–6). What the poem calls 'true works' (an ironic parenthesis explains 'to wit / Sordello's dream-performances that will / Be never more than dream'), by their gaps and flaws show 'a passion and a knowledge far / Transcending' what they actually articulate (III, ll. 606–8, 611–12). This reverses Sordello's retrospective interpretation of his winning performance as a matter of supplying the gaps and chasms in Eglamor's song 'Elys'. Sordello now fantasizes a rapt audience watching for 'evidence' as he plays, 'some slight weariness, a looking-off / Or start-away. The childish skit or scoff' which would prove to them the continuity of life before and beyond literature (III, ll. 615–16). Sordello wants to believe that the traces of poetry are visible breaks of concentration, not startling breaks of consciousness.

When a break of consciousness interrupts Book Three, a spirit comes to the rescue. Politics and authorship come together in a strange muse, 'the sad disheveled ghost' that plucks at the poet (III, l. 674). Browning wrote to Fanny Haworth, who had asked him to explain the lines addressed to her beginning 'My English Eyebright, if you are not glad / That, as I stopped my task awhile, the sad / Disheveled form . . . / Renewed me . . . (III, ll. 941–5):

> 'What are you to be glad of?' Why that as I stopped my task awhile, left off my versewriting one sunny June day with a notion of not taking to it again in a hurry, the sad disheveled form I had just been talking of, that plucked and pointed, where in I put, comprize, typify and figure to myself Mankind, the whole poor-devildom one sees cuffed and huffed from morn to midnight, that, so typified, she may come at times and keep my pact in mind, prick up my republicanism, and remind me of certain engagements I have entered into with myself about that same, renewed me, gave me fresh spirit, made me after finishing Book 3d commence Book 4th, what is involved here?[15]

She 'may come at times', this disfigured reminder of republican sympathies: is she not the fragmented reflex of the spirit of radical Shelley who was told 'come not now' in Book One? What inhibits as a pure phenomenon inspires as a disfigured one: 'care-bit, erased / Broken-up beauties ever took my taste / Supremely' (III, ll. 721–3). Shelley was told that disaster would strike the poem 'wert thou to hear': the sad ghost is instructed to 'hear / Me out' (III, ll. 745–6). And bringing this antithetical breaking-up to the level of words, the epithet 'disheveled' is a disheveled version of the precursor's name.

The sad ghost's face and body are broken up, as the pure light of lyric is 'broken into prismatic hues' in Browning's account of his own poetry.[16] As a ghost her very being is a lie or symbol in which 'form' claims to represent the 'Life' of Venice or the political convictions of a living author. What the poet in *Sordello* knows is that the 'secret' of finding the ghost (or of letting her find you, as the 1863–88 text has it) lies in deception and disguise. 'Rough apparel' and a hesitant style like Sordello's might lure her: 'sing now and now glance aside' (III, ll. 730, 735). This must refer to Browning's way of writing in *Sordello*. The ghost represents language's figurative power, its resources of indirectness and disguise: the poet cannot clothe her in life. He must become elusive, solitary and ragged like her until it is uncertain which has priority over the other. Which has something to give the other? Alms and inspiration are not like proper gifts: the poet asks the form, asks Shelley, asks poetry: 'whom but you / Dare I bestow your own upon?' (III, ll. 744–5). This is a political question about the distribution of resources, but only because it was primarily a creative question. Browning's poetry is addressed to ghosts who influence it, it is written so as to discompose and dishevel the reading mind into a ghostly state. The audience of lovers, those who are not dead poets already, must be astonished out of themselves, dissolved.

3
Drama, Macready and Dramatic Poetry

In the 1840s Browning characterized the imaginative space where he worked in terms of what it excluded. He told his friend Alfred Domett that to write he needed 'partial retirement and stopping the ears against noise outside' or – Domett had recently emigrated – a metaphoric version of *'going to New Zealand'*.[1] Writing required that he should leave himself behind and undertake a private emigration into what Browning called at about this time a poetry 'always dramatic in principle' (Penguin I, p. 347 n. 3).[2] This chapter maps Browning's creative development as he abandoned the form of the early narratives and moved through playwriting to his first experiments with dramatic lyric and dramatic romance, his names for the forms that sustained his most intense poetic achievement from *Bells and Pomegranates* through *Men and Women, Dramatis Personae, Pacchiarotto and How He Worked in Distemper* to the *Dramatic Idyls* (1879 and 1880) and some poems in the last collection, *Asolando*. Browning's relations with the actor-manager William Macready provide a chance to explore the workings of sympathy and drama in Browning's literary life.[3]

Passing identifications

Drama inspired young Browning: Edmund Kean's performance of Richard III moved him to begin writing *Pauline*. Kean's Richard had been deeply admired by Keats, Byron and Hazlitt late in the Regency, but the actor was now capable of his former grandeur only in 'bursts'.[4] *Pauline* cultivates a 'wondrous sympathy' for all sorts of life-forms, and thus dramatizes a self that is outside or beside itself. Mill, expecting a central character who knew who he was, found the poem disturbing. What is 'a poetry always dramatic in principle'? It challenges the idea that one can know who one is, that one can find oneself, in relation to a poem or a play. It was the play of identifications in dramatic performance that interested Browning. A great tragedian like Kean or Macready appropriated Richard III or Othello by losing himself in the alien life, the language, of the character, and inviting the audience to come out of itself also. It seems to have been tragedy, the dramatic form that draws sympathy closest to the obliteration of the self in suffering, madness and death, that especially attracted Browning in the theatre.

His three early narratives are also in their way tragedies in which the central character with whom other characters and the reader identify suffers and dies. Various tendencies oppose the determinism of form in each poem. In *Paracelsus*, for instance, Browning wrote a dramatic poem that had to meet the 'sympathy and intelligence' of the reader in order to come into being. That poem's preface puts the reader on stage, and makes reading a drama in its own right. But only with *Pippa Passes: A Drama* (1841) did Browning begin to find a way for his title characters to survive.

Pippa is a silk-weaver, but not on the day of the poem. It is her holiday from being Pippa: 'am I not, this day, / Whate'er I please? What shall I please today?' (ll. 104–5). The poem is not interested in the development of Pippa's soul, which is unremarkable for powers of sympathy or insight. She does, however, have a sense of responsibility to the 'choices or ... chances' of her day, and a sense of that day's particular responsibility to her. She addresses it anxiously: 'for, Day, my holiday, if thou ill-usest / Me, who am only Pippa, – old-year's sorrow, / Cast off last night, will come again tomorrow' (ll. 31–2). She does not plan to spend the day as herself, she plans to identify with the four happiest people in Asolo: 'I may fancy all day – and it shall be so – / That I taste of the pleasures, am called by the names / Of the Happiest Four in our Asolo!' (ll. 111–13). She decides 'I am no less than Ottima, take warning!' then thinks of the couple Jules and Phene, asking 'Why should I not be the bride as soon / As Ottima?' then wonders 'what prevents / My being Luigi?' (ll. 116, 133–4, 166–7). Ruskin complained that 'Every now and then poor Pippa herself shall speak a long piece of Robert Browning.'[5] Pippa is also like Browning in her preparedness, her need on this day, to be other than herself. She is spared the inner conflict that preoccupies the protagonists of the early narratives; the poem's tragic elements lie in the stories of each of the characters Pippa passes (all their futures seem blighted and Ottima, Sebald and probably Luigi will die). Pippa has a confident faith in God and the future despite her closeness to terrible things. Her passing is a passing by, through and on, not a passing away.

The relative failure of Browning's plays in performance opens the way to great dramatic poems which stage evasion, deflection and various shifty devices associated with 'poetry, make believe / And the white lies that it sounds like' (*The Ring and the Book* I, ll. 455–6). Victorian theatre did not respond to Browning's exploration of psychological and poetic difficulty. After he had finished with the stage, in the 1850s, he clearly knew that in order to write he needed imaginary readers who might engage with complex *textual* staging. Browning understood himself as a writer for imagined audiences made up of living and dead lovers of literature. His poems are responsive to pressures inherent in poetic language; they were not made primarily to communicate with a contemporary audience. Yet he also wished to experiment with new, real audiences. The advertisement in *Pippa Passes* introduces the cheap pamphlet series known as *Bells and Pomegranates* with this thought:

> Two or three years ago I wrote a Play [*Strafford*], about which the chief matter I much care to recollect at present is, that a Pit-full of goodnatured people applauded it: – ever since, I have been desirous of doing something in the same way that should better reward their attention. What follows I mean for the first of a series of Dramatical Pieces, to come out at intervals, and I amuse myself by fancying that the cheap mode in which they appear will for once help me to a sort of Pit-audience again.
>
> (Penguin I, p. 1070n.)

Browning did not offer *Pippa Passes* to Macready and risk '"mettre du gêne [putting constraint]" in a friendship which I trust I know how to appreciate, by compelling you once more to say "No", where you would willingly say "Yes."'[6] Macready had already turned down *King Victor and King Charles* and *The Return of the Druses*. The plays were too complex and elusive, too ravelled in inwardness, for the immediacy of dramatic performance as Victorian production, embodied in Macready, could conceive of it.

Elizabeth Barrett wrote to Browning about the limited resources of the modern theatre in 1845, when Browning's career as a stage dramatist was virtually over:

> You are not to think that I . . . ever thought of exhorting you to give up the 'solemn robes' & tread of the buskin. It is the theatre which

vulgarizes these things ... And also, I have a fancy that your great dramatic power would work more clearly & audibly in the less definite mould.[7]

Strafford, and Browning's vexed dealings with the actor-manager William Macready show how Browning's dramatic experiments clarified the different resources of dramatic poetry. The early dramatic lyric, 'The Laboratory' (1844), is a specimen of a major change in Browning's work. First, however, are some thoughts on the relation of drama to composition from Henry James.

Henry James on Browning and dramatization

James knew the older Browning as a London figure and he pays the poet two critically impressive tributes, the memorial oration 'Browning in Westminster Abbey' (1890) and the centenary address 'The Novel in *The Ring and the Book*' (1912) (for discussion of these see my Introduction and Chapter 6). The tale 'The Private Life' and its preface (1893) dramatize the personal confusion Browning causes James. He is faced by the emphatically ordinary, certain, social Browning and still remains perturbingly conscious of the extraordinariness of the poetry. The lack of correspondence between public life and the 'life' of poetry is a major theme in Browning, who in his writing, if not in his confident, cheerful social persona, goes ahead of James as a researcher into this area. The early narratives *Pauline*, *Paracelsus* and *Sordello* take the forms of confession and historical biography and infuse them with the vitality that comes from poetic language rather than from life itself. This vitality often appears in particular relation to death. Death in each of the early poems is a narrative culmination and a form of triumph: the poet in *Pauline* promises 'I shall be / Prepared', not to live, but to die (ll. 974–5). Paracelsus welcomes death as reunion with the dead poet Aprile and the chance for a future purged of error. Sordello dies with a 'triumph lingering in the wide eyes' rather than choose between his poetic and political vocations (VI, l. 613).

The preface to 'The Private Life' tells of a voice prompting James to change his narrative of self-regarding fascinated bewilderment over Browning by transforming it into a literary conceit: 'Dramatise it! Dramatise it!'[8] The genesis of his story is a 'wondering sense' of discrepancy between Browning's personality and his genius. He sees the poet as an ordinary man haunted by his own creative spirit. For

James it was Browning's peculiarity 'to bear out personally as little as possible (at least to *my* wondering sense) the high denotements, the rich implications and rare associations, of the genius to which he owed his position and renown' (p. xiii). James's research into Browning's personality and literature also explores the effects of personality in his own writing. Indeed, he suggests in the preface that even one's own writing is foreign territory. Writing can unsettle the enigmas that composition was intended to clarify, and resist being appropriated by the author's consciousness:

> I find myself so fondly return to ground on which the history even of small experiments may be more or less written. This mild documentation fairly thickens for me, I confess, the air of the [tale]; the scraps of records flit through that medium, to memory, as with the incalculable brush of wings of the imprisoned bat at eventide.
>
> (p. xii)

James's experiment is a dramatization, which apparently moves a creative predicament into a figurative creation. The preface progresses from the initial attempts of a personality to understand what precisely lies beyond the limits of personal experience: '*my* wondering sense', 'one's own applied measure', repeatedly asking question of 'myself':

> One may go, naturally, in such a connexion, by one's own applied measure; and I have never ceased to ask myself, in this particular loud, sound, normal, hearty presence, all so assertive and so whole, all bristling with prompt responses and expected opinions and usual views, radiating all a broad daylight equality of emphasis and broad impartiality of address (for most relations) – I never ceased, I say, to ask myself what lodgement, on such premises, the rich proud genius one adored could ever have contrived, what domestic commerce the subtlety that was its prime ornament and the world's wonder have enjoyed, under what shelter the obscurity that was its luckless drawback and the world's despair have flourished.
>
> (p. xiii)

The preface goes on from the ceaselessly baffled self to a voice, impersonal, external: 'the ever-importunate murmur "Dramatise it! Dramatise it!"' The dramatization produces the tale of Clare Vawdrey, but still James remains curious about Browning. His narrative does not do away with the strangeness of the familiar London poet. James affirms 'I have never ceased to ask myself ... I never ceased, I say, to ask myself ...' The notions that the experiential self is primary and that its perceptions are the precondition of the tale are effects of a 'history' that is only 'more or less written' into narrative form. The 'ground' on which this uncertain writing takes place is not that of experience. James's narrative dramatization is the diachronic form of the synchronic structure of irony. The question of what lodgement existed for genius on the premises of Browning's 'loud, sound, normal, hearty presence' cannot be resolved. Like the fluttering of the bat at eventide, the relation of that presence to its haunting poetic creativity is ironic. Browning is figured as incompatible with himself, producing displacements that overwhelmingly disturb judgement, what James calls 'one's own applied measure'. James recounts an allegory of reading Browning in which personality is foreign to but, still more disconcertingly, not separable from poetic genius.

Hard work and experimentation

If Browning, like James, loved to experiment, he was also passionately dedicated to the daily effort of his poetic work. Aged about 18 he dropped his classes at University College London and definitely decided to be nothing but a poet. He proceeded to read Johnson's *Dictionary* from cover to cover. At the time of the publication of *Bells and Pomegranates*, despite the slow growth of his reputation, he told his friend Alfred Domett something of his thoughts about 'real' effort. He was now 34 and seemed prepared to write his earlier productions off as preparation for a genuine work that might lie ahead. Still, his account of a man cutting his way through woodland suggests that this hacking is also imaginative space-clearing:

> At this moment [the summer of 1846, with five plays behind him] I feel as every body does who has worked – 'in vain'? No matter, if the work was real: it seems disinspiriting for a man to hack away at trees in a wood and at the end of his clearing come to rocks or the sea or whatever disappoints him as leading to nothing .. but still, turn the man's face, point him to new trees and the true direction, and who will compare his power arising from experience with that of another who has been confirming himself all the time in the belief that chopping wood is incredible labour and that the first blow he strikes will be sure to jar his arm to the shoulder without shaking a leaf in the lowest bough? I stand at present and wait like

such a fellow as the first of these – if the real work should present itself to be done, I shall begin at once and in earnest .. not having to learn first of all how to keep the axe-head from flying back into my face; and if I stop in the middle .. let the bad business of other years show that I was not idle nor altogether incompetent.[9]

Making his way he knows not where the hacker comes 'at the end of his clearing ... to rocks or the sea or whatever disappoints him as leading to nothing.' The forest has no particular name or location, no familiar landmarks. Perhaps Browning's blind cutting follows what Bloom calls the hidden roads that go from poem to poem.[10] A letter to Elizabeth Barrett also in 1846 tells her that 'the little I *have* written, has been an inconscious scrawling with the mind fixed somewhere else.'[11] Although his route may be determined, it is by something outside his consciousness. Browning accepts this and confidently waits for a change of direction to 'turn [his] face, point him to new trees and the true direction.'

   This combination of hard work and passivity was an immense gamble, with Browning's daily activity, year after year, as the stakes. Interruptions for more public literary business were frustrating, whether the business was visiting Edward Moxon, his new publisher, or the practicalities of getting his plays performed. We get some idea of the real work Browning undertook after *Sordello* from a letter to Domett written four years earlier in 1842. Domett had just emigrated to the New Zealand, where he would carve out a political career for himself:

> Of me: a couple of days after you left, I got a note from Macready – the disastrous issue of the Play you saw of Darley's brother, had frightened him into shutting the house earlier than he had meant. Nothing new this season, therefore, but *next*, &c. &c. &c. So runs this idle life away!. while *you* are working! – I shall go to the end of this year, as I now go on – shall print the Eastern play you may remember hearing about – finish a wise metaphysical play (about a great mind and soul turning to ill) – and print a few songs and small poems – which Moxon advised me to do for popularity's sake – These things done (and my play out) I shall have tried an experiment to the end, and be pretty well contented either way.[12]

The experiment was not a literary one but a secondary project to set Browning's work before a wider public. Nothing was written 'for popularity's sake', but Browning had now begun to engage with the possibilities of packaging and presenting the work he had already begun to make. The next dozen years were highly productive: between 1842 and 1854 he published *King Victor and King Charles*, an essay on Chatterton and *Dramatic Lyrics* (1842), *The Return of the Druses* and *A Blot on the 'Scutcheon* (1843), *Colombe's Birthday* (1844), *Dramatic Romances and Lyrics* (1845), *Luria* and *A Soul's Tragedy* (1846), revised much of his previously published work (although not *Sordello*) for a collected *Poems* brought out by Chapman & Hall, and published *Christmas-Eve and Easter Day* (1850) and an essay on Shelley (1852). In 1845–6 he also wrote, with Elizabeth Barrett, a magnificent private correspondence. What sense can be made of Browning's prediction in the same letter to Domett that he didn't expect to do 'any real thing' until ten or a dozen years later? He stipulates the conditions needed to write, 'partial retirement and stopping the ears against noise outside'. The lonely imaginative pioneer had to coexist with the social man.

Browning and theatre: *Strafford*

Browning's literary business in the late 1830s and 1840s sometimes clashed with the different timing of his poetic career. Drama was not only a genre in which Browning's vocation led him to write; it was a necessary component in his articulating his own thoughts about writing. In order to explain his poetic ambitions to Domett he resorted to dramatizing the act of writing. Still, an exploration of Browning's relation with the dramatic must begin with the drama proper: Browning's first five plays were intended for the stage and all but the first failed. *Strafford* played for five nights at Covent Garden in 1837, a tragedy about Hippolytus feverishly imagined in 1841 reached paper only as the fragment 'Artemis Prologuizes', Macready rejected *King Victor and King Charles* and *The Return of the Druses* in the early 1840s and conclusively fell out with Browning over *A Blot in the 'Scutcheon* which ran for just three performances at Drury Lane in 1843. 'Macready has used me vilely,' Browning complained.[13] Charles Kean turned down *Colombe's Birthday* which was published in 1844. So much for the 'bad business' which prepared the irrepressible Browning for what he called 'new trees and the true direction'. *Luria* and *A Soul's Tragedy* were closet dramas, as were the classical 'transcriptions' of the 1870s, Euripides' *Alcestis* and *Heracles* and Aeschylus' *Agamemnon*.[14] By this late point Browning's creative concerns were remote from actors, producers, theatres and audiences (although he was pleased by the performance of *Colombe's Birthday* with Helen

Faucit in 1853, and helped prepare the play text of *Strafford* for Emily Hickey's production in the 1880s). The immediate context of his 'transcriptions' placed more emphasis on issues of poetic communication, either through the social function of drama – the Euripides plays were embedded in the story of *Balaustion's Adventure* (1871) and the aesthetic debate of *Aristophanes' Apology* (1875) – or, in the case of the *Agamemnon* and its preface, through the theory and practice of translation which I treat in Chapter 6.

Why didn't Browning's stage plays succeed? One decisive element was that William Macready, Browning's distinguished contact in the theatre, had no genuine sympathy for Browning's dramatic project. The actor's desperate enthusiasm for Browning, whom he had fantasized as the ennobler of modern drama, went hand in hand with a complete failure to recognize what was new and distinctive about Browning's plays. The dramas served an overwhelming imaginative purpose and could not at the same time make happy contact with Macready's familiar London audience. A clash of expectation eventually drove Browning and Macready apart.

The historical tragedy *Strafford* can be used as a test case. The play was written as relief from the arduous composition of *Sordello* and staged in 1837. At this stage Browning had made a few experiments with dramatic lyric, notably 'Porphyria' and 'Johannes Agricola' (later 'Porphyria's Lover' and 'Johannes Agricola in Meditation') but he apparently remained committed to the fragmented lengths of his dramatic narrative, deeply influenced by Shelley's *Alastor* and Keats's *Hyperion*. *Strafford* is concerned with political life at the time of England's Civil War. There is a strong literary side to Browning's political interests and affiliations, which go back through Shelley, and the younger Wordsworth, to Milton, who held office as Latin Secretary under Cromwell's Protectorate until the Restoration of the monarchy in 1660, when he resumed work on *Paradise Lost*. 'The Lost Leader' (1845) gives a genealogy of the imaginative left, lamenting Wordsworth's drift towards conservatism: 'Shakespeare was of us, Milton was for us,/Burns, Shelley, were with us – they watch from their graves!' The subject-matter of *Strafford* overlaps with Shelley's fragment of a play *Charles I*, which was published in the *Posthumous Poems* of 1824. *Charles I* includes several of the same characters (Strafford, Hampden, Pym and Vane) and takes a similar pro-Parliamentary position. The bicentenary of the English Civil War (1642–51) and the significant political events preceding it was in any case approaching. The Civil War, and the political struggle between

Parliamentarians and the monarchy before it, had been a crucial reference point for radical pamphleteers, anti-government agitators and opponents of censorship through the Regency (1811–20). By the 1830s the emphasis was on democratic reform rather than the urgent resistance of oppression: the French Revolution of 1789 had not overthrown monarchy throughout Europe. Browning thought of himself as a Republican, yet in his writing he remained fascinated by the failure of democracy.

Strafford focuses on the self-destructive loyalty the former Parliamentarian Wentworth bears towards King Charles I. Historically, Wentworth allied himself with Parliament early in his career, to limit the power of the monarchy and support the 1628 Bill of Rights. He did not, however, support the transfer of power from the monarch to Parliament, and fell out with his former Parliamentary allies over Charles's right to demand forced loans from his subjects in time of extreme national crisis. In 1640 Charles gave Wentworth the title Strafford, and the same year Strafford was accused by Parliament of planning to use an Irish army on the King's behalf against the English population. Historically and in the play Charles emerges as an unreliable and vacillating figure who does little to help Strafford. Despite mounting an extremely resourceful self-defence against Parliament's charges, Strafford was found guilty and executed in 1641. The naming of Browning's play by the new title *Strafford* foregrounds the question of conflict between earlier and later affiliations which are crucial to the hero's divided identity. Browning heightens this by adding the feature that as Wentworth, Strafford had been a close friend of the man who led the final attack on him, the Parliamentarian John Pym. Despite its overt concentration on a public political theme, 'the advancing good of England', the most intense moments in *Strafford* derive their energy from private and psychological sources in the characters (Act I, Scene I).

It is the person of Strafford himself upon whom the dramatic interest centres, but he functions for much of the play as a lay figure whose attributes and powers exist in the words of other characters: alienated Parliamentarians, fickle King Charles, his lost friend Pym, his unrequited lover Lucy Carlisle. Browning seems more interested in the processes through which character emerges and conflicts with itself than in dramatic exposition. Macready was worried that Forster's admiration of the play grew out of prior knowledge of the characters. He wrote in November 1836: 'I fear he [Forster] has such an interest in the individual characters, the biographies of whom he has written, that he is misled as to its dramatic power; character *to* him having the interest of action. *Nous verrons!*[15] The change of Strafford's name is typical of Browning's poetry of displacements and shifts, playing fast and loose with the idea of given and inalienable truths of experience. Still, the change of name obstructed communication between stage and audience. Browning did not answer the need for dramatic exposition in those who don't know that Strafford was not called Strafford until late in his career.

The first scene uses the name Wentworth to yoke Wentworth/Strafford to England's historical progress: this character above all others is the meeting point for the play's private and public concerns. Browning at once complicates this emblematic device as characters argue about it. The Puritan Vane finds it 'too bitter' that '[a]ny one man's mere presence should suspend/England's combined endeavour.' He also claims that Wentworth's 'single arm' has reversed historical progress: 'Rolled the advancing good of England back.' Hampden then asks 'Is hating Wentworth all the help [England] needs?' The debate over the power of one man's presence and arm to thwart the nation's fate foregrounds rhetoric as much as constitutional history. Browning challenges Carlyle's assertion that history is the biography of great men and suggests that the notion of an individual creating history by clearing his path through events is fictive. Strafford emerges in the context of 'combined endeavour' and of national progress. The Parliamentarians are conscious that their deeds create history. By contrast Charles upholds the timeless divine right of kingship. Through the play Strafford is caught between an impulse to unchanging loyalty and self-conscious participation in national transformation.

Pym, Strafford's one-time friend, emerges as the play's most powerful character, yet this strength is made strange. He has an extraordinary voice. The King's man Holland, asked to recount a crucial political speech of Pym's, can only imprecisely convey its effectiveness: 'I've a vague memory of a sort of sound/A voice, a kind of vast unnatural voice' (Act III, Scene I). Pym is also a canny enough rhetorician to ask 'What if Wentworth's should be still/That name' which could save England? This hyperbolic Wentworth could change sides a second time and wield his exaggerated powers for Parliament as well as against it. But Pym reckons without Strafford's pervasive will to fail, perhaps the play's most notable common feature with *Paracelsus* and *Sordello*. When Wentworth enters in the play's second scene, his much-vaunted body is supported by Lucy Carlisle and weakened by 'horrible fatigue'.

It is this weakness and susceptibility that Herbert Tucker links with the theme of influence, as 'A weakness, but most precious' (Act II, Scene II). Tucker describes Browning's plays as 'variations on a central action – a holding action, a dramatised version of the tactical delay that figures so importantly in Browning's early narratives'.[16] Strafford's love for an unworthy Charles I scarcely covers a blind unerring drive to his own martyrdom which has little relation to declared political goals or human attachments.

Browning was much attracted to the martyrological quality in John Lilburne, who succeeded in being imprisoned by every political faction before, during and after the English Civil War, refused to be silenced and who was consequently nicknamed the 'self-afflicter' in chapbook and ballad literature (see Chapter 7). A similar martyrological urge is a recognizable feature in the central characters in *Pauline*, *Paracelsus* and *Sordello*. Tucker reads Strafford's capacity to 'undermine his own defenses and explode his own images' in terms of the maintenance of an appropriately ruinous site for imaginative work (p. 135). When Strafford speaks of himself as early as Act II, Scene II, it is in antithetical comparison to the hero of a quest-romance:

> All knights begin their enterprise, we read,
> Under the best auspices; 'tis morn,
> The Lady girds his sword upon the Youth
> (He's always very young) – the trumpets sound
> Cups pledge him, and, why, the King blesses him –
> You need not turn a page of the romance
> To learn the Dreadful Giant's fate.

Strafford's beginning is all decline and belatedness. His aim in seeking out 'real strife' is not victory but the achievement of dying first. His dramatic identity moves from an absent Goliath in Act I, Scene I, to a pathetic spectacle in Act IV, Scene II, where 'we see, forsooth,/ Not England's foe in Strafford, but the man/ Who, sick, half-blind ...' – the description peters out, interrupted by the sight of the King's hand behind a curtain. Strafford Agonistes cannot even achieve full blindness, Samson's triumph in death would not interest him. The truncated description recalls Shelley on George III in 'Sonnet: England in 1819', 'An old, mad, blind, despised and dying king', the first in a catalogue of disastrous political circumstances which make up an unforeseen national resource of 'graves from which a glorious Phantom may/ Burst'.

Ultimately Browning would find such creative ruin not in his state of England play, but in the assorted crooks, lunatics, phonies and losers of the dramatic lyrics. The fascinating shiftiness of the dramatic lyrics would never have emerged without the plays: their failure before the public was necessary to Browning's development.

Strafford never bursts out, a glorious Phantom, to illumine Browning's play with deathly deeds or defiant words. When he submits to a treason trial, he accepts the letter of the law's procedure and his defence does not attempt to appropriate the law by misprision: 'Law,/I grapple with their law! I'm here to try/My actions by their standard, not my own!' (Act IV, Scene II). The passivity of his martyrdom could not be further from the plain-speaking triumphs of Browning's hero John Lilburne before Star Chamber. Pym, more of a satisfying dramatic hero, finally defeats Strafford in the same scene by improperly going beyond law (Vane says to Pym):

> You cannot catch the Earl on any charge, –
> No man will say the law has hold of him
> On any charge; and therefore you resolve
> To take the general sense on his desert,
> As though no law existed, and we met
> To found one.

Pym refuses to tolerate lack of power and will 'make occasion serve' in the acknowledged absence of a 'real charge'. Once condemned Strafford has found his moment: his defences are not laid against any opposing Giant but against his own survival. The play's last scene takes place inside '*The Tower*', the goal of Strafford's quest which he has conquered by becoming prisoner. Even there Strafford takes the condemned man's enemy, Time, for a friend 'Who in the twilight comes to mend/All the fantastic day's caprice (Act V, Scene II).

Pym the rhetorician understands the productivity of conflict and knows that reconciliation ('to walk once more with Wentworth – my youth's friend/Purged from all error, gloriously renewed') remains only a thought which must not delay action. In the closing moments of the play Strafford attempts an unambivalent move towards the future by cursing his former friend Pym. Yet Strafford curses in his own confused way, in anticipation and belatedly:

What if I curse you? Send a strong curse forth
Clothed from my heart, lapped round with horror till
She's fit with her white face to walk the world
Scaring kind natures from your cause and you –
Then to sit down with you at the board-head,
The gathering for prayer ... O speak, but speak!
... Creep up, and quietly follow each one home,
You, you, you, be a nestling care for each
To sleep with, – hardly moaning in his dreams,
She gnaws so quietly, – till, lo he starts,
Gets off with half a heart eaten away!

> (Act V, Scene II)

Even this final threat, apparently meant to deter Pym from 'helping' (influencing) England, is already well known to Pym. The curse describes a feeling Pym has already had, the effect of the thought of killing Strafford. Pym tells his colleague Fiennes in Act IV, Scene II, 'I have made myself familiar, ... / With this one thought – have walked, and sat, and slept, / This thought before me. I have done such things, / Being the chosen man that should destroy / The traitor.' Channelled through Pym's own influence at 'board-head' and 'prayer', Strafford's curse will make nothing new happen and its afflictions only affirm Pym's authority as 'the chosen man'.

Strafford's failure repeats the drift of the early narratives with its close reflection of the young poet's stance in relation to poetic history. Browning's dramas had a certain efficacy as a way of handling indebtedness, but their clear drive towards lack of achievement was bad for the action, dramatic tension and conflict needed on the stage. Browning's experiments eventually had to find a new form. The theatrical realization of Browning's dramatic ambitions was fraught with conflict. Two main factors obstructed the audience's identifying with his characters and entering imaginatively into the narrative of their actions. One was Browning's alteration of Aristotle's precept that character framed by dramatic action was crucial to tragedy: his plays took character as the framework within which action was staged. The other was the habitual reserve of his central dramatic characters: they have trouble with unambiguous action, remaining deliberately unclear to themselves and others. Tensions and contradictions are not only played out between characters, but operate in terms of formal deceptions at the heart of identity. Strafford havers, betrayed by his loyalty to a disloyal friend, the King. In *The Return of the Druses*, deception is an essential, as the Druses themselves, the Palestinian sect of the title, must appear to court assimilation: 'live/As Christian with the Christian, Jew with Jew,/Druse only with the Druses' (Act I, Scene I). All this lying, self-deception and dislocation thwart the immediate pleasure of an audience's identification with human drama. Questions of dramatization take precedence over character in action or even the exposition of action in character. Dramatic irony takes precedence over dramatic representation or *peripetia*.

Browning's plays make it very difficult for the reader or spectator to know what they have witnessed, because they are so concerned with what is veiled, with deceptive statecraft, with political conflict that cannot be represented on stage because it arises from the disjuncture of characters' relations with each other. Sometimes this takes the form of some kind of fall and an examination of the contrast between before and after. In *Strafford* the friendship between Wentworth and Pym becomes the tortured alienation between Strafford and Pym. A similar pattern occurs between Anael and Djabal in *The Return of the Druses*, and in the crisis caused between father and son in *King Victor and King Charles* by Victor's abdication in favour of the reluctant heir Charles, and Victor's subsequent desire to return to the throne. Other dramatic relationships are unstable because of vacillation (King Charles and Strafford), or deliberate deception (Loys and Djabal in *The Return of the Druses*). Constant, honest characters such as Polyxena in *King Victor and King Charles* have little power to affect events and appear most clearly in differentiation from opportunists like the scheming politician d'Ormea. In *Strafford* Lucy Carlisle is kept marginal; the play's action does not require her at any point – she only marks the intensity of Strafford's attachment to Charles. Remarks addressed to the audience tend to reveal caprice or deceptiveness: the reader of asides and soliloquies by King Charles, King Charles of Savoy, d'Ormea or Djabal may wonder whether these characters are describing their dramatic situation or are passively being spoken by it. It is often hard, as Tucker points out, to distinguish between psychological action and plot.

Macready

Towards the end of the experiment with stage plays, in 1842, Browning admitted to Domett: 'what men require, I don't know – and of what they are in possession, know nearly as little.'[17] Part of the experiment of the late 1830s and 1840s had been to establish closer contact with one who, apparently, did know. Browning's letters to the

actor-manager William Macready have some of the flattering forward-
ness of his first communications with Elizabeth Barrett:

> My mind is made up to believe that you comprehend me as
> you comprehend Macbeth or Ion, – that while you understand
> how intensely I feel, you see a reason for the little I say, and are
> satisfied with that little. I shall be at no pains, therefore, to set
> advantageously forth the proposition I am about to make, – in
> perfect faith that you know why 'nice affection' should 'scorn
> meaner hands' and be far removed from presumption while it
> aspires most earnestly.[18]

The 'proposition' was that Browning should write a tragedy for Macready
on 'any subject [that] shall suggest itself to you'. Macready was thrilled
by the offer and wrote in his diary 'I found a note from Browning. What
can I say upon it? It was a tribute which remunerated me from
the annoyances and care of years: it was one of the very highest, may I
not say the highest, honour I have through life received' (Diaries I,
p. 321). Presumably he did not recognize Browning's reference to 'nice
affection' as a garbled line from Book One of Spenser's *The Fairie Queene*.
Browning's dealings with the 'real' Macready veil the poet's true engage-
ment with the great figures of the poetic past. Had Macready spotted the
allusion, it would have wounded his delicate pride, for the poem outra-
geously contradicts the letter's idealization of the relation between the
dramatist and the actor.

The letter seems to say that Browning and Macready are on such
good terms that Browning will not hesitate to write the actor-manager
a tragedy. Spenser's poem says something very different from the gist
of the letter; Browning was always a free quoter of his own and others'
work, and he takes Spenser's parenthesis '(Entire affection scorneth
nicer hands)' from a context of quest and rescue. In *The Faerie Queene*,
Book I, Canto VIII the successful quester Redcrosse (George) has
defeated the Gyant, captured Duessa and now turns to the Gyant's
Prisoner. Browning was a regular visitor to Macready's dressing-room
after performances. Re-read through Spenser's words these visits take
on a dark slapstick quality. The young poet enters:

> he rent that yron dore,
> With furious force, and indignation fell;
> Where entred in, his foot could find no flore,
> But all a deepe descent, as darke as hell,

> That breathed ever forth a filthie baneful smell.
> But neither darkenesse fowle, nor filthy bands,
> Nor noyous smell his purpose could withhold.
> (Entire affection hateth nicer hands)
> But that with constant zeal, and courage bold,
> After long paines and labours manifold,
> He found the meanes that Prisoner up to reare;
> Whose feeble thighs, unhable to uphold
> His pined corse, him scarse to light could beare,
> A ruefull spectacle of death and ghastly drere.
>   (Book I, Canto VIII, Stanza xl)

Macready the Prisoner, with 'feeble thighs' and 'pined corse', was no admired figure from whom to learn about the drama. Browning 'after long paines and labours manifold' would save him, and save the stage from its aesthetic decline.

The letter more obviously continues the strain of mock-chivalry in an earlier note where Browning humorously compares Macready's hospitality to an intercession between questing Browning-Quixote and his imaginary enemies: 'If the *offer of a bed* be equivalent to the chasing-away of all Quixote's Giants, – surely the *direction to the Stage-coach* amounts to the not leaving him a solitary windmill to shake a spear at.'[19] The playful apparition of Shakespeare's name in 'shake a spear' gives a glimpse of Browning's orientation towards the Giants of the canon. At the same time the identification with Quixote echoes the beginning of *Sordello* and Browning's self-deprecating description of the poem as 'a Quixotic attempt' in the 1863 headnotes.

Shakespeare 'the inventor of *Othello*' appears as the typical 'objective poet' in Browning's 'Essay on Shelley' (1852). Unlike Browning this poet understands his public and is 'so acquainted and in sympathy with its narrower comprehension as to be careful to supply it with no other materials than it can combine into an intelligible whole'. Still, Shakespeare is much more than a symbol for Browning; perhaps his best known conception, that of the 'good minute', evolves in relation to the very bad minutes in Act 5 of *Othello*, when the Moor is meditating the murder of Desdemona: 'When I have pluckt the rose, / I cannot give it vital growth again, / It needs must wither: – I'll smell it in the tree. – [*Kissing her*]' (Act V, Scene II). 'Two in the Campagna' also recalls Othello's 'Perdition catch my soul, but I do love thee' in its phrasing as it describes the irreversibleness of time: 'I kiss your cheek, / Catch your soul's warmth, – I pluck the rose / And love it more than tongue can speak – / Then the good minute goes.'

John Forster was an influential drama critic who knew Browning and Macready well, as did the successful dramatist Thomas Noon Talfourd. Circumstances looked promising for Browning's *début* as a popular dramatist. However, the warm feeling generated by mutual idealization was not strong enough to overcome the conflict between Browning's steady pathbreaking through the forest, heading he knew not where, and Macready's insistence on dramatic power and action. Macready's diary comments on Talfourd's *Ion* succinctly give an impression of the actor's criteria for successful drama: 'where some of the most poetical passages are omitted, it is difficult to persuade an author that the effect of the whole is improved; but imagery and sentiment will not supply the place of action' (I, p. 246). Macready admired *Paracelsus* in 1835; his diary records, 'Read *Paracelsus*, a work of great daring, starred with poetry of thought, feeling and diction, but occasionally obscure; the writer can scarcely fail to be a great spirit of his time' (I, p. 265). Macready had not recognized the full scope of Browning's 'daring'. The diary entry echoes a reference to stars and constellation in the preface to *Paracelsus*: 'were my scenes stars it must be [the reader's] co-operating fancy which, supplying all chasms, shall connect the scattered lights into one constellation – a Lyre or a Crown.' Macready unfortunately misses the sense of the metaphor as Browning stages it. For Macready Browning's deliberate bid for interaction with his readers was mere darkness.

The actor's strong liking for *Paracelsus* may have been influenced by another part of the preface where Browning makes a forceful distinction between poetry and drama, and calls the poem an 'experiment':

> an attempt, probably more novel than happy, to reverse the method usually adopted by writers whose aim it is to set forth any phenomenon of the mind or passions by the operation of persons and events; and ... instead of having recourse to an external machinery of incidents to create and evolve the crisis I desire to produce, I have ventured to display somewhat minutely the mood itself in its rise and progress, and have suffered the agency by which it is influenced and determined, to be generally discernible in its effects alone, and subordinate throughout, if not altogether excluded: and this for a reason. I have endeavoured to write a poem, not a drama ...   (Longman I, p. 113)

If Macready inferred from this that Browning could if he chose direct his creative powers to write a drama of outward action, he was wrong.

Macready's journal is eloquent about the financial anxieties of life in the theatre and Browning better understood his friend once selections from the diaries were published in 1875. In the late 1830s the poet's readiness to be affected by the actor's performance continued to fuel false hopes of compatibility. Browning continued to think of a tragedy, and Macready's diary continued to idealize:

> He said that I had *bit* him by my performance of Othello, and I told him I hoped I should make the blood come. It would indeed be some recompense for the miseries, the humiliations, the heart-sickening disgusts which I have endured in my profession if, by its exercise, I had awakened a spirit of poetry whose influence would elevate, ennoble and adorn our degraded drama.
>
> (I, p. 277)

Theatre in the 1830s was indeed becoming less literary and more spectacular. Mixed shows, including animal acts, panoramas, light comedy and melodrama, were increasingly popular. The actor's idealization of influence seems a long way from Browning's earthy trope of being bitten by the mad dog or vampire of Macready's Othello. When Forster praised *Strafford* to him in 1836 Macready saw Browning as a rescuer. The author of *Paracelsus* was to save the drama. But Browning's spirit of poetry could not be cast into such a role: by May 1837 a disappointed Macready concluded in his diary that *he* had helped *Browning* through a risky venture with *Strafford:* 'Without *great assistance* his tragedy could never have been put in a condition to be proposed for representation ... nor without great assistance could it ever have been carried through its "perilous" experiment' (I, p. 393). And then there was *Sordello*. When the poem came out in 1840, Macready was among the many who found it unreadable.

Drama and sympathy

Something new was to be staged, and Browning depended on the readiness of Macready and the audience to acknowledge this without needing much explanation from him. As that first letter to Macready put it, Browning hoped 'that while you understand how intensely I feel, you see a reason for the little I say, and are satisfied with that little.' The preface to *Strafford* maintained a clear priority: 'Action in

Character rather than Character in Action' (Ohio II, p. 9). This reversed the classical formulation in Aristotle's *Poetics*, where tragedy centres on the imitation of external action. Macready, whether or not he had read the *Poetics*, was a popular Aristotelian. The chapters on tragedy illustrate the classical assumption that tragedy is primarily about events, not moods or states of mind:

> Tragedy is an imitation, not of *men*, but of *actions* – of life, of happiness and unhappiness: for happiness consists in action, and the supreme good itself, the very *end* of life, is *action* of a certain kind – not *quality*. Now the *manners* of men constitute only their *quality* or *characters*; but it is by their *actions* that they are are *happy*, or the contrary ... the *action* and the *fable* are the *end* of Tragedy ...[20]

The preface to *Paracelsus* appears to be written against the *Poetics*. It confides that persons and events are *excluded* from the poem, a manoeuvre at the heart of Browning's failure as a dramatist and success as a dramatic poet. To use rhetorical terminology, these exclusions give the poem a metonymic structure. The poem's 'mood' stands for and replaces an account of the 'agency which influenced and determined' that mood, substituting effect for cause. No drama could be read at such a remove and satisfy the Aristotelian criterion that without 'a proper fable and contexture of incidents', strongly-marked manners, well-turned language and sentiments were not enough (I, pp. 119–20). The poem, made up of unstaged 'scenes', was to work precisely in ways which no stage production could encompass. Browning wanted to keep open two doors at once: the absences in the text determine the reader's space of performance, and the reader's fancy is less than free in its responsibility to cooperate with the poet's work. Yet, still, the text depends on the individual reader's intelligence and sympathy and the name of its completed form is left undecided: would it become 'a Lyre or a Crown'?

Sympathy is also a faculty of acting. In a letter to Macready written after the actor had rejected *The Return of the Druses*, Browning assimilates Macready's remarkable non-verbal acting style to his own creative process. He describes imagining the actor's performance during composition, as a way of supplying a support his writing lacks. Westland Marston's descriptions of Macready as master of mime emphasize his strong presence, a silent quality alongside whatever lines he spoke: 'The power of expressing states of feeling by gesture and attitude is, of course, necessary to every actor. With Macready it rose into a special endowment.'[21] Macready was described as capable of becoming the medium of a 'strong sympathy' between audience and character (p. 99). Browning's letter uses the notion of sympathy to describe the relation between written character and reading actor, shifting its field from the public and spectacular to the private and literary. As he elaborates the actor's imaginary place in the poet's secluded work, Browning implicitly dismisses the actual Macready as superfluous. He becomes a chasm in which Browning's imagined Macready, oddly fused with the tragic heroine Penthesilia, appears:

> I *did* rather fancy that you would have 'sympathized' with Djabal in the main scenes of my play; and your failing to do so is the more decisive against it, that I really had you here, in this little room of mine, while I wrote bravely away – *here* were you, propping the weak, pushing the strong parts (such I thought there might be!) – now majestically motionless, and now 'laying about as busily, as the Amazonian dame Penthesile' – and *here*, please the fates, shall you again & again give breath and blood to some thin creation of mine yet unevoked – but *elsewhere* – *enfonce*![22]

The Penthesile reference garbles another moment in *The Faerie Queene* when Britomart, on her way to rescue her lover Artegall, fights and defeats the Amazon Radigund: 'Full fiercely layde the Amazon about / And dealt her blows unmercifully sore' (Book V, Canto VII, Stanza xxxi; Spenser puts 'bold Penthesilee' first among the women of 'Antique glory' in Book III, Canto IV, Stanza ii). Sympathy, literally feeling with another, reaches a point in this passage where it is difficult to tell who does what '*here*, in this little room of mine'. Is the warrior figure the poet, 'writing bravely away'? Is Browning the one who alternates between motionlessness and laying about busily? Or is the 'propping ... pushing' Macready the one who strikes the attitudes of stillness and fighting? Browning's 'little room' is the first and only stage for his ever (Mac)ready muse: '*here*, please the fates, shall you again and again give breath and blood to some thin creation of mine yet unevoked'. The closet-drama of composition has become an end in itself; something is happening there that cannot happen anywhere else. Despite his disappointment in Macready's lack of sympathy, Browning recuperates theatrical failure by opposing it to the continuing and somewhat vampiric or sacrificial ('shall you again and again give breath and blood') renewal of his own inspiration by a privately available Macready.

The Return of the Druses was not the last attempt to collaborate with Macready, who received the romantic tragedy *A Blot on the 'Scutcheon* late in 1841 and kept it until January 1843 when he summarily revised it. He cast Mr Phelps in the play's lead rather than himself, and organized a first reading featuring the theatre prompter, a lowly employee. Macready told Browning that the play was on this occasion 'laughed at from beginning to end'. Only afterwards did he explain to him that the comic effect was produced by the looks of the prompt, in Browning's words 'a grotesque person with a red nose and a wooden leg, ill at ease in the love scenes' (Orr, *Life*, p. 172). When Browning discovered Macready's financial difficulties in 1875 he still could not understood why his friend 'so disguised and disfigured them' with various ruses to avert or spoil the appearance of Browning's tragedy. Two changes by Macready particularly dismayed the author: Macready retitled the tragedy a 'play' and added 'two lines of his own insertion to avoid the tragical ending' (p. 174). A break with the tragical endings of his earlier work was coming at this time. Browning was beginning to write dramatic poetry that shifted the burdensome themes of desire and death onto everyday psychic life. In Ann Wordsworth's words Browning 'realigned his material, displacing it onto all the substitutes, imitations, travesties of vatic intensities which flicker in and out of ordinary life – erotic and religious fantasies, deathbed reveries, self-projections, narcissisms.'[23] To see the tragic end of *A Blot* ... cosmetically altered at this transitional phase of his creative development must have been a deep outrage.

'The Laboratory'

There is no record of Macready's opinion of Browning's shorter dramatic poems. The earliest ones to be published came out in a new periodical, *Hood's Magazine*, in June 1844. The timing was accidental; when Thomas Hood fell ill the acting editor of the magazine, Frederick Ward, asked a number of Hood's friends to send in work for the first issue. The first piece Browning sent was called 'The Laboratory'. The poem later appeared in *Dramatic Romances and Lyrics* paired with 'Confessional' under the heading 'France and Spain'. Its scenario – a woman goes to buy poison to kill her rival in love – shows Browning's poetry taking up a new relation to death. The woman in 'The Laboratory' is not a creative type, heading for suicide. She is delight-edly amateur, even a dilettante, thrilled by the chemical material in the pharmacist's workshop. Instead of the gasping openness of the embrace with Pauline, she covers herself with a glass mask and finally offers the pharmacist: 'You may kiss me, old man, on the mouth if you will.'

Pauline, *Paracelsus* and *Sordello* take their names from characters in the poem. The title of 'The Laboratory' directs attention to a particular place and the subtitle, *'Ancien Régime'*, to a particular time. The laboratory is a private stage for fantasy and projection and so is the poem itself. It prefigures other private spaces: artist's studio, death-bed scene, church loft or music-filled salon, which Browning's dramatic poems momentarily conjure up for life and death to work in. This place apart is accompanied by a specific historical reference, recently evoked in Carlyle's *The French Revolution* (1837), to the *ancien régime*, the name given to the state apparatus of the French monarchy when it was destroyed by the uprising of 1789.

The poem refers to a social world that will be lost: the church, court, dancing at 'the King's'. For the woman who wants to buy poison the church and the court are the absolute spiritual and temporal powers from which she must keep her purchase secret. The title reminds us that her small murderous intrigue will be subject to history's revenges. *Ancien régime* is also a good name for tradition in general, within which the laboratory acts like a hidden pocket of inventive resistance. And within the laboratory is the poison, volatile, deadly and liable to escape. For the poem to find its own moment, its 'now', the dangerous fumes must be kept out of the speaker's body. She is a woman with a mission to send death to others: the poison is immediate and indiscriminate in its effects. Her first line constitutes a defence: 'Now I have tied thy glass mask on tightly.' The mask remains in place until the last seven or eight lines when it is boldly removed.

The names given to the poem's fantasized victims suggest that Browning is also playing with the *ancien régime* of his own earlier work and its apocalyptic response to influence. 'The Laboratory' does not go in for suicide or the oedipal solution of poisoning the King. The King provides the setting for her planned attack on rival women in the court, 'Pauline' and 'Elise'. These are women's names from Browning's own earlier work, one the title of his first published poem, the other the title of Sordello's only surviving fragmentary song, a development of Eglamor's 'Elys'. Browning, through his poisoner, plays with the idea of a later poem destroying earlier ones: 'Soon, at the king's, but a lozenge to give / And Pauline should have just thirty minutes to live! / To light a pastille, and Elise, with her head, / And her breast, and her arms, and her hands, should drop dead!' The characteristics of

'Pauline' at the beginning of the earlier poem are picked off one by one. The 'gold oozings' of tree resin in the pharmacist's mortar echo Sordello's three-times-repeated description of Elys's blonde hair against her head 'the few fine locks / Coloured like pale honey oozed from topmost rocks' (II, ll. 152–5; V, ll. 883–7; VI, ll. 863–5). The woman in 'The Laboratory' likes her poison colourful: 'gold', 'exquisite blue', 'enticing and dim'. These manifest the 'prismatic hues' into which Browning spoke of breaking the fearful pure white light of (Shelleyan) lyric.[24]

George Herbert's devotional poem 'Virtue' (1633) presents a more straightforward relation between poetry and death: 'Sweet Spring, full of sweet days and roses, / A box where sweets compacted lie. / My music shows ye have your closes, / And all must die.' Browning takes up Herbert's implicit image of the poem itself as a closed form, a 'box where sweets compacted lie', in a way that emphasizes the sheer variety and uncontrollableness of poetic language. The woman covets 'a wild crowd of invisible pleasures – / To carry pure death in an earring, a casket, / A signet, a fan-mount, a filagree-basket!' Small everyday decorative objects discreetly enclose death. To use the literary terms adopted by New Criticism, the woman has found suitable 'vehicles' to carry her 'tenor' or meaning (death); her pleasure is comparable to aesthetic satisfaction. But death has a way of getting out of what carries it. Herbert insists that '*all* must die': the woman's pleasures are 'a wild crowd' and 'invisible'. The language that carries 'pure death' is not structured like a vessel, but discloses as well as encloses the power that it bears.

Shelley's love poem *Epipsychidion* was a clearly apparent influence on *Pauline*. In 'The Laboratory' its influence is more oblique; a passage in *Epipsychidion* describes a woman who is a natural producer of poison: 'One, whose voice was venomed melody'. She exudes an immediate vaporous seductive contagion without laboratory, mask, or phial and leaves those in her presence no time to 'sit ... and observe'. She

> Sate by a well, under blue nightshade bowers;
> The breath of her false mouth was like faint flowers,
> Her touch was as electric poison, – flame
> Out of her looks into my vitals came,
> And from her living cheeks and bosom flew
> A killing air ...
>
> (ll. 256–62)

Browning's poem situates fatal power in more palpable forms and fascinatedly notes poison's physical properties: 'That in the mortar – call you a gum?/Ah, the brave tree whence such gold oozings come!/And yon soft phial, the exquisite blue,/Sure to taste sweetly – is that poison too?' Browning's little 'minion' can only dream of the radiant uncontained power that exudes 'killing air'.

Tennyson and Elizabeth Barrett found the poem hard to take on metrical grounds, especially its first line. Barrett criticized its obtrusive rhythm: 'I object a little to your tendency .. which is almost a habit .. & is very observable in this poem I think .. of making lines difficult for the reader to read .. see the opening lines.'[25] Her advice led to revision, but Tennyson still found that the first line 'lacked smoothness, that it was a very difficult mouthful'.[26] In the end '... that I tying thy glass mask tightly' trips and gasps even more than the earlier version '... tied thy glass mask on tightly'. Elizabeth Barrett judged 'Where we have not direct pleasure from rhythm, & where no peculiar impression is to be produced by the changes in it, we shd be encouraged by the poet to *forget it altogether*, should we not?' But what if the odd rhythm and assonance in this line are a reminder of an aspect of poetic language that cannot be reduced to 'direct pleasure' or a well-defined impression, yet which Browning does not want his readers to forget?

The indirect effects of experiments with poison can be particularly dangerous. At the end of the poem the woman tells the pharmacist to 'brush this dust off me, lest horror it brings/Ere I know it – next moment I dance at the King's!' She has painted a very clear picture of the desired effect on others of the poison she has come to buy. She imagines her dying rival, the poison disfiguring her face: 'Let death be felt and the proof remain;/Brand, burn up, bite into its grace./He is sure to remember her dying face!' After the victim's suffering, the visible proof of death will be left. The 'dying face' will become a memorial not only of the victim but, indirectly, of the murderer herself. She intends to use poison to brand her mark on her rival's face, which will in turn brand itself on the man's consciousness. So far, so good. But poison, like poetic textuality, is not entirely safe to use as an instrument. Poetic language takes unexpected and enticing forms, but the poem suggests that its power is not confined to the spectacular colours and the obvious effects. There is danger in the faint, scarcely perceptible presence of dust, waste, remains. The closing lines of the poem acknowledge that its defences are still incomplete. With her mask untied the woman is open to the horror of being taken quietly by surprise. The 'Essay on Shelley' describes the subjective poet as struggling towards the 'seeds of creation lying burningly on the Divine Hand'. That image develops Shelley's description of the creative mind as a fading coal in the *Defence of Poetry*. 'The Laboratory's uncontainable deadly white fumes and almost imperceptible poisoned dust are the stuff of creation.

Courtship drama: 'the less definite mould'

By the time 'The Laboratory' was being revised for publication in *Bells and Pomegranates* VII, Browning had begun his correspondence with Elizabeth Barrett. As a beginning the first letter makes much of its own discontinuity: 'this is no off-hand complimentary letter that I shall write, – whatever else, no prompt matter-of-course recognition of your genius, and there a graceful and natural end of the thing.'[27] No indeed: Browning does not articulate his reading of the poems, he assimilates them:

> I have been turning and turning again in my mind what I should be able to tell you of [the] effect [of your poems] upon me [...] – but nothing comes of it all – so into me it has gone, and part of me it has become, this great living poetry of yours, not a flower of which but took root and grew – oh how different that is from lying to be dried and pressed flat, and prized highly and put in a book with a proper account at top and bottom, and shut up and put away .. and the book called a 'Flora,' besides!

Browning did keep to the end of his life, pressed in a book, a dead flower from Shelley's grave.[28] Shelley's remains animated Browning's entire writing life from *Pauline* to *Asolando*. Yet Browning receives Barrett's poetry as living immediacy, even allows it to grow in him, and does not put it in a book. In his imaginative economy her 'great living poetry' cannot be substituted, translated or exchanged into other words. It is itself. As Daniel Karlin has put it: '[t]he question of what Browning found to admire in Elizabeth Barrett's poetry can ... be answered in a word: nothing.'[29] In Browning's words, 'nothing comes of it all': to his poetic imagination Elizabeth Barrett is a living, organic representation of the lyric made safe, a lyricism without the troublesome parts of Shelley's legacy. Yet imagination contains incompatible elements: to the extent that Barrett and Shelley are also alike for Browning, the nothing turns into something.

Or in the idiom of Shakespeare's Sonnet 53 ('What is your substance, whereof are you made, / That millions of strange shadows on you tend?') the strange shadow of Shelley attends Elizabeth Barrett as Browning loves and writes her.

By contrast Elizabeth Barrett's interpretation of Browning's dramatic experiments sets him in the context of the past, Renaissance tragedy or Greek sacred play, and sees the work, phantom because as-yet-unread, in place of the man she had not yet met: 'in the meantime, I seem to see "Luria" instead of you; I have visions and dream dreams. And the "Soul's Tragedy," which sounds to me like the step of a ghost of an old Drama!' 'A step of a ghost', visions and dreams are not the only supernatural touches in this winning letter which I also quote at the beginning of the chapter. She asks 'Who told me of your skulls and spiders? Why, couldn't I know it without being told? Did Cornelius Agrippa know nothing without being told? ... if I were to say that *I heard it from you yourself*, how would you answer? *And it was so*. Why are you not aware that these are the days of mesmerism and clairvoyance?' In the next paragraph a tender animism reaches back to infuse Barrett's imagined glimpses of 'Luria' and 'A Soul's Tragedy' in place of their author with subtle physical promise:

> I have some sympathy in your habit of feeling for chairs and tables. I remember, when I was a child & wrote poems in little clasped books, I used to kiss the books & put them away tenderly because I had been happy near them, & take them out by turns when I was going from home, to cheer them by the change of air & the pleasure of the new place. This, not for the sake of the verses written in them, & not for the sake of writing more verses in them, but from pure gratitude. Other books I used to treat in a like manner – and to talk to the trees & flowers, was a natural inclination ...[30]

Ghosts, clairvoyance and mesmerism, animism and sympathy: in the 1850s Barrett's literal interpretations of these improbable phenomena led to discord with 'infidel' Browning, who hated seances and table-rapping. But at this early stage Barrett's terminology, interspersed with literary thoughts and confidences, remains open and suggestive as a way of approaching Browning's work.

Daniel Karlin comments that even after Browning began to call regularly on Elizabeth Barrett, on Saturday 8 November 1845, the letters remain remarkably self-contained (p. 76). Yet as the courtship develops, so the available literary space of the letters appears to diminish. Actions rather than thoughts and moods come to the fore. The uncertain promise of the correspondence is displaced by another kind of bond. Browning wrote to Elizabeth Barrett about the marriage licence and arrangements on 10 September 1846. Although letters continued to be exchanged until September 19 and departure for Le Havre, that letter gives the impression that marriage will mark a shift in the unconventional verbal performances between them: 'It seems as if I should insult you if I spoke a word to confirm you, to beseech you, – relieve you from your promise, if you claim it.'[31] Confirmation, beseechment, promise and, for that matter, insult are performatives, acts of language that do things. The figures of imaginative containment in 'The Laboratory' suggest that Browning's poetic power comes through by his adoption of very definite dramatic moulds, out of which it emerges and escapes as indirect effects.

4
Browning's Now versus Carlyle's Today

We are now to see our Hero in the ... character of Poet; a character which does not pass.[1]

No sooner had Browning settled into his literary career and the character of an acknowledged poet, than a new kind of misunderstanding faced him. In 1836 Landor and Wordsworth had toasted 'the youngest poet of England' over a literary dinner at Talfourd's house. By the early 1840s Browning had also attracted admiration from Dickens, R. H. Horne and Forster. Thomas Carlyle, author of *Sartor Resartus* (1833) and *The French Revolution* (1837), met Browning in 1836. The satiric inventor of the 'Philosophy of Clothes' noticed that the young man was dandaical to a fault, but thought the poetry worth encouragement (Carlyle I, p. 4). Their friendship was to last over forty years, during which time Carlyle began by thinking that Browning had immense promise, if only he would express himself more plainly, and ended by feeling acutely disappointed in what he saw as the banal content and the riddling form of Browning's late works. In between lay a period of acceptance in the 1840s and 1850s: Carlyle particularly praised the 'Essay on Shelley' and *Men and Women*. Browning loved Carlyle dearly but never took his views on poetry to heart. Carlyle's personality could be loved and understood like that of the subjective poet in the 'Essay on Shelley': together his writing and personality made something singular and extraordinary. This chapter explores the Carlyle–Browning relationship with emphasis on Browning's particular way of writing about the present. Browning's 'now' differs from Carlyle's historical sense of 'today'.

'Ghosts ... patched with histories'

Sordello was Ezra Pound's model for his own epic or 'poem including history', the *Cantos*, but this was not because the poem provided a model historicism or theory of history.[2] Histories were only repairs in the poem's more significant spectral movements. The draft of Canto I (1917) addresses Browning:

> And half your dates are out, you mix your eras;
> For that great font Sordello sat beside –
> Tis an immortal passage, but the font? –
> Is some two centuries outside the picture.
> Does it matter?
>   Not in the least. Ghosts move about me
> Patched with histories.[3]

Those last two lines show Pound courting the ragged and dishevelled ghostly muse that haunts Book Three of *Sordello*, symbolizing Browning's political inspiration. Ghosts are by their nature untimely: neither 'immortal' as Pound, with a disciple's exaggeration, calls the passage about the font, nor in any familiar sense historical. In Browning's poem the font is a place of mourning where Sordello memorializes what he cannot remember, the death of his mother. It is a 'font-tomb', a 'vault', a 'crypt' (VI, l. 630; I, ll. 406, 438). Sordello's evening vigils at the font, sharing in fantasy the penance of the stone caryatids, are examples of a sense of present responsibility that goes beyond the strictly contemporary. Sordello's sense of relationship to the caryatids is peculiar to him: they are a memorial of his mother and of his own future death and burial at the font, but their significance does not stop there. In them he communes with various women who are not there, set apart as entombed vestals or walled-up nuns. His being with them evening after evening is the beginning of a sense of political responsibility that later draws him to the Guelf cause, broadly identified with the suffering and ghostly 'people'. Browning's 1863 dedication insists that the 'historical decoration was purposely of no more importance than a background requires; and my stress lay on the incidents in the development of a soul: little else is worth study' (Longman I, p. 353n.). But the development of Sordello's soul involves a strange sense of political responsibility, shared by Browning, to an idea of mankind or humanity that includes those not presently alive and to a notion of the present that includes what is not present.

Since Pound, Browning's poetry has become associated with literary modernism and with modernity in general, as if his work might be better understood in a context of later ideas and formal concerns.[4] It is tempting to think that criticism does a better job with the passage of time, but Browning himself was more inclined to think of time in terms of ghosts and the whirligig of revenge. 'Time's Revenges' (1845) is the title of a poem Browning designated in 1863 a dramatic romance, and which, oddly for the form, has no plot to speak of. Instead it focuses on states of mind in the manner of a dramatic lyric and especially emphasizes unrequited attachment and dissymmetry between relationships. The poem takes place in the present tense and describes two figures that, as it were, belong to the speaker: 'I've a friend, over the sea; / I like him, but he loves me; / It all grew out of the books I write': this friend admires the speaker's work. 'And I've a Lady' who 'calmly would decree / That I should roast at a slow fire / If that would compass her desire' (she is loved more than the friend and more than 'all my genius, all my learning'). The poet-speaker is alone in his garret and imagines the different behaviour towards him of the friend, the lady and the reader. However, these remain imaginings: the sick poet does not call his friend to nurse him, the lady does not ask him to be roasted, the reader does not provoke fury by questioning the poet's devotion to the lady. Nothing happens, destiny seems suspended and time revenges itself through intentions and imaginings that do not come to pass rather than through acts of retribution.

History, for Carlyle, manifested the possibility of crucial interventions in its narrative on the part of rare, gifted individuals. Amid the chaos it was possible to identify Destiny. The true Poet was a seer: Browning was, Carlyle initially hoped, such a poet. Browning's appeal for Carlyle was built on a certain theory of history and of contemporaneity. The friendship between Carlyle and Browning stretched from the late 1830s to the 1880s, but it was haunted by Browning's failure to respond to what Carlyle saw as the imperative of the present. Poetry, as Pound and Browning knew, is a space where ironies play and ghosts appear. Poetry accordingly allows access to a notion of history where time is not at one with itself. The present was extremely interesting for Browning, but his poems do not simply exist in shared historical time. They produce another 'now' that can be distinguished from the universal present. For example, Sordello's returns to the font allow him to imagine a past moment of another's forbidden sexual love followed by penance that lasts 'for ever' and is still happening in his own times (I, l. 426). His imagining responds to the pulsing tactile quality of the marble caryatids who bear the font.[5] They are 'Of just-tinged marble like Eve's lilied flesh / Beneath her Maker's finger when the fresh / First pulse of life shot brightening the snow' (I, ll. 413–15). They are 'just', barely, life-coloured, they were given life only a moment ago and are untarnished by original sin. Immediately lovely, they shrink under the weight of the font itself, which young Sordello reads as a penitential burden. The caryatids are absolutely new and historical at once.

'The good minute'

The 'good minute' is perhaps Browning's most memorable temporal figure. 'Two in the Campagna' (1855) from Carlyle's favourite Browning collection, *Men and Women*, describes the experience in terms of sexual love. The poem incorporates two different relations to time in its account of the touch of sexual experience.[6] One of its inter-pretations of the privileged moment recognizes the secondariness of literature. The poem 'knows itself', in the words of Paul de Man, 'to be mere repetition, mere fiction and allegory, forever unable to partici-pate in the spontaneity of action or modernity'.[7] For example, the feeling of brushing against an old thought in the second stanza:

> For me, I touched a thought, I know,
> Has tantalised me many times,
> (Like turns of thread the spiders throw
> Mocking across our path) for rhymes
> To catch at and let go.

Still, de Man points out, literature is also persistently tempted 'to fulfil itself in a single moment' (p. 152). In the tenth stanza the poem artic-ulates such a desire, such a close touch or near thing:

> ... I yearn upward – touch you close,
> Then stand away. I kiss your cheek,
> Catch your soul's warmth, – I pluck the rose
> And love it more than tongue can speak –
> Then the good minute goes.

Sordello is perhaps Browning's fullest narrative development of this conflict, dramatized in the career of Sordello from the heady moment of composition that launches his public life as a minstrel, but which is in fact a repetition of a 'sometime deed', through his attempt to initiate and theorize a poetic language simultaneously. Sordello dies, unable to choose between his vocation as a poet and his inherited destiny as leader of the Ghibellin party he spent most of his life opposing.

In Browning criticism, *Browning's Beginnings* by Herbert Tucker definitively charts the movements of a will to modernity in early and mid-period Browning. Tucker shows the linguistic and thematic paths that link Browning's distinctive initiatives to the past, particularly to Shelley. It's a pattern that is not confined to any particular phase of Browning's career: perhaps its most intense lyric expression is in 'Now', from the last collection, *Asolando* (1889):

> Out of your whole life give but a moment!
> All of your life that has gone before,
> All to come after it, – so you ignore
> So you make perfect the present, – condense,
> In a rapture of rage, for perfection's endowment,
> Thought and feeling and soul and sense –
> Merged in a moment which gives me at last
> You around me for once, you beneath me, above me –
> Me – sure that despite of time future, time past, –
> This tick of our life-time's one moment you love me!
> How long such suspension may linger? Ah, Sweet –
> The moment eternal – just that and no more –
> When ecstasy's utmost we clutch at the core
> While cheeks burn, arms open, eyes shut and lips meet!

So strong is the poem's condensed resistance to narrative and history that it seems somewhat perverse to investigate the perfect moment that it calls for. Still, lyric invocation opens up a distance between the poem's 'now' and the simple present. 'Now' does not take the present tense, active voice: it takes the vocative, initially urging 'give but a moment!' Making perfect the present in a simple kiss requires several supplementary processes: condensation, merging, enveloping and clutching. In the course of being prefigured in words, the relation between the 'you' implied from the first line and the 'me' that appears repeatedly in the second half of the poem undergoes extreme distortion. The question 'How long such suspension may linger?' holds off the verb to the end of the sentence, reminding the reader that the time of reading is not identical with the resolved narrative that the poem describes. Indeed, as the poem is addressed to the prospective partner in the 'moment eternal', by its very being 'Now' holds off the meeting with the desperately desired 'core' of being, even as it seductively tries to bring it on. The phrase 'clutch at the core' is haunted by the rhyming phrase 'clutch at a straw'. 'Now' suggests that physical passion is not the direct route to the core, rather a gesture in relation to it. It may be that the blazing, blindly groping, mute passion of clutching is where an authentic relation to the core lies, not in the grasp which wants to lay hold of it and resolve matters.

'Two in the Campagna' also suggests that the nucleus of temporal experience cannot be apprehended. The core is the name of something absolutely elusive, no matter how close you come. 'Where does the fault lie? what the core / Of the wound, since wound must be?' The poem leaves us to wonder what the core of a wound is. Is it a kind of font-tomb, the traumatic inward source of generativity, producing or resonating with the obvious mark or scar at the surface? When the surface heals over, does the core remain within it, still a wound? In 'Now' there is a momentary fantasy that 'you' takes on the function of a periphery to the core that is 'me': 'You around me ... beneath me, above me'. Cheeks, arms, eyes and lips do their stuff but these surrounding shell-phenomena provide no definite access to what is really being clutched at in the moment of ecstasy. This sense of something at once inside, outside and beside the self recalls a profoundly Shelleyan moment, the Poet's narcissistic dream of a veiled girl in *Alastor*, in a formative passage for Browning's notion of sexual love:

> her outspread arms now bare,
> Her dark locks floating in the breath of night,
> Her beamy bending eyes, her parted lips
> Outstretched, and pale, and quivering eagerly.
> His strong heart sunk and sickened with excess
> Of love. He reared his shuddering limbs and quelled
> His gasping breath, and spread his arms to meet
> Her panting bosom: ... she drew back a while,
> Then, yielding to the irresistible joy,
> With frantic gesture and short breathless cry
> Folded his frame in her dissolving arms.
> Now blackness veiled his dizzy eyes, and night
> Involved and swallowed up the vision; sleep,
> Like a dark flood suspended in its course,
> Rolled back its impulse on his vacant brain.
>
> (ll. 177–91)

In Browning's poetry also, sexual desire has something subtly impossible about it. His love poetry encompasses a temporal conflict within literature. Literature may be considered to be fiction and allegory, condemned to non-fulfilment, but it is also a performative language that fulfils itself in a single moment. 'Now' creates 'you', demands that the reader 'give me at last / You around me for once, beneath me, above me' to make the perfect reading, the perfect embrace. But the embrace dissolves as it enfolds.

One might compare with this Browning's development of the idea of his life as a work of art, 'R. B. a poem', in a letter to Elizabeth Barrett. Her previous letter asked him to 'teach me yourself' and his reply says that when he has finished *Luria* and 'some Romances and Lyrics, all dramatic', he will do as she bids:

> *then*, I shall stoop of a sudden under and out of this dancing ring of men & women hand in hand, – and stand still awhile, should my eyes dazzle, – and when that's over, they will be gone and you will be there, *pas vrai*? – For, as I think I told you, I always shiver involuntarily when I look .. no, glance .. at this First Poem of mine to be – 'Now' – I call it – what, upon my soul, – for a solemn matter it is – what is to be done *now*, believed *now*, so far as it has been revealed to me – solemn words, truly, – and to find myself writing them to anyone else! Enough now.[8]

I do not read the 'First Poem of mine to be' simply as a reference to a future literary work, the real work he writes about to Elizabeth Barrett and Alfred Domett. The capitalization and the context suggest that Browning is thinking along the lines of Aprile in *Paracelsus*: 'God is the PERFECT POET, / Who in his person acts his own creations' (II, ll. 601–2). This poem is to be lived rather than penned. Browning writes about abandoning dramatic poetry for life as poetry; it is the meeting with her, outside the dance of his own creations, which he calls 'this First Poem of mine to be'. Browning's letter holds off the solemnity of responsibility to the present, the encounter with the pure white light of lyric love. He finds himself pausing on a step, the punning *pas vrai* or true step away from the dance of his dramatic poetry.[9] This *pas vrai* also addresses EBB: 'you will be there', is it not so? and hints, very far ahead, at the solemn and unpoetical performative language of eternal vows.[10] He shivers and is able to say 'Enough now': enough of that for now, but also that's enough of now, let's go back to the unaccountable deferrals of writing.

Political differences

Carlyle disliked Shelley for his deathliness and had a gloomy attitude to the complications of modernity. Browning read *Sartor Resartus* in 1837, met Carlyle in 1839 and attended the lectures *On Heroes and Hero-Worship* in 1840. At this relatively politicized phase of Browning's career, the poet enthused to Domett: 'the intensity of [Carlyle's] Radicalism ... is exquisite.'[11] But this was a Tory radicalism that valued authority, the antithesis of Shelley's politics. Browning shared some of Carlyle's sympathies and had helped him research his *Oliver Cromwell's Letters and Speeches* (1845). 'Cavalier Tunes'[12] (1842) and the marching song for the other side, 'Fife, trump, drum, sound!' in the *Parleying* 'With Charles Avison' (1887), are a Carlylean combination of history, revolution and rousing music. Yet Browning's belief in liberty and his political liberalism had nothing in common with, say, the extreme racism that found expression in Carlyle's pro-slavery intervention 'On the Nigger Question' (1849). Browning wrote to Elizabeth Barrett: 'All men ought to be independent, whatever Carlyle may say.'[13] Browning's identification with the unrepresented masses, like Shelley's, extended to identification with the dead. He represents his republicanism to himself as a ghost in *Sordello*, and 'Saint Martin's Summer' (1876) associates march music with haunting: 'why should ghosts feel angered?/Let all their interference/Be faint march-music in the air!' Browning and Carlyle were contemporaries, but at the same time their work diverges over the meaning and significance of modernity and contemporaneity.

Carlyle wanted Browning's allegiance and attempted, unsuccessfully, to take up Browning's writings into his own sense of the present. He wrote that the Hero as Poet or Man of Letters was 'sent hither specially that he may discern for himself, and make manifest to us, [the] Divine Idea: in every generation it will manifest itself in a new dialect' (Carlyle V, p. 156). Poets should communicate much-needed and otherwise inaccessible truths to their fellow men. Carlyle did not value poetry as a literary genre but as a phenomenon in events. Early in his *History of Frederick the Great* (1858–65) he suggests that the poet ultimately tends to become a historian: 'the man of rhythmic nature will feel more and more his vocation towards the Interpretation of Fact; since only in the vital centre of all that, could we once get thither, lies all real melody; and ... he will become, he, once again the Historian of events' (Carlyle XII, p. 19). The kind of Fact that summons the poet comes from times of faith, spirituality and idealism, and modern Britain lacked the necessary qualities to provide poets with 'real melody'.

For Carlyle poetry was a kind of thought that articulated a hidden or inward melodic structure in an otherwise chaotic reality. The 'inarticulate unfathomable speech' of music exceeds logic but nonetheless lets the reader 'gaze' into the 'Infinite'. 'The Hero as Poet' elaborates that:

> A *musical* thought is one spoken by a mind that has penetrated into the inmost heart of the thing; detected the inmost mystery of it, namely the *melody* that lies hidden in it; the inward harmony of coherence which is its soul, whereby it exists, and has a right to be, here in this world. All inmost things, we may say, are melodious; naturally utter themselves in Song.
>
> (Carlyle V, p. 83)

Carlyle distinguishes genuine musical thought from contrived poetizing: 'What we want to get at is the *thought* the man had, if he had any: why should he twist it into jingle, if he *could* speak it out plainly?' (Carlyle V, p. 90).

Browning had attended the lectures on *Heroes and Hero-Worship*, and heard via Richard Monckton Milnes that Carlyle had praised *Sordello*.[14] Carlyle wrote to Browning the following year:

> Fight on: that is to say, follow truly, with steadfast singleness of purpose, with valiant humbleness and openness of heart, what best light *you* can attain to; following truly so, better and ever better light will rise on you. The light we ourselves gain, by our very errors if not otherwise, is the only precious light. Victory, what I call victory, if well fought for, is sure to you.[15]

His exhortations closely, flatteringly, resemble the description of Dante's creative struggle that Browning would have heard in the third lecture 'The Hero as Poet'. Of Dante's composition of *The Divine Comedy* in exile, Carlyle says:

> No Florence, nor no man or men, could hinder him from doing it, or even much help him in doing it ... 'If thou follow thy star, *Se tu segui tua stella*,' so could the hero, in his forsakenness, in his extreme need, still say to himself: 'Follow thy star, thou shalt not fail of a glorious haven!'   (Carlyle V, p. 90).

Browning and Carlyle shared a belief in the steadfast pursuit of creative destiny through hard work. For Browning this came from his poetic vocation: work would equip him for the moment when he happened upon his proper direction. This policy sustained him through many difficulties, but his private star was not a constant guiding light, but changeable in colour and form: 'My star that dartles the red and the blue!/Then it stops like a bird; like a flower, hangs furled' ('My Star', 1855).

'I never minded what Carlyle said of things outside his own little circle' Browning told William Allingham shortly after Carlyle's death in 1881, drawing a circle in the air with his forefinger. '[W]hat was it to me what he thought of Poetry or Music?'[16] Given the massive scale of Carlyle's writing, Browning's circle in the air is a wonderfully bold device. The poet's studied inattention was not only due to the temperamental contrast between the two men that left Carlyle wondering: 'He seems very content with life, and takes a great satisfaction in the world. It's a very strange and curious spectacle to behold a man in these days so confidently cheerful.'[17] Browning's poetry plays with time in complex ways. It also, as the 'Essay on Shelley' begins to spell out, takes its movements from powerfully invested temporal relationships with earlier poetry and with the future. 'How It Strikes a Contemporary' has been read as a portrait of Carlyle, and it provides a chance to think about Browning's idea of contemporaneity. His poetry resisted and still resists belonging exclusively to any present: it also continues to strike contemporaries with considerable force. This force is not a force of communication: in 'How It Strikes A Contemporary' (1855) the poet is, finally, distinguished from the town-crier 'Who blew a trumpet and proclaimed the news,/Announced the bull-fights, gave each church its turn,/And memorized the miracle in vogue!'

Carlyle read the nineteenth century as a dramatic epic in which he wanted to enlist contemporaries as protagonist/interpreters. His notion of 'the riddle of Destiny' suggests he was a forgetful reader of Greek drama, where Oedipus correctly answers the riddle of the Sphinx but goes on to catastrophically mistime his understanding of the riddle of his own life.[18] If today seemed unintelligible, Carlyle wished England to interpret it until it became clear. *Past and Present* (1843) represents the strange and new as a test of sense and courage. England must puzzle out the meaning of its present:

> With Nations it is as with individuals: Can they rede the riddle of Destiny? This English Nation, will it get to know the meaning of *its*

strange new today? Is there sense enough extant, discoverable anywhere or anyhow, in our united twenty-seven million heads to discern the same: valour enough in our twenty-seven million hearts to dare and do the bidding thereof? It will be seen!

(Carlyle X, pp. 7–8)

Compare with this Browning's 'Memorabilia' (1855), which responds with excitement and surprise to something that happened 'once' in the past but remains able to originate, to shock: 'Ah, did you once see Shelley plain, / And did he stop and speak to you? / And did you speak to him again? / How strange it seems and new!' For Carlyle enigma evokes a quest for understanding; 'Memorabilia' on the other hand links surprise to forgetting. Where Carlyle looks for valour in the hearts of the nation, 'Memorabilia' substitutes for a heart an almost weightless bit of discarded plumage: 'there I picked up on the heather / And there I put inside my breast / A moulted feather, an eagle-feather – / Well, I forget the rest.'

The feather is a very light relic and recalls the longing to be blown about in Shelley's 'Ode to the West Wind': 'O lift me as a wave, a leaf, a cloud!' Shelley's and Browning's capacity for conscious passivity in relation to the shocks of time contrasts with Carlyle's appeals to human steadfastness. For Carlyle poets should perceive and reveal to others the meaning of a 'today' characterized by confusion and degeneration. He more than once uses the archaism 'rede', meaning 'interpret'. Browning also uses the phrase in his long poem about Napoleon III's London retirement, *Prince Hohenstiel-Schwangau, Saviour of Society* (1871). The Prince describes himself as Sphinx, who encounters a female Oedipus in Leicester Square and longs to tell his secrets to her. The Sphinx has grown 'sick of snapping foolish people's heads, / And jealous for her riddle's proper rede' (ll. 10–11). Yet over two thousand words later the Prince has found it impossible to surrender the truth of his secret: 'But, do your best, / Words have to come: and somehow words deflect / As the best cannon ever rifled will' (ll. 2132–4). These facts about words may themselves be formative of history. The Prince holds a sealed letter: its contents are unknown but possibly of immense historical significance (perhaps a promise of support for the Italians in their war for freedom from Austria, according to the Penguin editors). The poem ends 'Double or quits! The letter goes! Or stays?' This unread letter figures the impossibility of getting 'to know the meaning' of Destiny, which is suffused with chance.

Carlyle and humanity

Elizabeth Barrett sent her poetry to Carlyle in the early 1840s, and wrote an essay about him (edited and revised by Horne, the praiser of *Sordello*) for a volume on *The New Spirit of the Age* (1844). Carlyle's sense of the timeless essence of humanity was important for her thinking about poetry. The essay greets Carlyle as a fellow of poets, according to an idealized account of the aim and end of poetry:

> 'The great fire-heart,' as [Carlyle] calls it, of human nature may burn too long without stirring ... and to emancipate the flame clearly and brightly, it is necessary to stir it up strongly from the lowest bar. To do this ... is the aim and end of all poetry of a high order, – this, – to resume human nature from its beginning, and return to first principles of thought and first elements of feeling; this, – to dissolve from the eye and ear the film of habit and convention, and open a free passage from beauty and truth, to gush in upon unencrusted perceptive faculties: for poetry like religion should make a man a child again in purity and unadulterated perceptivity.[19]

Poetry should have the effect of poking a fire, of washing your face, of becoming a child again. Browning's thoughts on the relation of poetry to the reader are at once less homely – 'A poet's affair is with God' – and cannier about resistance – 'It is all teaching, and the people hate to be taught' (Woolford and Karlin, p. 258). His poems figure reading poetry as a strange kind of growing up, – 'nothing ever will surprise me now', claims the hero of *Pauline*, after his first experience of books. At the other end of Browning's career the aged speaker of 'Development' (1889) still finds reading difficult but at least no longer crumples or defaces what he reads 'boy's way'.

Past and Present refers to a transcendent Eternity behind 'fearfully emblematic' reality, to the '*human*' identified by its relation to the truth, to Genius as 'the clearer presence of God most High in a man' (Carlyle X, p. 292). Barrett and Horne's essay celebrates the power of Carlyle the historian-magician to bring truth gushing in, to bring back 'his man from the grave of years ... with all his vital flesh as well as his thoughts about him' (pp. 243–4). The essay describes how, in the process of this dramatic writing, Carlyle conjures up the dead into a 'now' that abolishes temporal difference:

The reproduced man thinks, feels, and acts like himself at his most characteristic climax – and the next instant the Magician pitches him into Eternity ... But his power over the man, while he lasts, is entire, and the individual is almost always dealt with as in time-present. His scenes of bygone years, are all acted now, before your eyes.

In Browning's 'now', mind and body are haunted by the effects of an alien 'core' which cannot be reduced to those outward effects. In different ways ghost poems such as *Sordello*, 'St. Martin's Summer' and 'Bad Dreams IV' (1889) show a sense of responsibility to the dead and to the future that would not allow Browning to casually pitch them into Eternity. He is all too aware of their claims and powers. Barrett's Carlyle is a master of the secrets of the past which he revives and uncovers. Browning's 'now' is powered by secrets which he has no interest in revealing: swing open the front of the poet's house and you will not see the wellspring of creativity ('House', 1876). The mages in Browning poems do not reproduce but create something new: roses in the 'shut house of life' ('"Transcendentalism"'), a tree made of fire (*Sordello*), a talismanic ring (*The Ring and the Book*). Nonetheless Elizabeth Barrett wrote to Browning the following year about 'the great teacher of the age, Carlyle, who is also yours and mine. He fills the office of a poet – does he not? – by analyzing humanity back into its elements, to the destruction of the conventions of the hour.'[20] Browning would have agreed with Carlyle and EBB about the essential independence of the writer from received opinion. Yet Browning's sense of the office of a poet goes beyond Carlyle's just as his relation to convention was less innocent than childlike 'purity and unadulterated perceptivity'.

Carlyle's ideal of poetry involved immediacy, clarity and truth, qualities that he found lacking in his own times. The present was a fallen time, not without hope but confused and corrupted, faithless and therefore aberrant in relation to a divine origin. Mrs Orr recounts the story of Carlyle and Browning walking together in Paris in the 1850s. They passed an image of the Crucifixion – 'and glancing towards the figure of Christ, [Carlyle] said, with his deliberate Scotch utterance, "Ah, poor fellow, *your* part is played out!"' (*Life*, p. 173). He wanted literature and literary language to take on religion's prophetic function. If literature was not true to the observed world, or clear to the reader, it was worthless. Browning told Elizabeth Barrett 'Carlyle thinks modern Italy's abasement a direct judgement from God'.[21] His letter to her gives the sense of Carlyle's argument as follows:

> Here is a nation in whose breast arise men who could doubt, examine the new problems of the Reformation &c – trim the balance at intervals, and throw overboard the accumulation of falsehood ... now is the time for the acumen of the Bembos, the Bentivoglios and so forth .. and these and their like, one and all, turn round, decline the trouble, say 'these things *may* be true, or they may not .. mean-time let us go on verse-making, painting, music-scoring' – to which all the nation accedes as if relieved of a trouble – upon which God bids the Germans go in and possess them ...

For Carlyle all art that did not orient itself in relation to the pressing historical and national questions of the day was an evasion.

Carlyle's account of the text of Jocelin of Brakelond's chronicle in *Past and Present* praises the editor Rokewood for his way of setting history straight. The description of Rokewood's work also refers to Carlyle's own task of deciphering and reproducing history, for the historian edits the product of a divine Author. 'Not only has [Rokewood] deciphered his crabbed Manuscript into clear print; but he has attended ... to the important truth that the Manuscript so deciphered ought to have a meaning for the reader. Standing faithfully by his text, and printing its very errors in spelling, in grammar or otherwise, he has taken care by some note to indicate that they are errors, and what the correction of them ought to be' (Carlyle X, p. 42). Carlyle's editorial device in *Sartor Resartus* is closer to Browning in its proliferation of disconcerting ironies. Poetry's teaching is not the same as correcting or pointing out the right way and Browning refuses to provide a correct version of his poems by subsequent commentary. 'Childe Roland to the Dark Tower Came' (1855) begins 'My first thought was, he lied in every word' and the heroic quest notably follows the wrong direction to the end.

Carlyle's ideas of poetry, prose and song

Carlyle, who had abandoned poetry in the 1820s after his courtship of Jane Welsh, liked to advise Browning and other poets to write in prose. The suggestion was not because of the peculiarities of Browning's far from plain poetic language; it came from Carlyle's overwhelming sense of the need to engage with a shared present. He argued that the modern world was hostile to poetry and unprepared for it.[22] Poetry was a matter of exaggerated common sense; it should be a truthful reception of the world rather than a twisting of language. He told Browning in his first extant letter to him in 1841:

> If your own choice happened to point that way, I for one should hail it as a good omen that your next work were written in prose! Not that I deny you poetic faculty; far, very far from that. But unless poetic faculty mean a higher-power of common understanding, I know not what it means. One must first make a *true* intellectual representation of a thing, before any poetic interest that is true will supervene. All *cartoons* are geometrical withal; and cannot be made until we have fully learned to make mere *diagrams* well. It is this that I mean by prose ...

He shocked Elizabeth Barrett by making a similar suggestion to her.

Browning resisted Carlyle's advice about poetry by evasion rather than confrontation. His letter to Elizabeth on the subject is anecdotal and indirect; like Browning's best poems it does not aim at bare conceptual argument. She was troubled by Carlyle's having thought of her 'putting away even for a season, the poetry of the world'.[23] Browning's response draws her into the intimacy he shared with the Carlyles and his warm ironic tone counters the high seriousness of Carlyle's exhortations. The point of Browning's stories is that Carlyle belongs to poetry despite himself, without knowing it. The Carlyle who interests Browning lives a relation to language through desire and erroneous interpretation. Browning wrote:

> I know Carlyle and love him – know him so well, that I would have told you he had shaken that grand head of his at 'singing,' so thoroughly does he love and live by it. When I last saw him, a fortnight ago, he turned from I don't know what other talk, quite abruptly on me with, 'Did you never try to write a *Song*? Of all things in the world, *that* I should be proudest to do.'[24]

Browning's letter does not dwell on Carlyle's critical definitions. His fondness for the strange Scot is reminiscent of the 'Essay on Shelley', which says of the subjective poet: 'in our approach to the poetry, we necessarily approach the personality of the poet; in apprehending it we apprehend him, and certainly we cannot love it without loving him.' The letter's loving observation of 'dear' Carlyle envelops and deflects his theories:

Then came his definition of a song – then, with an appealing look to Mrs. C., – 'I always say that some day *"in spite of nature and my stars"* I shall burst into a song' (he is not mechanically 'musical,' he meant, and the music is the poetry, he holds, and should enwrap the thought as Donne says 'an amber-drop enwraps a bee') and then he began to recite an old Scotch song, stopping at the first rude couplet – 'The beginning words are merely to set the tune, they tell me' – and then again at the couplet about – or, to the effect that – 'give me' (but in broad Scotch) 'give me but my lass, I care not for my cogie.' *'He says,'* quoth Carlyle magisterially, 'that if you allow him the love of his lass, you may take away all else, – even his cogie, his cup or can, and he cares not' – just as a professor expounds Lycophron.

This affectionate glimpse of Carlyle at home nonetheless marks the limitations of his critical sensibility. Despite his magisterial tone, Carlyle can do little more than repeat the lines that have impressed him.[25] Older Browning's own handling of the classics was very unlike academic exposition in its concern, not with verbal music, but to translate the turns of the original in all their difficulty. No wonder that the professorial Carlyle was baffled by Browning's *Agamemnon* in the 1870s.

Having unsettled Elizabeth Barrett's sense of Carlyle's authority in literary matters, Browning illustrates the power of words to move the sage even against his own political inclinations:

Did I not hear him croon, if not certainly sing, 'Charlie is my darling' ('my *darling*' with an adoring emphasis) and then he stood back, as it were, from the song, to look at it better, and said 'How must that notion of ideal wondrous perfection have impressed itself in this old Jacobite's "young Cavalier" – ("They go to save their land, and the *young Cavalier*!") – when I who care nothing about such a rag of a man, cannot but feel as he felt, in speaking his words after him!' After saying which, he would be sure to counsel everybody to get their heads clear of all singing!

Song can dictate and produce feelings alien to the hearer or the performer. Browning does not point out Carlyle's contradictory attitudes to belittle him; he delightedly recognizes the unaccountable power of song at work in Carlyle's life.

Carlyle, however, was not above disparaging Browning. When Bronson Alcott, an American vegetarian friend of Emerson's, visited

London in 1842, he recalled: 'The third time we met, little Browning *Paracelsus* was there, a neat dainty little fellow, speaking in the Cockney-quiz dialect; to whom poor Alcott's vegetable-diet concern was as ridiculous as it could be to most.'[26] Browning corroborated the event in a letter to Domett:

> Carlyle I saw some weeks since: a crazy .. or sound asleep .. not dreaming .. American was with him – a 'special friend' of Emerson's – and talked! I have since heard, to my solace, that my outrageous laughters have made him ponder seriously of the hopelessness of England – which he would convert to something or other.[27]

The outrageousness of Browning's laughters would probably have endeared him to Carlyle, who loved hearty laughing. But the hilarity and Browning's vagueness about the American's pet project cover a memory that Browning may have wished to keep from Carlyle. Browning had himself experimented with vegetarianism in emulation of Shelley, whom Carlyle found unmanly and morbid. A year of bread and potatoes in his late teens had meant near disaster for his health. Carlyle nicknamed Alcott 'Potato-Quixote', a name that would have been unkindly apt for the author of *Sordello*: the poem begins with an allusion to Cervantes' novel. Browning, it seems, never came so near to reducing his friend's strangeness to mere eccentricity.

Carlyle followed Browning's career with interest in the 1840s and said 'wonderfully kind things' about the latest number of *Bells and Pomegranates* in April 1846. In May the Barrett–Browning letters return to Carlyle, 'the present age', 'art' and (Elizabeth Barrett's word) 'Humanity'. Barrett had disagreed with her friend the writer Anna Jameson, saying: 'art surely, if art is anything, is the expression, not of the characteristics of an age except accidentally, .. essentially it is the expression of Humanity in the individual being.'[28] Browning's reply does not take up the idea of 'expression of Humanity in the individual being'. More negatively, his hopeful 'green bough inside a truss of straw' would be 'some unbeliever' who would be unable to participate in the acknowledged struggles of the day.[29] He responded:

> All you write about Art is most true. Carlyle has turned and forged, reforged on his anvil that fact that 'no age ever appeared heroic to itself' .. and so, worthy of reproduction in Art by itself .. I thought that after Carlyle's endeavours nobody could be ignorant of *that*, –

nobody who was obliged to seek the *proof* of it *out* of his own experience .. The cant is, that an 'age of transition' is the melancholy thing to contemplate and delineate – whereas the worst things of all to look back on are times of comparative standing still, rounded in their impotent completeness – So the Young England [Tory] imbeciles hold that 'belief' is the admirable point – *in what* they judge comparatively immaterial![30]

Elizabeth Barrett's decidedly modern *Aurora Leigh* (1856) repeats the message a decade later: 'Ay; but every age / Appears to souls who live in't (ask Carlyle) / Most unheroic' (V, ll. 155–7). The project of *Past and Present* was to edit and write about the past of England in order that men might 'know Wisdom, Heroism, when they see it' and live accordingly (Carlyle X, p. 38). Browning's poetry, whatever its historical setting, throbs with dramatic interpersonal and political action because of his interest in incompleteness.

In 1852 Carlyle greeted Browning's 'Essay on Shelley' as properly 'human' speech:

> I liked the Essay extremely well indeed; a solid, well-wrought, massive, manful bit of discourse; and interesting to me, over and above, as the first bit of *prose* I have ever seen from you; – I hope only the first of very many. You do not know how cheering to me the authentic sound of a *human* voice is! I get so little except ape-voices; the whole Universe filled with one wide tempestuous Cackle.[31]

The human voice achieved by Browning in the 'Essay' emerges between Shelley's voice which, for Carlyle, 'has too much of the *ghost*', and the goose-voices of a cackling modern public. (Perhaps it was Carlyle who inspired the older Browning to name two pet geese 'Edinburgh' and 'Quarterly'? Their fondness for him contradicted Carlyle's estimate of human geese as cackling defenders of convention.) Carlyle found Shelley 'Hades-like'. Shelley's devoted reader Browning was the man of the hour:

> Give us some more of *your* writing, my friend; we decidedly need a man or two like you, if we could get them! Seriously, dear Browning, you must at last gird up your loins again; and give us a right stroke of work: ... Nor do I restrict you to Prose, in spite of all I have said and still say: Prose or Poetry, either of them you can still

master; and we will wait for you with welcome in whatever form your own *Daimon* bids. Only see that he *does* bid it; and then go with your best speed ...

The 'Essay on Shelley' makes frequent reference to the 'human': but the notion of humanity is not central to Browning's theory of literary creation and literary history. Beginning with the 'objective poet, as the phrase now goes' , Browning sets 'the manifested action of the human heart and brain' with 'the phenomena of the scenic universe' as examples of the 'things external' that the objective poet reproduces. Moreover the objective poet, unlike the subjective, makes appeal to and refers to 'the aggregate human mind', a phrase Browning uses twice to denote the remaining 'raw material' upon which 'spiritual comprehension' must operate. Browning describes the contrasting figure, 'the subjective poet of modern classification' as having to do '[n]ot with the combination of humanity in action, but with the primal elements of humanity ... and he digs where he stands'. (The phrase 'primal elements of humanity' is reminiscent of Barrett and Horne's description of Carlyle 'analyzing humanity back into its elements'. However, they see analysis of humanity as the aim and end of poetry whereas for Browning humanity is part of a more extensive poetic process.) The subjective poet 'does not paint pictures and hang them on the walls, but rather carries them on the retina of his own eyes: we must look deep into his human eyes, to see those pictures on them'. The human is less an absolute value, than a vehicle for poetry's pictures. Those pictures constitute a dislocated glimpse of the external: the eyes reveal not the inwardness of a soul, but a 'reflex', a reflection of divine intuitions. Likewise according to the 'Essay', Shelley's soul aspired 'to elevate and extend itself in conformity with its still-improving perceptions of no longer the eventual Human, but the actual Divine'. Browning even argues that Shelley, had he lived, 'would have finally ranged himself with the Christians'. Shelley's poetry is, for Browning, 'a sublime fragmentary essay towards a presentment of the correspondency of the universe to Deity, of the natural to the spiritual, and of the actual to the ideal'. The 'Human' of Carlyle and Barrett is too simple and positive a value to allow these negotiations between fragment and whole, past and present.

In its discussion of Shakespeare 'The Hero as Poet' asks: 'poetic creation, what is this ... but *seeing* the thing sufficiently?' – the thing being human life (Carlyle V, p. 104). And in these terms Browning wins high praise:

I shall look far, I believe, to find such a pair of *eyes* as I see busy there inspecting human life this long while. The keenest insight into men and things; – and all that goes along with really good *insight*: a fresh valiant manful character equipped with rugged humour, with just love, just contempt, well carried and bestowed; – in fine a most extraordinary power of expression; such I must call it, whether it be 'expressive' *enough*, or not.

> (*Carlyle to Mill, Sterling and Browning*, p. 298)

The chief value of *Men and Women* for Carlyle was Browning's observation of a shared contemporary scene. Carlyle also sees a 'dark side to the picture' in Browning's 'unintelligibility', yet now he no longer identifies articulate clearness only with prose:

A writing man is there to be understood: let him lay that entirely to heart, and conform to it patiently; the sooner the better!

I do not at this point any longer forbid you *verse*, as probably I once did. I perceive it has grown to be your dialect, it comes more naturally than prose; and in prose too a man can be 'unintelligible' if he like! ... Continue to write in verse, if you find it handier. And what more? Aye, what, what! Well the sum of my ideas is: If you took up some one *great* subject, and tasked all your powers upon it for a long while, vowing to heaven that you *would* be plain to mean capacities, then – ! – But I have done, *done*. Good be with you always dear Browning; and high victory to sore fight!

> (pp. 299–300)

When Browning produced *The Ring and the Book*, its subject did not fit Carlyle's notion of greatness. He said it was 'all made out of an Old Bailey story that might have been told in ten lines and only wants forgetting'. He reduced the poem's elaborate relation between fragmentary fact and poetry to a joke. Allingham records his comment: 'But the whole is on a most absurd basis. The real story is plain enough on looking into it. The girl and the handsome priest were lovers' (*Diary*, p. 207). In *Red Cotton Night-Cap Country* (1873), a poem influenced by the red Cap of Liberty in his own *French Revolution*, Allingham notes that Carlyle found 'ingenious remarks here and there; but nobody out of Bedlam ever before thought of choosing such a theme' (*Diary*, pp. 224–5). Browning had described the recent events upon which the poem is based as 'a capital brand-new subject'.[32]

A verbal portrait, Carlyle felt, was the product of human sympathy and discernment. It therefore revealed as much about the writer as the subject:

> Find a man whose words paint you a likeness, you have found a man worth something; mark his manner of doing it, as very characteristic of him. In the first place, he could not have discerned the object at all, or seen the vital type of it, unless he had, what we may call, *sympathised* with it, – had sympathy in him to bestow on objects.
> (Carlyle V, p. 93)

'Portrait-painting' was according to 'The Hero as Poet' Shakespeare's particular greatness, the revelation of the 'inmost heart and generic secret' of the thing he looked at. Browning's objective poet, the poet of Othello, also painted portraits and hung them on the walls, but the 'Essay on Shelley' describes another kind of poetry, a different kind of secret. The subjective poet is a 'particular describer' and 'we must look deep into his human eyes to see [the] pictures on them'. His inmost heart and generic secret is a landscape: 'those external scenic appearances that strike out most abundantly and uninterruptedly his inner light and power.'

'"Transcendentalism"'

'"Transcendentalism"' takes up the Carlylean idea of a poet who writes prose, offering 'thoughts' fit for 'grown men'. Its title adopts a term used pejoratively by *The Athenaeum*, which claimed that *Sordello*'s obscurity of thought 'carries us too far into the regions of transcendentalism to offer any certainty of a satisfactory solution'.[33] Browning sets up transcendentalism in opposition to the creative immediacy of magic words, his examples being the German visionary Jacob Boehme (1575–1624) who, like the Wordsworth of the '"Intimations" Ode' (1807), converses with flowers, and John of Halberstadt, who lived the century before Boehme and used words to conjure up roses in his room. Despite his rational refusal to believe in table-rapping spiritualism Browning understood poetry's closeness to the occult. The poet in Browning is often an initiate to some kind of secret knowledge, and the crafts practised by the armour maker in *Sordello* or the goldsmith in *The Ring and the Book* are partly magical. Browning also sometimes represents magical phenomena as strange visionary versions of natural objects. *Sordello* III, ll. 595–607 briefly entertains the notion that the poem is a fierily beautiful tree (a 'transcendental platan') conjured up by an arch-mage to court a 'novice-queen'. His mimesis is only temporarily impressive, however. The tree fades into flinders and dust, the mage goes to sleep and the woman looks on in 'uncontrolled delight'. The tree has not transcended her defences and the mage's mastery has been overcome. But what does 'transcendentalism' mean? What happens when the movement of transcendence (from the Latin 'to pass over or beyond') is domesticated into a doctrinal '-ism'?

In Kant's philosophy, the transcendental is opposed to and prior to the empirical; it grounds the possibility of the sensory experience which British empiricism (Mill, for instance) claimed was the only possible ground for all knowledge. In nineteenth-century Anglo-American literary culture the word crops up in diverse contexts, notably in connection with the group surrounding the poet Emerson in New England in the 1840s and 1850s. The term crossed out of theory and into the rigours of widespread usage. This may be one reason that the term interested Browning; he did not write a poem called 'Utilitarianism' or 'Benthamism'.[34] Carlyle's work subjects 'transcendental' and its cognate terms to varied treatment. He uses the term to mean surpassing ordinary experience: Teufelsdrockh's anxiety is called transcendental in *Sartor Resartus* (Carlyle I, p. 113). *The French Revolution* states that 'Very frightful it is when a Nation, rending asunder its Constitutions and Regulations which were grown dead cerements for it, becomes *trans*cendental; and must now seek its wild way through the New, Chaotic' (Carlyle IV, p. 2). Dante and Shakespeare in their perfection are transcendental according to 'On Heroes and Hero-Worship'. The word can also be a term of abuse: 'To such length can transcendental moonshine, cast by some morbidly radiating Coleridge into the chaos of a fermenting life, act magically ...' (Carlyle XI, p. 96). Barrett and Horne quote Carlyle's swingeing abuse of -isms in his preface to Emerson's *Essays*:

> In a word, while so many Benthamisms, Socialisms, Fourrierisms, *professing* to have no soul, go staggering and lowing like monstrous mooncalves, the product of a heavy-laden moon struck age; and in this same baleful 'twelfth hour of the night' even galvanic Puseyisms, as we say, are visible, and dancings of the sheeted dead – shall not any voice of a living man be welcome to us, even because it is alive?

These -isms profess to be without soul and are nothing but apparitions and ghosts. Their pretensions to scientific method and system horrify Carlyle for whom 'soul' was an essential component of thought. The magnificent grotesquerie of this passage prompts Barrett and Horne to identify Carlyle with life against death.

In Browning the living mingle inseparably and disturbingly with the dead. An audience of brother-poets and critics, quick and dead, are called to witness the opening of *Sordello*. There is horror at the thought that the poem might be heard by one dead poet in particular. Shelley's silent power to hear is potentially devastating for *Sordello* and for poetic language in general. '"Transcendentalism"' is spoken by one brother poet to another – it could be Browning to Carlyle, or in the poetic line from Browning to Wordsworth: 'Stop playing, poet! May a brother speak? / 'Tis you speak, that's your error. Song's our art.' But the relation to Wordsworth surpasses the intended reproach that he is prosy; '"Transcendentalism"' is, as Ann Wordsworth puts it, 'remorselessly charged with Wordsworth's '"Intimations" Ode'.[35] 'In its creative resistance to Wordsworth's chronicle of loss and gain, Browning's poem dissolves its own surface, taking the reader down into a play of writing that has no external or literal equivalences' (p. 16). The 'pure face' that threatened all articulate language at the opening of *Sordello* now has a correspondingly disembodied and disturbing voice. We could say that the poem is spoken by a phantom Shelley, reproaching Browning for his attachment to dramatic speech and psychology. But the phantom voice discomfits any notion of belonging: Shelley seems to represent something that resists appropriation.

The sudden rising of a deadly Shelleyan face upon *Sordello* becomes in '"Transcendentalism"' a deliberate breaking-in, to tell the story of the apparition of a 'sudden rose' which has sunlike qualities. *Sordello* suggests that such unlikely materializations also occur in history. The earlier poem links the Carlylean theme of the emergence of heroes into history with the surprising apparition or disappearance of cities, phantoms and flowers. The Longman editors relate the poem's treatment of the hero appearing amid collective humanity to Carlyle's early work, and find in Book V of *Sordello* an uncertainty implicit in Carlyle: whether great men precipitate historical change or represent change collectively accomplished by the multitude.[36] Perhaps this question of agency arises because of the way that the hero appears. *Sordello* suggests that uncertainty about the priority of the individual or the multitude is a response to discontinuous apparition or sudden flowering: 'That loose eternal unrest – who devised / An apparition i' the midst? the rout / Who checked, the breathless ring who formed about / That sudden flower' (V, ll. 118–21).

The originations in '"Transcendentalism"' and *Sordello* are not modelled on natural processes but on the way that language can posit something entirely new without the delays of organic growth. *Sordello* puts poetry aside to investigate beginning in literature through the poet himself, only to find that he is not himself:

> Who began
> The greatnesses you know? – ay, your own art
> Shall serve us: put the poet's mimes apart –
> Close with the poet – closer – what? a dim
> Too plain form separates itself from him?
> Alcama's song enmeshes the lulled Isle,
> Woven into the echoes left erewhile
> Of Nina's, one soft web of song: no more
> Turning his name, now, flower-like o'er and o'er!
> (V, ll. 96–104)

The poet's self cannot be closed with, it turns out to be haunted by a 'dim / Too plain form' of his precursor: Alcama's song is a text woven into his precursor Nina's making 'one soft web of song'. Poetry flowers, but not in the way that flowers flower. The soft web has the poets' names woven into it and to call poetry the 'poet's mimes' reinforces the sense of dispossession at the inseparableness of the names of individuals from the knitted films of text. A mime is a movement that does not belong to the mimic who performs it. Mime also engages negatively with the objective world because it makes visible objects that are not there.

The gesture of turning a flower-like name recurs in a letter to Elizabeth Barrett in 1845. The flower is a mimosa, the mimic plant, on Browning's table. He has just learned Elizabeth's nickname 'Ba': 'I TRIED (– more than *wanted* –) to call you *that* on Wednesday! I have a flower here – rather, a star, a mimosa, which must be turned and turned, the side to the light changing in a little time to the *leafy* side, where all the fans lean and spread .. so I turn your name to me, that side I have not last seen'.[37] The name is an object of fascination for Browning, and in the case of 'Ba' there is no impediment to Browning's passionate onomatophiliac gaze at its leaning and spreading as it turns from side to side. 'Ba' is a private domestic name and not the name on Elizabeth Barrett's books. Poetry both makes the poet's name and renders it inseparable from the dim forms and echoes of writing. It takes up the poet's voice and name into a web of song from which it cannot be plucked.

Browning is delighted that Elizabeth Barrett Barrett will remain 'my EBB' even after marriage has made her Elizabeth Barrett Browning. This easy turning of one name into another is not possible in poetry: in *Sordello* the haunted hero is never whole, and mankind is more than once typified as a phantom or phantasm (III, ll. 677ff.; V, l. 114). The mimosa is of course also known as the sensitive plant. The plant is often taken to be a synonym for Shelley himself, after the poem of that name.[38] Shelley, the mimic plant that turns and turns: not a self, but after all, a name for a movement of writing.

The untimely supernatural flowering in '"Transcendentalism"' represents the strange way that literature relates to time. The rhymes of fifteenth-century John of Halberstadt manage to be contemporary; his roses cover Boehme's book although Boehme did not write it until after John of Halberstadt's death. The mage

> with a 'look you!' vents a brace of rhymes,
> And in there breaks the sudden rose herself,
> Over us, under, round us every side,
> Nay, in and out the tables and the chairs
> And musty volumes, Boehme's book and all,–

This rhymed rose is strange. It does not grow organically but 'breaks' like the dawning sun. As the rose appears it takes up the word 'sun', breaks and buries it: the '*sudden* rose'. The association of sun and poet began with *Pauline*'s 'Sun-treader' and is implied in the letter to 'Ba' where the mimosa is her name, turning to Browning like a heliotropic plant seeking sunlight. A magical possibility of signification as 'flesh / Composed of suns' appears in the *Parleying* 'With Bernard de Mandeville', Browning's last engagement with Carlyle. '"Transcendentalism"' develops the allusion strangely and in a way that owes nothing to Wordsworth's 'clouds of glory' in the '"Intimations" Ode'. The rose / sun's shut-in brightness entombs as it illuminates: 'Buries us with a glory, young once more, / Pouring heaven into this shut house of life.'

The apparent aim of the last six lines resembles Carlyle's objective in *Past and Present*: to teach contemporaries by pointing to a more authentic past:

> So come, the harp back to your heart again!
> You are a poem, though your poem's naught.

The best of all you showed before, believe,
Was your own boy-face o'er the finer chords
Bent, following the cherub at the top
That points to God with his paired half-moon wings.

Authentically good work comes from a human relation to the Divine, glimpsed in the playing poet's young face. But the boy-face becomes poetic and points to God only by following the cherub carved at the top of his harp in an act of unconscious imitation. The 'boy-face' that denotes a boyish desire for 'images and melody' is not anyone's 'own'. Shelley, the lyric poet dead at 29, and Chatterton the 'marvellous boy' here blend with Browning the 'oddish sort of boy' who has never grown up into prose. The double look that simultaneously concentrates on the finer chords of the harp, and follows the cherub whose wings point to God, avoids facing the dead Shelley who terrorized *Sordello*. The self-overcoming in '"Transcendentalism"' is a deflection and articulation of anxiety about the facelessness and voicelessness of poetry's sights and sounds.

How it struck a contemporary

Carlyle promised Browning that he would read *Men and Women* with attention:

> As indeed I perceive all manner of intelligent people are diligently doing. Such is the fact; beyond doubt, in this bottomless, shoreless, vilely fermenting mud-lake and general reservoir of Human Nonsense, which is called the 'Literary Public' ... Brutal Delirium only *seems* to be the King of this world: and is not in reality.[39]

The poet is, must be, ahead of his contemporaries. Browning's dramatic lyric 'How It Strikes a Contemporary' was admired by Carlyle, but suggests that almost *nothing* to do with poetry strikes the poet's contemporary. The poem details unreliable observations and some speculation about the person of the poet: 'this, or something like it, was his way.' Browning's poet is a 'a man of mark' and the poem is full of marking, cognizance, taking account and re-marking. It is also full of error and misinterpretation. The narrator's father points out the poet as a Corregidor, judge or literally corrector. His son is wrong in identifying the town-crier as the poet: 'We were in error; that was not the man.'

The poet's observable life appears to be full of mistakes: he and his dog 'turned up ... the alley.../That leads nowhither' and they took the air 'just at the wrong time', unlike the speaker who heads out 'to make the most of time' at the end of the poem. The narrator doesn't know that writing verse is making the most of time: he would not have understood Sordello's waiting with the patient caryatids at Goito. In the absence of a perceptible identity for the poet the narrator attributes uncanny life to his clothes. His 'cloak/Had purpose, and the ruff, significance'. He wears a 'scrutinizing hat' and 'the ferrel of his stick' tries the mortar as if by its own volition. The poet is a man who remarks, watches, sees without staring and he is marked in turn by gossip and imagining. The neighbour 'marked the shameful and notorious fact' that he was a 'recording chief-inquisitor'. He is also disturbing to look at: 'you stared at him,/And found, less to your pleasure than surprise,/He seemed to know you and expect as much.' And his look haunts the looked-at, in a wonderful backwards formulation of how literature strikes or touches: 'there wanted not a touch,/A tang of ... well, it was not wholly ease,/As back into your mind the man's look came'.

Can religion put the poem straight? References to the poet's work for 'our Lord the King' suggest that he is close to God. Browning wrote to Ruskin in 1856 that 'A poet's affair is with God, to whom he is accountable, and of whom is his reward'. But this relation, as Browning understands it, cannot be observed by a third party, so for his contemporaries this poet appears to be a kind of mysterious angelic spy. The poet's true business eludes the narrator, who sees only the narrative content of his life. In this sense 'How It Strikes' is a counter-poem to '"Transcendentalism"', one poem being curiously drained of colour where the other is flooded with it.

Carlyle's response to *Balaustion's Adventure* (1871) ends by describing Browning and his poetry in terms rather like those used in 'How It Strikes a Contemporary'. Allingham's *Diary* records the verdict:

> I read it all twice and found out the meaning of it. Browning most ingeniously twists the English language into riddles – 'There! there is some meaning in this – can you make it out?' I wish he had taken to prose. Browning has far more ideas than Tennyson, but is not so truthful. Tennyson means what he says, poor fellow! Browning has a meaning in his twisted sentences, but he does not really go into anything, or believe much about it. He accepts conventional values.
>
> (p. 205)

Carlyle disliked late Browning perhaps because of the shift to nineteenth-century settings, characters and stories, or perhaps because Browning continued with his poetic project regardless of accusations of unintelligibility. Carlyle read each poem promptly on publication, only to damn it. Of *Prince Hohenstiel-Schwangau* (1871), which takes on his own notion of destiny, Carlyle wrote to his brother John that it was Browning's 'worst hitherto'.[40] Two years later the emphatically contemporary and anecdotal *Inn Album* (1875), full of topical references to high and popular culture, all the 'noise' of London that Carlyle so loathed, was judged in a letter of 16 February 1876 'the worst of all he has given us'. The suggestion that Browning ought to translate the Greek also led to disappointment. In 1877 *The Agamemnon of Aeschylus* was offered in dedication to Carlyle as 'commanded' by him and dignified by 'the insertion of his dear and noble name'. But Carlyle found the translation unreadable.

A last parleying

Browning quarrelled with Carlyle only in his poems. The nature of these poems means that the conflict did not take the form of logical dispute. '"Transcendentalism"', 'How it Strikes a Contemporary' and 'With Bernard de Mandeville' are less philosophical arguments (which would require shared assumptions and a common language) than ironic displacements of Carlyle's position and his critical authority. These intended criticisms occur en route to a more general and radical displacement of subjectivity in writing. In the *Parleying* 'With Bernard de Mandeville' Browning called on the eighteenth-century author to 'confute for me / This parlous friend'. Carlyle had died in 1881; after years of advice how pleasurable to teach *him* that although he sees '"No sign ... / No stirring of God's finger to denote / He wills that right should have supremacy / On earth, not wrong! ...",' there is a purpose at work. Yet the intention to correct Carlyle is only actualized in his absence, and in the absence of Mandeville also. Browning routinely wrote for and to the dead.

The title *Parleyings with Certain People of Importance in Their Day* takes up a moment in Dante's *Vita Nuova* first developed by Browning in 'One Word More' (1855). In 'One Word More' Dante is drawing an angel for his dead love Beatrice, when the dead and damned from the *Inferno* break in on him and haul him back to writing:

> Dante standing, studying his angel, –
> In there broke the folk of his Inferno.
> Says he – 'Certain people of importance'
> (Such he gave his daily dreadful line to)
> 'Entered and would seize, forsooth, the poet.'
> Says the poet – 'Then I stopped my painting.'

Dante is admired because, like Carlyle and Browning, he knew how to hate: 'loved well because he hated, / Hated wickedness that hinders loving'. The *Parleying* 'With Bernard de Mandeville' returns to questions of good and evil which are, in the dead writer's case, introduced through reading. Browning does not ask Mandeville for 'new gainings from the grave'. He tells Mandeville: 'I ask no more / Than smiling witness that I do my best / With doubtful doctrine'. Mandeville's book, *The Fable of the Bees: Or, Private Vices, Publick Benefits* (1724) is a satire, dealing in the doubtful doctrine of irony.

The way of reading that the first section of 'With Bernard de Mandeville' describes is totally different from Browning's own as suggested in his poems and dedications, and as it is explicitly expressed in his correspondence with Ruskin. It puts forward a practice that the poem itself confutes. Lines 1–10 adopt a depth–surface model of interpretation and describe moving through 'turbidity' down to a profound harmony. They espouse 'logic' and do not mention the loving attention that Browning felt was essential to reading. The subtle reader of Mandeville's counsels

> Could, through turbidity, the loaded line
> Of logic casting, sound deep, deeper, till
> It touched a quietude and reached a shrine
> And recognized harmoniously combine
> Evil with good, and hailed truth's triumph – thine,
> Sage dead long since, Bernard de Mandeville!

In addition to the circumstantial evidence that this subtler skill of reading is not the kind of reading Browning wanted for his own poems, the language of the passage hints at the limitations of the model it proposes. The image of measuring depths by 'casting' the 'loaded' line of logic, pulls the plumbline out of true by simultaneously suggesting the casting of loaded dice. Logic cheats by denying the chances of reading what literature can say outside logic's linguistic assumptions and conventions. A poem in the next collection,

'Inapprehensiveness' (1889) also uses the notion of touching quietude, and there, 'quietude' is an inapprehensive misnomer for an immense unpredictable possibility contained in a hidden germ or generative core: 'You let your eyes meet mine, touch what you term / Quietude – that's an universe in germ'.

Browning's lesson to Carlyle also concerns reading, and the figure of a 'ground-plan' in section VII of his poem parodies Carlyle's letter to him years before about the need to learn how to make a diagram (prose) before going on to the freehand drawing (poetry). The *Parleying* takes as its first example of signification a ground plan of Goethe's estate in Wiemar (Carlyle loved and translated Goethe). The plan is marked with letters A to Z to show the function of the build- ings. In a tone of strained patience Browning asks Carlyle: 'Do you look beyond / The algebraic signs, and captious say / "Is A. the House? But where's the roof to A., / Where's Door, where's Window?"' This folly resembles a 'mortal purblind' error in reading, 'seeking in the symbol no mere point / To guide our gaze through what were else inane, / But things – their solid selves'. But, as the second section of the poem argues, error is inevitable: 'foiled darings, fond attempts back-driven, / Fine faults of growth, brave sins which saint when shriven'. The poem began with the promise to review Mandeville's teaching 'not as fools opine / Its purport might be'. Section VII sets up literal interpretation as 'folly' and the province of 'simple ones' who ask: 'Is, joint by joint, / Orion man-like, – as these dots explain / His constellation? Flesh composed of suns – / How can such be?' This poetic question about signification attracted the notice of Jacques Lacan, who quotes it in his 1953 report 'The function and field of speech and language in psychoanalysis' published in *Ecrits* (1966). Immediately after the quotation Lacan comments: 'Such is the fright that seizes man when he unveils the face of his power that he turns away from it even in the act of laying its features bare.'[41] Apprehension, a favourite Browning word, names both fear and understanding. Perhaps the folly of literal interpretation is inevitable and there is no way of not falling victim to apprehensiveness in one form or another, reading an ironic text like Mandeville's *Fable of the Bees*. In this context a parleying would mean both a conversation and the negotiation of an implied conflict.

Browning repeats the lesson of 'Two in the Campagna', 'Must I go / Still like the thistle-ball, no bar, / Onward, whenever light winds blow, / Fixed by no friendly star?' Reading is always 'Off again!' – or as 'With Bernard de Mandeville' puts it:

> Look through the sign to the thing signified –
> Shown nowise, point by point at best descried,
> Each an orb's topmost sparkle: all beside
> Its shine is shadow: turn the orb one jot –
> Up flies the new flash to reveal 'twas not
> The whole sphere late flamboyant in your ken!

The starry points are not consistently present in space: they are produced as momentary discontinuous flashes. The turning that reveals these flashes is figuratively the movement of language, poetic troping as well as the spinning orbit of star or planet. The new flash thus produces a new but finite understanding of all that has gone before. And again, the language is that of Browning's description of 'the spheric poetic faculty of Shelley, as its own self-sufficing central light, radiating equally through immaturity and accomplishment, through many fragments and occasional completion, reveals it to the competent judgement'.

When the Carlyle-figure in 'With Bernard de Mandeville' responds 'What need of symbolizing?' the poem turns to myth. What it mythologizes is a troubled relation to 'influence': the old theme returns on a cosmic scale. In the last sections of the *Parleying*, the sun is Shelleyan in its suddenness, joy and erotic power. It leaps up, as does the sun at the beginning of Shelley's *Triumph of Life* (1824): 'the Sun sprang forth / Rejoicing in his splendour' and 'the mask / Of darkness fell from the awakened Earth'. Section IX of Browning's poem begins: 'Boundingly up through Night's wall dense and dark, / Embattled crags and clouds, outbroke the Sun / Above the conscious earth ...' Browning's conscious earth does not share man's apprehensions. She can 'acknowledge Sun's embrace sublime' at the same time as ecstatically thrilling to it. Creation laughs and is glad at the dawn, but in an anticipation of the vocabulary of 'Now', man wishes to 'condense / – Myself – Sun's all-pervading influence / So as to serve the needs of mind'. Man longs to 'see, / Touch, understand' an 'outside mind'. But despite Carlyle's admonitions that Browning must unfold his thought into articulate clearness: 'All in vain / Would mind address itself to render plain / The nature of the essence.' The core remains within, hidden.

Browning's 'man' does not seek confrontation between himself and the Creating mind: 'Drag what lurks / Behind the operation – that which works / Latently everywhere by outward proof – / Drag that mind forth to face mine? No!' He wants a conscious, willed and skilful relation to influence, just 'one spark/Myself may deal with ...' He is like the subtler reader at the beginning of the poem, or the one in '"Transcendentalism"' who seeks 'subtler meanings of what roses say'. He lacks Browning's customary audacity. Inverting the phrase that the 'Essay on Shelley' uses about the subjective poet, this little man turns to what man sees, not what God sees. Man works with a burning-glass on the 'pin-point circle' of sunlight. The poem ends: 'Little? In little, light, warmth, light are blessed –/Which, in the large, who sees to bless? Not I/More than yourself: so, good my friend, keep still/Trustful with – me? with thee, sage Mandeville!' It would be unwise to trust the reduction. In Browning's poetry irony is more than a restriction of understanding – it can expand in joyous impersonal laughter. A poet is more than a man, more than human. The myth began with something much grander and more beautiful than a domestic fire in the hearth. The passage is reminiscent of '"Transcendentalism"' and 'Thamuris Marching' in its overflowing laughter and gladness:

> outbroke the Sun
> Above the conscious earth, and one by one
> Her heights and depths absorbed to the last spark
> His fluid glory, from the far fine ridge
> Of mountain-granite which, transformed to gold
> Laughed first thanks back ...
> Everywhere
> Did earth acknowledge Sun's embrace sublime
> Thrilling her to the heart of things: since there
> No ore ran liquid, no spar branched anew,
> No arrowy crystal gleamed, but straightway grew
> Glad through the inrush ...

The injunction to Carlyle that he should trust Mandeville where he did not trust Browning is a joke and a belated attempt to teach the dead and the living something about irony. Carlyle wrote in *Sartor Resartus* that 'no man who has once heartily and wholly laughed can be altogether irreclaimably bad' (Carlyle I, p. 26). Browning takes laughter further – it is the eruption into consciousness of something other than consciousness. Yet as 'thanks' and in its very gladness, laughter is as much a response and a kind of responsibility as Sordello's vigil by the font in Goito.

5
Browning and Ruskin: Reading and Seeing

Ruskin wrote in the third volume of *Modern Painters* (1856) that 'the greatest thing a human soul ever does in this world is to *see* something, and tell what it *saw* in a plain way. Hundreds of people can talk for one who can think, but thousands can think for one who can see. To see clearly is poetry, prophecy, and religion – all in one' (Ruskin V, p. 33). Seeing doesn't happen this 'plain way' in Browning's poetry: not for the characters in poems and not for the reader. When a Browning poem appears to contemplate the visual in the form of scenery, a face or a painting, that same poem will embrace the possibilities of hallucination, phantom presences and delusion. This interest in half-presences does not correspond with Ruskin's ideal of observed reality, nor with the transcendent category of vision by divine revelation. Where there is clarity in Browning's poetry it does not necessarily establish confidence in the evidence of one's eyes. For example, the dramatic lyric 'My Last Duchess' (1842) begins with a line that turns the poem into a painting: 'That's my last Duchess, painted on the wall'. Or in 'Memorabilia' (1855) the speaker puts seeing in a context of a figure from the past appearing, like a ghost: 'Ah, did you once see Shelley plain,/ And did he stop and speak to you?/ And did you speak to him again?/ How strange it seems, and new!'

The collection in which 'Memorabilia' appears, *Men and Women* (1855), was intended to make readers experience more than they might expect from reading. Browning told Joseph Milsand 'I am writing – a first step towards popularity for me – lyrics with more music and painting than before, so as to get people to hear and see'.[1] In the context of Browning's emphatically verbal art, simple sensory responses become strange and new. Such poems produce uncertainty about the kind of experience it might be to read poetry, although there is nothing vague or tentative about the work itself.

Shades

The melancholy Ruskin is consciously haunted by the sublime shadiness of modern aesthetic experience, and constantly compares it with the bright untroubled luminosity of medieval imagination. By contrast, Browning's death-seeking heroes and dodgy characters positively flourish under the storm cloud of the nineteenth century. Perhaps all literature is somewhat shady: the term suits both Browning's and Ruskin's writing, despite temperamental differences in their relation to shadowiness. *Shade* indicates the effects of influence as the overshadowing of a belated poet by a mountainous precursor figure. Shade also describes Ruskin's idea of the dark cast of modern imagination in 'the ages of umber' (Ruskin V, p. 321). Browning exploits the vivid and apparently more innocent possibilities of shade as coloration: especially in a poem famously interrogated by Ruskin, 'Popularity', where influence is troped as a beautiful shade of blue. Breaking light into different shades and colours may also protect someone from the undifferentiated dazzle of too much brightness. A letter to Elizabeth Barrett discusses these two related kinds of shading. She has asked Browning to tell her any faults he sees in her work, and he replies by discussing poetry as painting. He describes the 'peculiar artist's pleasure' of deciphering the writer's intentions by seeing where she has laid the paint on too thick:

> An instructed eye loves to see where the brush has dipped twice in a lustrous colour, has lain insistingly along a favourite outline, dwelt lovingly in a grand shadow – for these 'too muches' for the everybody's-picture are so many helps to the making out the real painter's-picture as he had it in his brain.[2]

In the next paragraph Browning delivers his famous comparison: 'You speak out, *you*, – I only make men and women speak – give you truth broken into prismatic hues, and fear the pure white light, even if it is in me, but I am going to try ...' The 'pure white light' associates Elizabeth Barrett with Shelley, the subjective poet whose work, like hers, is 'the very radiance and aroma of his personality'.

Browning's self-diagnosed photophobia is fear and love of the power of a pure poetry; witness the apparition of a terrifying 'pure face' that threatens to halt *Sordello* at the beginning of Book One. In *Pauline* the detractors of Shelley are like the spider disturbed from his web by the dangerously attractive 'lit torch' of the poet's renown (ll. 147–9). Elsewhere Browning wrote to Elizabeth Barrett of his fondness for 'sculls and spider-webs'.[3] Contemporary accounts of her appearance in the 1840s vary and photographs and other portraits show slightly eerie looks. His very first letter to her compares his almost visiting her once to being 'close, so close, to some world's-wonder in chapel or crypt'.[4] I began thinking about shade by mentioning the shadow of past poetic achievement, but for Browning some poetry, and his own poetic inspiration, has a blinding sunlike quality, requiring to be broken into colours in order to be seen at all. Finally, and still in connection with the precursor, a shade is a ghost or apparition. Between the living and the dead there is room for various kinds of official traffic: entombment, commemoration, bereavement. For Ruskin these more or less ritualized acts found a pensive aesthetic of belatedness. Browning's poetry insists that there are also illegitimate relations between life and death – confusions, necrophiliac embraces, hauntings without feature or visual form.

Browning and Ruskin are part of a poetic tradition of influence in which imagination may be bereft of itself by that which, according to common sense, should nourish and inspire. However, they disagree about what it means to be a seer. According to Ruskin, Turner and Scott are the exemplary great modern seers: each possessed of 'a right understanding of what *he* can do and say, and the rest of the world's sayings and doings', the manner of their work 'necessitated by the feelings of the men, entirely natural to both, never exaggerated for the sake of show', and, at work, capable of great results with '*no effort*' (Ruskin V, pp. 332–3). In literature, Ruskin specifies that Seers are superior to Thinkers (too often lacking in practical purpose) and to writers of 'sentimental literature, concerned with the analysis and description of emotion' (p. 334). He prefers what he calls Creative to 'sentimental' writers such as Byron, Tennyson or Keats: 'generally speaking, pathetic writing and careful explanation of passion are quite easy, compared with [the] plain recording of what people said and did, or the invention of what they are likely to say and do' (p. 335).

Browning had spent much of the first half of the 1850s thinking about sight. 'Memorabilia' suggests that 'plain' sight may not be plain at all. His great work on modern landscape 'Childe Roland to the Dark Tower Came' was written at Paris in the summer of 1852, during the composition of the 'Introductory Essay' to Moxon's

Letters of Percy Bysshe Shelley (1852). The 'Essay on Shelley' develops Browning's own theory of the seer. Browning's elaborately worked piece clashes with Ruskin's clearer, but less subtle and differentiated, statements about creativity. Ruskin depends on the notions of seeing clearly and telling plainly, and does not distinguish between the circumstances in which works of art are produced and received. Browning's particular imagination, as well as his personal experience of repeatedly failing to second-guess public taste, led him to ponder deeply the ironic gap between the perceptions of an artist in composition, and the effect of the work upon readers. For Browning, poetry exists in relation to readers and is affected by their knowledge and desires. Faced with newly discovered letters by Shelley (these were, in fact, soon revealed as forgeries, and the book withdrawn) Browning immediately thinks about what readers might want of biographical information about poets. Browning's understanding of these desires of the 'auditory' are not formed by universal assumptions about the nature of creativity, as Ruskin's are. Readers 'accept gladly', 'covet' or 'must' read the biography of a certain kind of poet because of the particular law forming the poet's genius. Shelley's letters are so important because his genius 'has operated by a different law'. The biography of the more objective poet, Shakespeare for example, is dispensable because he pitches his writing at the limited capacities of his fellow men. Browning associates dramatic inventiveness with the objective poet, the fashioner whose poetry 'will of necessity be substantive, projected from himself and distinct'. His 'endeavour has been to reproduce things external [...] with immediate reference, in every case, to the common eye and apprehension of his fellow men'.

For Browning, the subjective poet produces less a work than an 'effluence' and this subjective poet is 'rather a seer ... than a fashioner'. No less perceptive than the fashioner, Browning's seer embodies 'the thing he perceives, not so much with reference to the many below as to the one above him, the supreme Intelligence which apprehends all things in their absolute truth, – an ultimate view ever aspired to, if but partially attained, by the poet's own soul'. He is harder to understand and is probably not going to be popular. Ruskin argues that 'to describe a separate emotion delicately, it is only needed that one should feel it oneself' (Ruskin V, p. 335). Browning is less literal about the self: 'the subjective poet, whose study has been himself' appeals 'through himself to the absolute Divine mind'. Shelley, Browning's seer, is therefore conceivably a Christian poet despite his avowed atheism because of his concern with 'the primal elements of humanity' and practice of digging in 'his own soul as the nearest reflex of ... absolute Mind'. There is no reason, Browning writes with disconcerting flexibility, why the objective/subjective distinction should be set up as absolute. The objective poet takes up the 'doings of men' and the subjective 'selects that silence of earth and sea in which he can best hear the beatings of his individual heart': this 'seems not so much from any essential distinction in the faculty of the two poets or in the nature of the objects contemplated by either, as in the more immediate adaptability of these objects to the distinct purpose of each'. The two poles of much of Ruskin's thinking about literature are the poet's mind and the nature of the object. Browning is more interested in poetic purpose and in objects as they are adaptable to it. As the opening of the essay puts it, readers require 'a right understanding of the author's purpose and work'.

When Browning takes up an argument with Ruskin about the 'Of Modern Landscape' section of *Modern Painters* III in a letter of 1 February 1856, it is to reassert the significance of his own relation with God in his work and to communicate a right understanding of his purpose in certain passages of *Sordello*. Browning, his essay makes clear, is not simply to be categorized as an objective or a subjective poet. It is not possible to decide a priori whether to let his work stand alone or to approach it through his biography. A 'mere running-in of one faculty upon the other, is, of course, the ordinary circumstance' and it depends upon readers' 'especial want' as to which kind of poet and which way of reading may be preferred. Browning more than once emphasized that his poetry was dramatic, but here is a clear instance of Browning as one of the subjective poets, communicating 'to us what they see in an object with reference to their own individuality'.

For Browning the man, individuality was inconceivable without a relation to God. The God of Browning the poet may be read figuratively, and is as much a name for a creative absolute as 'Shelley' is. Using the general terms of the essay on Shelley, Browning's letter to Ruskin provides the essential biographical information to reveal the 'moral purpose' which inspires certain passages of *Sordello*. A great purpose must animate great work 'even where it does not visibly look out of the same'. Unprecedentedness risks non-recognition, and Browning repeatedly identifies poetry with a movement beyond what is currently held to be ultimate, 'looking higher than any manifestation yet made of both beauty and good'.

The influence of the dead

Ruskin's main precursor is Wordsworth, who 'in all things / ... saw one life, and felt that it was joy' – a gift that 'is yours / Ye mountains, thine O Nature' (*The Prelude*, 1799 version, II, ll. 549–60, 491–2). Harold Bloom notices that the personal experience of failing visual powers described in a letter to Walter Brown is scripted in idea and phrase by Wordsworth's '"Intimations" Ode'.[5] The relevant passage even begins with the same words as the ode, 'There was a time': 'For instance, there was a time when the sight of a steep hill covered with pines, cutting against a blue sky, would have touched me with emotion inexpressible [...] Now I can look at such a slope with coolness, and observation of *fact*.'[6]

Browning's chief shade is Shelley, in the later dramatic poems as much as the earlier, more evidently *Alastor*-like doomed quest narratives. Browning's tone differs greatly from Shelley's: nothing in the earlier poet's 'Adonais: An Elegy on the Death of John Keats' (1821) sounds quite like Browning's blunt question in 'Popularity': 'What porridge had John Keats?' It will emerge in the course of this chapter how different tracing literary influence can be from drawing up a family tree of poets. I will be exploring effects of reading that resemble a gathering of untimely ghosts more than the affirmation of a father-to-son canonic line. The relation between Ruskin and Wordsworth in the letter to Walter Brown is straightforward enough: whole phrases are repeated along with a Wordsworthian argument about imaginative loss. But influence can also be illicit, disturbing and cryptic in relation to language. Browning's grotesque diction is formed in reaction to the lyrical beauty of Shelley's, and Browning poems display Shelleyan tropes in perverse and ingenious ways, as well as memorializing and hiding Shelley's name across their lines.

Browning poems are full of cross-border activity between the living and the dead: my last Duchess is dead but the spot of joy on her painted cheek still disturbs and contradicts the drift of the speech that tells of her demise. In 'Love Among the Ruins' (1855) the imagined past of those grass-covered stones competes very powerfully with the imagined embraces of the living, and the strongly anticipated climactic encounter is itself a promise of blinding mutual extinction. The girl in 'Evelyn Hope' (1855) is dead, but her lover makes his first declaration and love-gift to her corpse, confident that she will wake and understand. These poems are neither elegiac nor tragic. In the words of *Modern Painters* V (1860) they 'indeed put more vitality into the shadows of the dead than most others can give the presences of the living' (Ruskin, VI, p. 446). Ruskin's tribute is to Browning as historical poet in 'The Bishop Orders His Tomb' (1845), but a later poem 'Childe Roland to the Dark Tower Came' (1855) achieves much more than a revival of the past when Roland's dead precursors return in a poem suddenly alive with light and sound. Day comes back – 'The dying sunset kindles through a cleft' and noise tolls 'Increasing like a bell. Names in my ears / Of all the lost adventurers my peers'. The dead gather 'To view the last of me, a living frame / For one more picture'. Browning's purpose sometimes seems to be a prolongation of the uncanny instant in *Adonais* when Urania's presence revives the corpse:

> In the death-chamber for a moment Death,
> Shamed by the presence of that living Might,
> Blushed to annihilation, and the breath
> Revisited those lips, and Life's pale light
> Flashed through those limbs, so late her dear delight.
>
> (ll. 217–21)

Browning's moments of life in death (like the Duchess's posthumous blushes) don't allow his readers to share Urania's innocent grief. The poems take interpretation – as viewing and as framing – to be part of the drama of life and death as writing. There is a contrast here with Ruskinian lament. A favourite of Ruskin's, 'The Bishop Orders His Tomb', aptly dramatizes this theme.

Ruskin's work on Renaissance tomb-sculpture in *The Stones of Venice* (1851–3) and his autobiographical account of the decline of his own visual powers are burdened by a melancholy sense of loss. What was the lost experience? In a diary entry for 3 June 1849 Ruskin describes an instance of the kind of imaginative effort which could transform sight from banal sensory perception to a poetic experience. The effort is straightforward, the willed exercise of human powers upon unre-markable scenery:

> ... I put my *mind* into the scene, instead of suffering the body only to make report of it; and looked at [the landscape] with the posses-sion-taking grasp of the imagination ... It required an effort to maintain the feeling: it was poetry while it lasted, and I felt that it was only while under it that one could draw, or invent, or give glory to, any part of such a landscape ... I felt that the human soul was all, the subject nothing.   (Ruskin V, p. xix)

That phrase 'the possession-taking grasp of the imagination', which describes Ruskin's own powers, might have a very different atmosphere if imagination were not a faculty under the dominion of the will, but a power that could itself hold and possess consciousness. What if a mountain could look at Ruskin, a strange look without a face, and even grasp him? This is the threat explored in the famous passage in Book I of *The Prelude* where Wordsworth remembers stealing a boat and seeing 'the huge cliff / As if with voluntary power instinct, / [Uprear] its head' and then as he rowed, it 'With measured motion, like a living thing / Strode after me' (1799 version, I, ll. 108–10, 113–14). Ruskin experiences no such imaginative anxiety. His 'feeling ... was poetry while it lasted', and this broad notion of poetry as a state of feeling is harder to sustain through a reading of Browning than a reading of Wordsworth. Browning's descriptions of the poet's experience, constituted in composition and performance, include the effects of what Wordsworth describes as a blackness or blankness inside thought. After being pursued by the mountain, Wordsworth writes that:

> for many days my brain
> Worked with a dim and undetermined sense
> Of unknown modes of being. In my thoughts
> There was a darkness – call it solitude,
> Or blank desertion – no familiar shapes
> Of hourly objects, images of trees,
> Of sea or sky, no colours of green fields;
> But huge and mighty forms that do not live
> Like living men moved slowly through my mind
> By day, and were the trouble of my dreams.
>
> (I, ll. 420–7)

Browning's career could be described in terms of constantly developing defences against misinterpretation of this undetermined sense of almost nothing. In the earlier poems there are footnotes, prefaces, suggestions on how to read; by the time Browning wrote *Men and Women* the interpretative swerve was more likely to be generated dramatically by events within the poem than imposed upon it through textual apparatus.[7] This makes the rhetorical pressure on the reader more difficult to resist. In contrast Ruskin's ideas about seeing characterize a way of thinking about poetry that is oriented by a language of images and positive immediate visual consciousness.

Ordering a tomb

'The Mountain Glory' section of *Modern Painters* IV (1856) famously assimilates Browning's 'The Bishop Orders His Tomb' into a Ruskinian critical project. Ruskin quotes large chunks of the poem, the dying words of a corrupt old man to his sons, as an example of the particular faults of later Renaissance Italy, revealed clearly in the increasingly evasive relation to death of its over-decorated tomb sculpture. Browning's poem does offer a study of evasion: but not only through the Bishop's patent failings or the decadence of his historical context. Another engagement with evasiveness takes place through an exploration of the linguistic performance of ordering. Ruskin's celebration of 'The Bishop Orders His Tomb' focuses on the poem's accurately observed corroboration of his own researches:

> Robert Browning is unerring in every sentence he writes of the Middle Ages: always vital, right and profound; so that in the matter of art, with which we have been specially concerned, there is hardly a principle connected with the mediaeval temper, that he has not struck upon in those seemingly careless and too rugged rhymes of his.   (Ruskin VI, pp. 446–7)

Ruggedness is itself a quality of stones that Ruskin describes in his extended discussion of 'Of Mountain Beauty' in *Modern Painters* IV as 'more pleasing to the modern than the medieval' (p. 365). *The Stones of Venice* reads stonework as a language that can reveal historical truths about Renaissance culture. In *Pauline* Browning makes the wild claim that words can actually be stones to damage the reader. Ruskin's literalness never dreams of such a thing. He cites 'The Bishop Orders His Tomb' as an instance of the way that Browning's perceptiveness outdoes even Shakespeare, the poet who was content to paint '*what he saw*' (p. 446):

> There is a curious instance ... in a short poem referring to ... tomb and image sculpture; and illustrating just one of those phases of local human character which, though belonging to Shakespere's own age, he never noticed, because it was specially Italian and un-English; connected also with the influence of mountains on the heart, and therefore with our immediate inquiries.
>   (p. 447)

The connection with the theme of influence is important. Mountains for Ruskin are often significant 'influences over the human heart', dispensing gloom as well as splendour (p. 418). The early essay *The Poetry of Architecture* (1837–8) as well as *Modern Painters* IV observes furthermore that 'a stone, when it is examined, will be found a mountain in miniature' (Ruskin I, p. 48; VI, p. 368). Stone shows the condensed influence of mountains within buildings and looking at stone structures uncannily recalls what is older and more powerful than architecture. Stones and mountains articulate the bind of *literary* influence: stone makes tombs and monuments possible, and yet every stone monument is haunted by the priority of the mountain from which it came. Words are also things, as Wordsworth says, discussing repetition in his note to 'The Thorn' (1800). The poem as a monument to human imagination is made up of material that withstands appropriation, whether that material be fallen and disordered (like the stones in Turner's drawings of northern English Rivers), worked with immense elaboration (as in Italian tombs of the late Renaissance), or just threatening to beat out your brains (as in the preface to *Pauline*).

As I discuss in my Introduction, Milton's 'Epitaph on the Admirable Dramatic Poet W. Shakespeare' recognizes also that to read literature is to take the risk of oneself becoming marble, the surface that receives and retains Shakespeare's name: 'Then thou, our fancy of itself bereaving, / Dost make us marble with too much conceiving.' Ruskin's recourse to idealized accounts of aesthetic emotion could be seen in this context as a defence against the loss of primary feeling which marks the imagination's profound encounter with literature. Keats describes this loss of primary sensual pleasure, and the encounter not just *in* but *with* an unimaginably ancient stone building that follows it in Book I of *The Fall of Hyperion* (1819) which I read as an allegory about the ascent from a naive to an imaginatively purged reading. Told 'If thou canst not ascend / These steps, die on the marble where thou art' (ll. 107–8), the dreamer experiences the numbingly cold and possession-taking grasp that Ruskin's determined association of the imagination with feeling shields him from:

> I heard, I looked: two senses both at once,
> So fine, so subtle, felt the tyranny
> Of that fierce threat and the hard task proposed.
> Prodigious seemed the toil; ...
>   ... suddenly a palsied chill
> Struck from the paved level up my limbs,

> And was ascending quick to put cold grasp
> Upon those streams that pulse beside the throat.
> I shrieked; and the sharp anguish of my shriek
> Stung my own ears. I strove hard to escape
> The numbness, strove to gain the lowest step.
> Slow, heavy, deadly was my pace; the cold
> Grew stifling, suffocating, at the heart;
> And when I clasped my hands I felt them not.
>
> (ll. 118–131)

Once the dreamer's foot touches the steps, 'life seemed / To pour in at the toes' but the near-death experience allows him to postpone his actual death and opens his quest towards a more profound understanding of the nature of poetry. Something in Ruskin's critical sensibility keeps him away from this kind of research and directs his attention towards the external world with reference to 'the common eye and apprehension of his fellow men', as Browning puts it. Ruskin is an appreciative reader of the Browningesque objective poet, for he possesses very strongly Browning's sense that 'it is with this world, as starting-point and basis alike, that we shall always have to concern ourselves: the world is not to be learned and thrown aside, but reverted to and relearned'.

Learning the world was vitally important to Ruskin but he was far less objective and more idiosyncratic in aesthetic matters than he wanted to be. The discussion of 'The Bishop Orders His Tomb' ignores both the Bishop's disparagement of inferior types of stone and his sense of a relation between the beauty of stone and that of the female body, cutting the relevant passages. Ruskin's idealized description of the feeling of the sculptor and the beholders for the stone that was the material of their architecture also glosses over the violence of quarrying and construction. 'The Mountain Glory' celebrates the 'admiration with which a southern artist regarded the *stone* he worked in; and the pride which populace or priest took in the possession of precious mountain substance, worked into the pavements of their cathedrals, and the shafts of their tombs' (Ruskin VI, p. 447). Yet the chapter on 'Roman Renaissance' in *Stones of Venice* III cites the historical development of Renaissance tomb sculpture as evidence of a change of feeling: it is difficult if not impossible to maintain the right relation to one's monuments: 'exactly in proportion as the pride of life became more insolent, the fear of death became more servile; and the difference in the manner in which the men of early and later days adorned the sepulchre, confesses a still greater difference in their manner of regarding death' (Ruskin XI, pp. 81–2). The tomb ordered by Browning's Bishop is not at Venice, but it does show the relation to ornament contemptuously described by Ruskin as 'a ghastly struggle of mean pride and miserable terror'. How very *un*idealized is this account of the creative process as the impulse to make monuments, compared with the descriptions of imagination as a glorious and momentarily unifying power elsewhere in Ruskin's work.

The undissolved talisman

Dante Gabriel Rossetti was outraged by the philistine cuts Ruskin made in 'The Bishop Orders His Tomb'.[8] Ruskin has no particular concern to assess the aesthetic qualities of the poem itself; he only praises Browning's historical insight:

> I know of no other piece of modern English, prose or poetry, in which there is so much told, as in these lines, of the Renaissance spirit, – its worldliness, inconsistency, pride, hypocrisy, ignorance of itself, love of art, of luxury, and of good Latin. It is nearly all that I said of the central Renaissance in thirty pages of the *Stones of Venice* put into as many lines, Browning's being also the antecedent work.   (Ruskin VI, p. 449)

The poem is a good piece of writing because it admits of generalization – yet the density of Browning's poetic language gives Ruskin pause. He describes it using the central figure from Walter Scott's novel *The Talisman* (1832). The

> worst of it is that this kind of concentrated writing needs so much *solution* before the reader can fairly get the good of it, that people's patience fails them, and they give the thing up as insoluble; though, truly, it ought to be to the current of common thought like Saladin's talisman, dipped in clear water, not soluble altogether, but making the element medicinal'
>
>   (Ruskin VI, p. 449).

Scott and Wordsworth are the most admired modern writers in Ruskin's literary criticism and *Modern Painters* III finds the 'excellence of Scott's work ... precisely in proportion to the degree in which it is sketched from present nature' (Ruskin V, p. 337). Yet the talisman itself is not actually seen in Scott's novel, which only describes the mysterious curative efficacy of 'a small silken bag made of network, twisted with silver, the contents of which the bystanders could not discover'.[9] The OED describes a talisman as a 'charm, amulet, thing supposed capable of working wonders; inscribed stone or ring supposed to ensure safety or good fortune'. Etymology links talisman with *telos* – end – and with ritual and completion. The eponymous objects in *The Ring and the Book* (1868–9) are both talismans to the poet. *Modern Painters* V associates the talisman with the safety and well being of 'common thought'. Poetic language may be difficult but if it is regarded as magical like a talisman difficulty need not be an absolute obstacle to poetry benefiting mankind. Altering the familiar image of readers dipping into books, Ruskin dips 'concentrated writing' into what he rather optimistically calls the clear waters of general thought.

As I argue in my introduction, the talisman, which is 'not soluble altogether', could also describe what, in Browning's oeuvre, marks it as his own. And like the talisman in Scott's novel, these marks aren't necessarily significant in themselves. Derrida would call these talisman effects, signatures. The phrases, sounds, motifs or emblems in which the singularity of Browning's oeuvre comes through might include the various versions of 'I ... fear the pure white light, even if it is in me', the tolling of a bell or the rhyming of a fantastic rhyme (Hobbs and Nobbs, Stokes and Nokes), the motif of imperfection and resistance to closure, the emblem of a drunken or unconscious bee, a ruined tower. Each of these affirms Browning's name and at the same time marks the effacement of his name, its absence from the work. He shuns pure subjectivity, he makes up names that belong to no one, he never finishes up, the bee knows nothing, the tower is incomplete and anyway belongs to Shelley, to Milton, or since God evicted mankind from Babel, to nobody.

Ruskin's commentary on 'The Bishop Orders His Tomb' emphasizes the historical accuracy and rightness of the poem, despite his sense that the poetic language refuses to liquefy and melt indistinguishably into ordinary discourse. Yet Browning's poem promises a future gone wrong and a tomb that may never be built, while it is concerned with *solution* as a threat to the Bishop's project of building a monument. Browning's dramatic writing becomes increasingly capable of triumph in the prospect of ruin because it invents a world and a self always in relation to language. Ruskin tends to lament ruin in himself and in the world and grieves for the loss of his capacity for intense visual pleasure. In *Modern Painters* IV he portrays modernity as a shadow-state of ruggedness, discoloration and loss. *The Stones of Venice* concerns itself with loss and ruin, its famous opening even prophesying the collapse of the British Empire which may fall like ruined Venice and like Tyre, of which 'only the memory remains' (Ruskin IX, p. 17). *The Stones of Tyre* would be impossible for Ruskin to write: Tyre represents the power of influence through a name, through words and inherited skills, without much in the way of remains for the modern onlooker to interpret.

Before looking at what Browning does with Tyre, I will stay a little longer with the Bishop and his tomb. Two senses of *order* emerge and come into conflict as the Bishop speaks. Firstly there is the order suggested by the precious substantialness of poetic language. This order is guaranteed by the hierarchy of more and less durable stones (basalt, peach-blossom marble, onion-stone, lapis lazuli, jasper, agate), and by the lines of genealogy and inheritance (the references to the Bishop's sons and to their mother). Against these monumental enduring qualities lies the risky verbal performance of ordering by the Bishop who wants to prepare a place for himself in the church, the poem's figure for the canon. He says 'I fought / With tooth and nail to save my niche'. The poem is a cliffhanger: can precious mountain substance be summoned at the Bishop's will and can its powers be put to the service of the Bishop's memory and name? Will the bastard sons be dutiful and carry out the Bishop's orders? Are they indeed his sons or his rival Gandolf's? And where are these orders coming from, for just when the place of death and the final resting place are being determined down to the last sumptuous detail, death becomes elusive.

The Bishop asks more than once 'Do I live, am I dead?' and refers to the book of Job – 'Man goeth to the grave, and where is he?' It is always possible to get the wrong kind of tomb made of the wrong kind of stone, with horrible consequences: 'Stone – / Gritstone, a-crumble! Clammy squares which sweat / As if the corpse they keep were oozing through'. Ruskin drops these lines in the extract reprinted in *Modern Painters* IV. He also excludes the reference to the uncut chunk of lapis lazuli which the Bishop wants as a protective talisman: 'Some lump, ah God, of *lapis lazuli*, / Big as a Jew's head cut off at the nape, / Blue as a vein o'er the Madonna's breast'. The sons must 'let the blue lump poise between my knees / Like God the Father's globe on both his hands'. The concentrated solidity of the stone, which the Bishop has kept buried in his vineyard, seems to guarantee the untranslatability of its qualities. It must stay out of circulation. Browning, Ruskin admiringly notices, anglicizes Italian *Nero Antico* into 'antique-black' and *cipollina* into 'onion-stone', thereby retaining the 'force of the foreign language', but Latin *lapis lazuli* remains untranslated and italicized (Ruskin VI, p. 448n.). A talisman exerts influence without losing shape and ceasing to be itself: it is distinctly 'cut off at the nape'. However, Browning's Bishop knows that stone can crumble, dissolve and compromise the clear distinction between, say, the corpse and the more enduring substance of the tomb.

'Last oozings': 'Popularity'

The blueness of the *lapis lazuli* is compared to living blood in a vein (in *Sordello* and 'Popularity' the colour blue is in liquid dye form). The Bishop speaks out of a confused togetherness of life and death, active ordering and passive submission to the prospect of death. He is in some sense already dissolving, his body failing, his consciousness hovering, his name scattered among half-acknowledged 'sons'. Ruskin argues that some degree of solution or translation is essential for poetry to be understood, but too much solution might mean the disappearance of idiom, distinctive identity, singularity or signature-qualities as they pass into the wider language. The Bishop's fears about gritstone suggest that a poem must hold the tendency of its language to 'ooze', to be translated into new words, together with the tendency of poetic language to retain its distinctiveness and particular shape, word for word in the reader's memory. The Bishop hasn't got much time left. Richard Rand's extraordinary essay on Keats's 'Ode to Autumn' (1820) suggests that the exemplary way to regard the trans-lations of poetic language is with Autumn's patient look: 'by a cyder-press, with patient look, / Thou watchest the last oozings hours by hours.'[10] As the Bishop knows, it's not so easy to keep this kind of unexcited watchfulness when it's you that's oozing through your tombstone, your name that's seeping away into the language. Sometimes, as Ruskin says, people's patience fails them.

Ooze is a favourite Browning word. In *Sordello* it blends, on three separate occasions, with another familiar Browning emblem, a woman's hair (featured in *Pauline*, 'Porphyria's Lover', 'A Toccata of Galuppi's' and elsewhere), to describe the unknown woman Elys in Sordello's only surviving lyric: her 'few fine locks / Coloured like honey oozed from topmost rocks'. The references to hair and honey recall Milton's 'Lycidas' (1638) where drowned Lycidas is described washing his hair in heaven: 'With nectar pure his oozy locks he laves' (l. 175). The sounds of 'Lycidas' echo in the name 'Elys', and for that matter in 'lapis lazuli', marking that which in writing resists appropriation by a voice. Book Three has not honey but water in the rock, struck forth by Moses: 'Mark ye the dim first oozings?' (III, l. 804). The lines on 'Elys' figure in the opening description of composition in *The Ring and the Book* (I discuss this connection at more length in Chapter 6.) The Elys song, originally Eglamor's subject, appropriated by Sordello, survives as 'some unintelligible words' which have all but lost their association with Sordello. These words, sung by a child at Asolo in Browning's own time, at once affirm and efface Sordello's name . The monument is fragmented, the inscription is illegible. At the same time the lines recall Milton through the revision of 'Lycidas' and in this movement perhaps also refer to Shelley's death by water. The child is one note, unconsciously part of a thundering chord of names. Contemporaneity is scattered and divided in a literary landscape where it is not possible to perform a solo, in time or space.

When Browning and Ruskin first met at Florence in 1852 they talked about Italy. Ruskin, an admirer of Elizabeth Barrett, was initially disappointed that 'only the husband was at home' but found Browning's grasp of Italian politics rational, if rather on the liberal side. In London in 1855 the Brownings visited Denmark Hill to have lunch and see Ruskin's collection of Turners. Both of them liked Ruskin 'very much' (Orr, *Life,* p. 203). At this time the Brownings also spent time with Ruskin's protégé Dante Gabriel Rossetti, and introduced the young painter Frederick Leighton to Ruskin. In November 1855 *Men and Women* came out and copies were sent to close friends and relatives of the Brownings, to Fox and Moxon and to fellow poets Bryan Waller Procter, Coventry Patmore, Rossetti and Tennyson. A copy also went to Ruskin, who spent a whole night reading it with Rossetti. Ruskin found the volumes 'a set of the most amazing Conundrums that ever were proposed to me' and wrote to Browning in protest choosing 'Popularity' as a 'fair example' of the volume's difficulty.[11] Browning rapidly replied with one of the most explicit statements of poetic principle he ever made, in which it emerges that he and Ruskin 'don't read poetry the same way, by the same law; it is too clear … You would have me paint it all plain out, which can't be' (Woolford and Karlin, p. 257).

'Popularity' is an ironic title; the poet in the poem is not popular, and Browning is concerned to account for this and to describe the movements of critical reception and poetic tradition. He does this in a characteristically elliptical way. In his own words to Ruskin 'by various artifices I try to make shift with touches and bits and outlines which succeed if they bear the conception from me to you'. This 'conception' which is borne in reading can, I think, be related to the excessive 'conceiving' brought on by reading Shakespeare in Milton's 'Epitaph'. The touches and bits and outlines in 'Popularity' – ruins purposefully created – describe the remembering and forgetting of a poet as effects of a movement of reading. The difficulties which strike Ruskin as insoluble conundrums, Browning might wish to correspond to the wonderful, astonishing Delphic qualities of Shakespeare's poetry as Milton describes it. Impressed on the hearts of readers, they 'make us marble with too much conceiving'. This drama is enacted between reader and text and also through 'Popularity's' fragmentary impressions of Shelley, Milton and Keats. 'Popularity' leaves a deep, if not always decipherable, impression on Ruskin and is itself the inscribed surface upon which the names and works of earlier poets are recorded. Ruskin recognizes something dangerous in it when he tells Browning:

> There is a stuff and fancy in it which assuredly is in no other living writer's, and how far this purple of it *must* be with in this terrible shell: and only to be fished for among threshing of foam & slippery rocks, I don't know. There are truths & depths in it, far beyond anything I have read except Shakespeare.
>
> (Woolford and Karlin, p. 255)

'Popularity' concerns the recognition of a poet by one who 'saw you, / Knew you, and named a star!' Ruskin quotes and questions it, almost line by line. He asks of the opening couplet: 'Does this mean: literally – stand still? or where was the poet figuratively going – and why couldn't he be drawn as he went?' (p. 253). Despite the promising relevance of the poem's theme, knowing a true poet, Ruskin cannot tell how to begin. His attitude of bold explicit enquiry into Browning's poetic method covers a steady resistance to the creative power that he is acknowledging. Creativity presents something new and must therefore teach – and part of what it has to teach is the fact that what has been created *is* new. Ruskin appeals to observation of a given reality, and to a firm relation between beholder and beheld.

> Stand still, true poet that you are,
>   I know you; let me try and draw you.
> Some night you'll fail us. When afar
>   You rise, remember one man saw you,
> Knew you, and named a star.

The poem cites the thoroughly Ruskinian notion that to know a phe-
nomenon, to really *see* it, it is necessary to 'try and draw' it. Yet
'Popularity' is disruptive to Ruskin's more conservative assumptions
about the supreme truth of visual experience. The poem is written in the
second person, addressing the 'true poet' who is already moving by at his
own speed. The peremptory command 'Stand still' – the precondition of
the poem – implies a movement that denies primacy to steady Ruskinian
observation. Before vision is possible comes an act of language that is not
figurative or imagistic. The hailing, like the Miltonic 'Hail, holy light',
marks a difference between sight and reading. Why couldn't the poet be
drawn as he went? In reply to Ruskin, Browning says:

> You begin 'Stand still, – why?' For the reason indicated in the verse, to
> be sure – *to let me draw him* – and because he is at present going on his
> way, and fancying nobody notices him, – and moreover 'going on' (as
> we say) against the injustice of that, – and lastly, inasmuch as one
> night he'll fail us … and I want to make the most of my time.
>
> (p. 257)

This issue of arrest and movement in relation to language disrupts the
motionless dualistic relation between reader/poem, speaker/true poet,
subject and object which Ruskin expects. For instance, he balks at an
ellipsis in the first line of stanza two, which creates a potential for
confusion between the poet and God:

> My star, God's glow-worm! Why extend
>   That loving hand of his which leads you,
> Yet locks you safe from end to end
>   Of this dark world, unless he needs you,
> Just saves your light to spend?

'The ellipsis of "Should He" [after "Why"] throws one quite out – like
a step in a floor that one doesn't expect' (p. 253). The poet's general
response to Ruskin is that he needs to learn to jump.

Observation carries in it a sense of guarding and keeping and stanzas
two (above) and three develop the notion of observation as a kind of
concealment and keeping for the future:

> His clenched hand shall unclose at last
>   I know, and let out all the beauty.
> My poet holds the future fast,
>   Accepts the coming ages' duty,
> Their present for this past.

God's loving hand holds onto the poet, keeping him to himself because he needs to and (because?) the poet is in turn holding onto the future. Ruskin writes of these stanzas:

> Yet locks you safe. How does God's hand lock him; do you mean – keeps him from being seen? – and how does it make him safe. Why is a poet safer or more locked up than anybody else? I go on – in hope. 'His clenched hand – beauty' – very good – but I don't understand why the hand should have held close so long – which is just the point I wanted to be explained. Why the poet *had to be* locked up.
>
>   'My poet holds the future fast.' How? Do you mean he anticipates it in his mind – trusts in it – I *don't* know if you mean that, because I don't know if poets *do* that. If you mean that – I wish you had said so plainly.   (p. 253)

Browning doesn't take up this point, except perhaps when he says 'you would have me paint it all plain out, which can't be' (p. 257). The word 'locks' silently forges a connection between looking and keeping beauty locked up 'in this dark world'. The safety of a Browningesque 'good minute' always 'goes': the figure of the poet combines arrest and move- ment 'from end to end'. And the poet is passively held and hidden by God. Browning's reply to Ruskin opposes idealization of the poet as a potent Orphic figure: 'It is all teaching, and the people hate to be taught. They say otherwise, – make foolish fables about Orpheus enchanting stocks and stones, poets standing up and being worshipped, – all non- sense and impossible dreaming' (p. 258). 'Popularity's' poet resembles a different, failed Orpheus. In the myth and in Browning's poem 'Eurydice to Orpheus' (1864) looking is absolutely unsafe and yet irresistible. Like light or wine, the poet is destined to be spent, scattered, consumed, dis- membered. 'Popularity' has not even begun to draw the poet when it voices the certainty that 'Some night you'll fail us'. Only *God's* hand suc- cessfully 'leads you, / Yet locks you safe from end to end / Of this dark world'. Orpheus's attempt to lead Eurydice up from the Underworld leaves him empty-handed. He doesn't wait for the prodigally radiant moment of looking at Eurydice. Browning's letter uses astronomic fact to explain the failure line to Ruskin, who was bothered by it: 'one night he'll fail us, as a star is apt to drop out of heaven, in authentic astronomic records, and I want to make the most of my time' (p. 257). This impa- tience is Orphic: Browning's look and his naming of the star will not wait for God to unclose his hand.

'Popularity's' promise to 'draw you as you stand' is fulfilled in terms not of what's seen but of what's *said*: 'I'll say – a fisher, on the sand / By Tyre the old, with ocean plunder, / A netful, brought to land'. 'Tyre' (in Hebrew and Phoenician 'the Rock') has at least three relevant connotations: the empire without much in the way of monuments that Ruskin mentions in *Stones of Venice*, the skill of navigation by the stars and Tyrian purple. The colour of 'Popularity' is not Ruskinian brown but a legendary blue.

> Who has not heard how Tyrian shells
> > Enclose the blue, that dye of dyes
> Whereof one drop worked miracles,
> > And coloured like Astarte's eyes
> Raw silk the merchant sells?

Ruskin the theorist of colour asks: 'Now, where *are* you going to – this is, I believe pure malice against *me*, for having said that painters should always grind their own colours'. This blue belongs with the bright pigments abandoned by modern painters. 'Who has not heard' also by now Shelley's name in the 'shells' that enclose the dye?

Dyeing mischievously alludes to death and 'Popularity' rewrites Shelley's great lament for Keats' assassination by hostile critics. *Adonais* laments for Shelley himself too and 'Popularity' absorbs Shelley into the Keats / Adonais figure who so oddly ends the poem: 'What porridge had John Keats?' There are also shades of Milton's 'Epitaph' in the lines:

> And each bystander of them all
> > Could criticize, and quote tradition
> How depths of blue sublimed some pall
> > – To get which, pricked a king's ambition
> Worth sceptre, crown and ball.

revising Milton's 'kings for such a tomb would wish to die'. Milton is describing the unparalleled magnificence of a monument made out of your very own stone reader. 'Popularity's' fluid depths of blue cloth displace the *Epitaph*'s solid marble tomb sculpture. Ruskin writes 'Was there ever such a fool of a King? – You ought to have put a note saying who' (p. 254). He also objected to the verb *sublimed*: 'I don't know what you mean by "sublimed". Made sublime? – if so – it is not English. To sublime means to evaporate dryly, I believe and has participle "Sublimated".' Ruskin's pedantry forgets relevant usages of the verb 'sublime' meaning 'to exalt' in Dryden, Burke and Macaulay, but to say this is to forget that Browning's 'not English' *is* new because its authority is not derived from tradition or history. 'Sublime' is a forcibly Miltonic adjective, which has also come to describe Milton's poetry itself, but Browning daringly transmutes Miltonic loftiness into intense depth.

Names

The speaker of 'Popularity' claims that his own singularity comes from being the 'one man' who 'saw you/Knew you, and named a star!' This move is hardly original: it occurs in *Adonais* and before that in *Lycidas* where the identification of another poet as a star takes place beside the sea. Browning looks down and catches influence in a net:

> ... there's the dye, in that rough mesh
>   The sea has only just o'erwhispered!
> Live whelks, each lip's beard dripping fresh,
>   As if they still the water's lisp heard
> Through foam the rock-weeds thresh.

A related passage in *Sordello* gives the whelk's lip's beard another name while describing Sordello being returned to his former self by Nature. Nature will wash away the stain of factitious influences from the bard:

> And turn him pure as some forgotten vest
> Woven of painted byssus, silkiest
> Tufting the Tyrrhene whelk's pearl-sheeted lip,
> Left welter where a trireme let it slip
> I' the sea and vexed a satrap ...
>   ... how the tinct loosening escapes
> Cloud after cloud!
>
> (III, ll. 11–18)

The byssus, an outgrowth of the lip of a shellfish, source of the precious murex dye, contaminates the purity of Shelley's name Bysshe by loosening the relation of the word to a single individual. The forgotten vest also recalls the pledge to memorialize Lycidas: 'He must not float upon his watery bier/Unwept, and welter to the parching wind' (ll. 12–13). 'Popularity' brings together the figurative representations of influence as guiding star and miraculous dye, textual intermovements between poems and the sibilant lisping murmur of name-parts. The whelks suggest mouths, female genitalia and ears, pleasurably responsive to the whispering and lisping of the sea. It isn't *Browning's* name that has been subjected to this dismemberment across the poem's invocation of the most potent aural pleasure and visual loveliness. The words fisher, ocean, shells, mesh, fresh, thresh, furnish, abyss, shone speak Shelley's name without speaking it, rinse it in what Browning calls o'erwhispering, or in visual terms give the effect of dye weltering, cloud after cloud, into the sea.

The bee that is a Browning emblem in *Sordello* comes back here too, in a scene that can no longer be read in terms of observation and Ruskinian fidelity to the natural. Browning mentions the bee in *Sordello* in a letter to Ruskin and an earlier one to Elizabeth Barrett. In those letters the bee is cited as evidence that a poet's affair is with God. The transcendency of God is by no means incompatible with the fact that a poet's affair is also with the magical names of other poets; their names also may not be spoken without serious consequences. Browning's late occasional sonnet 'The Names' (1884) again rewrites Milton's 'Epitaph'. It suggests that silence is the fit companion for naming and that the issue of Shakespeare's name is to be left to sight. The movements I have been trying to convey are a way of 'voic[ing] the other name' silently, fragmenting and monumentalizing the names of poets:

> Shakespeare! – to such name's sounding, what succeeds
> > Fitly as silence? Falter forth the spell, –
> > Act follows word, the speaker knows full well,
> Nor tampers with its magic more than needs.
> Two names there are: That which the Hebrew reads
> > With his soul only; if from lips it fell,
> > Echo, back thundered by earth, heaven and hell,
> Would own 'Thou didst create us!' Naught impedes
> We voice the other name, man's most of might,
> > Awesomely, lovingly: let awe and love
> Mutely await their working, leave to sight
> > All of the issue as – below – above –
> > Shakespeare's creation rises: one remove,
> Though dread – this finite from that infinite.

The sonnet's closing reference to the finite and the infinite recalls Browning's reply to Ruskin in 1855: 'I *know* that I don't make out my conception by my language; all poetry being a putting the infinite within the finite' (Woolford and Karlin, p. 257). God's is the ultimately proper name, capable of giving a voice to everything so that Creation will 'own' (acknowledge) him. Shakespeare's name works in silence, its issue may be hard to place ('below – above –/Shakespeare's creation rises') and therefore hard to attribute to a source, but it is finite. 'Popularity' and the reply to Ruskin suggest that the 'infinite' authorship of God (associated with the assured correspondence between the spoken name and a universal echo) coexists with the finitude of literary creativity figured by Shakespeare and associated with sight.

In *Sordello* the bee as an observed natural phenomenon is Browning's tribute to God's presence in the world. Yet this transaction passes unnoticed by readers until Browning draws attention to its significance in a letter to Ruskin in 1856. The bee in its anonymity does not magically echo back 'Thou didst create me' at the sound of Browning's name. In 'Popularity' a bee comes in stanzas nine and ten where dismembered fragments of the name Bysshe Shelley are scattered and repeated: perhaps most beautifully when falling into the intensely coloured nothingness of an 'abyss of blue':

> Enough to furnish Solomon
>> Such hangings for his cedar-house,
> That, when gold-robed he took the throne
>> In that abyss of blue, the Spouse
> Might swear his presence shone
>
> Most like the centre-spike of gold
>> Which burns deep in the blue-bell's womb,
> What time, with ardours manifold,
>> The bee goes singing to her groom,
> Drunken and overbold.

The natural process under observation in these stanzas is pollination, an excessive, prodigal movement that runs counter to the monogamous union of 'Spouse' and 'groom'. Ruskin, always interested in proper female behaviour, writes:

> I don't think Solomon's spouse swore – at least not about blue-bells. I understand this bit, but fear most people won't. How many have noticed a blue-bell's stamen?

'Bee to her groom' I don't understand. I thought there was only one Queen-bee and *she* was never out o'nights – nor came home drunk or disorderly. Besides if she does, unless you had told me what o'clock in the morning she comes home at, the simile is of no use to me.   (Woolford and Karlin, p. 254)

The bee enters the abyss or womb of the flower, but never just the one. Her ardours are 'manifold': and as the flower contains both male 'spike' and female 'womb' it is impossible to observe whether she enters the abyss of blue to collect pollen from the stamen or deliver it to the stigma. The bee bears a seed that is also, the verb 'burns' suggests, in Shelleyan terms, a spark or an ash. Browning entertains the thought that the survival of the blue of poethood depends on a kind of a-human promiscuity rather than spousal or filial fidelity to tradition.

This astonishing passage gives way to a satirical account of the craft needed to extract the blue dye from the byssus:

> Mere conchs! not fit for warp or woof!
> Till cunning come to pound and squeeze
> And clarify, – refine to proof
> The liquor filtered by degrees,
> While the world stands aloof.

To this Ruskin asks: 'Mere conchs – [art?]. Well, but what has this to do with the Poet. Who 'Pounds' *him*? – I don't understand' (p. 254). Ruskin still looks for a person, a poet or a fisherman: what 'Popularity' has done is to translate the Poet into figures and syllables. Proper names and signatures are worked to the point of oozing. Names have been disguised as things (the murex, the insect) and broken up into a series of sounds and common nouns. The safekeeping of God's hand is just a temporary delay before he lets out the other poet in his full beauty. 'Meantime', the beauty of 'Popularity's blue comes from the pounding and squeezing and clarifying of names dissolved almost beyond recognition.

The last two stanzas suddenly take on a note of indignation at the exploitation of the poet by his inferiors. A different notion of the promiscuity of poetic textuality emerges in stanzas twelve and thirteen; others can profit from the work of the truly deserving originator:

> And there's the extract, flasked and fine,
> > And priced and salable at last!
> And Hobbs, Nobbs, Stokes and Nokes combine
> > To paint the future from the past,
> Put blue into their line.
>
> Hobbs hints blue, – straight he turtle eats:
> > Nobbs prints blue, – claret crowns his cup:
> Nokes outdares Stokes in azure feats, –
> > Both gorge. Who fished the murex up?
> What porridge had John Keats?

Ruskin is bewildered by this reduction: '"Flasked & fine." Now *is* that what you call painting a poet. Under the whole and sole image of a bottle of Blue, with a bladder over the cork? The Arabian fisherman with his genie was nothing to this.' The bottle takes us back to the question 'Why is a poet safer or more locked up than anyone else?' which could be answered: 'Because poems house or flask his memory and name in terms of things in general and language in general, or as Browning would have said in terms of God's creation'. Poems are the ultimate address of poets and there is no way back to the 'whole and sole' *image* of a poet from the oozy processes of distillation and solution which Browning and Ruskin teach us to recognize as creative.

'A poet's affair is with God'

The relation to God as the anonymous (because sole) author of everything was crucial to Browning's understanding of his own authority. This may explain his powerful response to Ruskin's claim that the writers of the modern age were unable distinctly to perceive God in the world. Alongside an active social life of visiting and showing his famous collection of Turners, Ruskin was absorbed by a quite different relation to contemporary culture: agonized and inspired by the failings of his age. He began writing *Modern Painters* to convince the world of the extraordinary value and significance of Turner's painting, but as the project grew volume by volume the painful sense of discrepancy between his own aesthetic convictions and those of mid-Victorian England only increased. In 'Of Modern Landscape' in *Modern Painters* III he writes:

Whereas all the pleasure of the medieval was in *stability*, *definiteness*, and *luminousness*, we are expected to rejoice in darkness and triumph in mutability; to lay the foundation of happiness in things which momentarily change or fade; and to expect the utmost satisfaction and instruction from what is impossible to arrest, and difficult to comprehend.

(Ruskin V, 317)

He found his own epoch lacking in the necessary faith to give glory to its subject-matter. He calls the nineteenth century '*sadder* than the early ones ... in a dim wearied way, – the way of ennui, and jaded intellect, and uncomfortableness of soul and body' (p. 321). This sadness speaks as discoloration. It was not, in the more ambivalent words of 'Andrea del Sarto', that a common greyness silvered everything. Ruskin found in modern landscape not the sombre illumination of silvering but, oddly enough, an embrowning.

'Of Modern Landscape' includes Mrs Browning, along with Byron, Keats, Tennyson and Wordsworth, in its account of contemporary poets' sense of separation from God. The section echoes with attacks on the current 'denial of the sacred element of colour' expressed in the ubiquity of brown. This brown is a signifier, all colour is a language. Old, mad Ruskin writes about the sky in *Fors Clavigera* VII (1877): 'The Word of God, printed in very legible type of gold on lapis-lazuli, needing no translation of yours, no colporteurship' (Ruskin XXIX, p. 56). Down on earth in the 1850s all was not so well. The Middle Ages had been 'the bright ages; ours are the dark ones. I do not mean metaphorically but literally. They were the ages of gold; ours are the ages of umber' (Ruskin V, p. 321). Contemporary painters tend 'continually to grey or brown' and 'paint our sky grey, our foreground black, and our foliage brown'. The problem extends beyond painting to daily life: 'we build brown brick walls, and wear brown coats, because we have been blunderingly taught to do so'. Where medieval life 'was inwoven with white and purple: ours is one seamless stuff of brown'. Beauty is banished under the 'system which reduced streets to brick walls, and pictures to brown stains'.

Ruskin ascribes the discoloration to 'our want of faith' and Browning's refutation of this claim comes from what might seem at first glance a similar religious background to Ruskin's. Both men were Nonconformists, educated in religion by Scottish Presbyterian mothers. Both had admired the preaching of Henry Melvill at the Congregationalist Camden Chapel in the 1830s. Both men's writings strongly show the influence of the King James Bible. The young Browning was fascinated by the devotional genre of the emblem book. He read Quarles's *Emblems* as a child and refers to them in his letters to Elizabeth Barrett. Ruskin remained, even during the loss of his religious faith in 1858–75, convinced of the sacredness of the visual imagination. Apart from a short period of atheism in emulation of Shelley when he was a teenager, Browning's faith in God was unshaken throughout his life, and his reply to Ruskin on *Men and Women* insists that 'a poet's affair is with God'. In a letter to Ruskin in 1856 he cites three passages from the sixth book of *Sordello* as evidence of his passion for natural detail as a reference to the work of God. That Browning's own name does not appear in Ruskin's chapter is an irrelevant technicality for a poet who sought to associate his poetry with nature in its very anonymity:

> You know what you say very energetically and reasonably about modern poets being 'without God in the world' 'an inherent & continual habit of thought which Scott shares with the moderns in general, being the instinctive sense of the divine presence, not formed into distinct belief: it creates no perfect form, does not apprehend distinctly any divine being or operation, but only an animation (slightly credited) in the objects of nature – this feeling (you sum up) is quite universal with us.' ... I look at this as requiring answer, if answer be to give – and, for one ... speak for myself out of the 'universally habituated.' Of all my things, the single chance I have had of speaking in my own person – not dramatically – has been in a few words in the course of 'Sordello' – a poem never *forgotten*, for a good reason, but printed sixteen years ago: here it is ... so I at once ask myself – knowing what my faith was, & immeasurably deeplier *is* – 'Did I then, if I needed to notice a natural object, really withhold my tributary two-mites tho' they do but make a farthing?' – I dip for & find these passages – now; do read them.
>
> [He quotes VI, ll. 619–28, 778–85 and 849–66.]

Seen in isolation the passages Browning picks out are indeed distinct descriptions of nature with reference to 'God in the world': they acknowledge nature as a divine creation and move towards the Seer's vision that looks to 'Not what man sees, but what God sees'. The letter insists on Browning's Protestant singularity; he wants to be able to speak *for himself* to God, and set himself apart from Ruskin's generalizations about universal tendencies. In narrative context another picture emerges also. The passages are moments when the poem moves away from Sordello's human story to sketch nature's indifference to it, a life that is not personal but which blithely exists in aching proximity to, and separation from, human creative struggles. The first passage Browning cites immediately follows, midline, Sordello's last moment. A little bee has calmly nibbled a leaf to fit or 'answer' its house:

> as Palma prest
> In one great kiss her lips upon [Sordello's] breast
> It beat. By this the hermit-bee has stopped
> His day's toil at Goito – the new-cropped
> Dead vine-leaf answers, now 'tis eve, he bit,
> Twirled so, and filed all day – the mansion's fit
> God counselled for.
>
> (VI, ll. 617–23)

The passage contains effects not ascribable to narrative content. There is an important coming together of visual images suggesting complementarity (the lips on the breast, the bee and the leaf) and strongly marked repetitious sound effects. 'It beat' echoes in 'hermit-bee', 'Goito' and 'he bit' (and a few lines later in the phrases 'soft small unfrighted bee' and 'font-tomb'). Is this combination of sights and sounds reiterating the sound, as well as the sense, of 'putting the infinite within the finite'?

A love letter to Elizabeth Barrett ten years before describes a bee making 'his nest, no doubt – or tomb, perhaps ... well, it seemed awful to watch that bee – he seemed so *instantly* from the teaching of God!'[12] The bee does not remember, feels no awe. He indifferently creeps off 'through the crevice' and 'leaves alone' the stone font where Sordello dies, which will become his 'font-tomb', and where as a boy he unconsciously mourned his mother Retrude. '[N]o remembrance racks' the bee which represents nature, the writing of God (VI, ll. 626–8). The poet also builds a nest or tomb, very different-looking from the one the Bishop ordered at St Praxed's. The ambition to remain is the same, but the materials are words bit, twirled and filed away. The final edifice is a poem that rather carelessly houses or entombs the poet's memory, leaving that bee to creep away from the 'stone maidens and the font of stone' which is the poem's most obvious location for death and mourning.[13]

The other two passages that Browning reminded Ruskin about also emphasize the indifference of nature to human tragedy. The memorial takes the form of the 'one tower left, a belfry', recalling Shelley's 'Julian and Maddalo' (1824). The tower is an important figure in Browning, most famously perhaps in 'Childe Roland to the Dark Tower Came', but also in *Sordello, The Inn Album* and *Asolando's* 'Inapprehensiveness' which are all closely associated with Ruskin.[14] I will follow Harold Bloom's example and quote the Shelley passage here:

> I looked and saw between us and the sun
> A building on an island; such a one
> As age to age might add, for uses vile,
> A windowless, deformed and dreary pile;
> And on the top an open tower, where hung
> A bell, which in the radiance swayed and swung;
> We could just hear its hoarse and iron tongue:
> The broad sun sunk behind it, and it tolled
> In strong and black relief.
>
> (ll. 98–106)

Maddalo interprets this sight and sound to Julian in a way that Browning would have found personally abhorrent in its association of faith with delusion and lack of genuine purpose:

> 'And such,' – he cried, 'is our mortality,
> And this must be the emblem and the sign
> Of what should be eternal and divine! –
> And like that black and dreary bell, the soul,
> Hung in a heaven-illumined tower, must toll
> Our thoughts and our desires to meet below
> Round the rent heart and pray – as madmen do
> For what? they know not, – till the night of death
> As sunset that strange vision, severeth
> Our memory from itself, and us from all
> We sought and yet were baffled.'
>
> (ll. 120–30)

The supernatural tolling in the Rù valley near Asolo recalls the 'coarse and iron tongue' of Shelley's bell on the Venetian coast. For Browning in *Sordello* the sound has an added significance as the memorial of a terrible series of events, the destruction of Alberic and his children.

The stubbornly repetitive sounds of 'cheruping' and chirring might also be said to mark 'the ravage' without knowing it:

> and I think grass grew
> Never so pleasant as in valley Rù
> By San Zenon where Alberic in turn
> Saw his exasperated captors burn
> Seven children with their mother, and, regaled
> So far, tied on to a wild horse, was trailed
> To death through raunce and bramble-bush: I take
> God's part and testify that mid the brake
> Wild o'er his castle on Zenone's knoll
> You hear its one tower left, a belfry, toll –
> Cherups the contumacious grasshopper,
> Rustles the lizard and the cushats chirre
> Above the ravage.
>
> (*Sordello* VI, ll. 773–85)

The last passage, also set at Asolo, brings together the dissolution of Sordello's first prize-winning song 'Elys' into 'some unintelligible words' sung by a boy on a hillside several centuries after Sordello's death. The words manage to 'beat the lark', Shelley's figure for the supreme poet, and leave that 'scorner of the ground' swooning at the boy's feet. The sublime loftiness of the tower is also grounded, 'Like the chine of some extinct animal / Half turned to earth and flowers'. These two Shelleyan symbols are ruined, become part of the 'heathy brown and nameless hill', which makes Browning's name an anonymous part of the landscape also:

> Lo, on a heathy brown and nameless hill
> By sparkling Asolo, in mist and chill,
> Morning just up, higher and higher runs
> A child barefoot and rosy – See! the sun's
> On the square castle's inner-court's green wall
> – Like the chine of some fossil animal
> Half turned to earth and flowers; and thro' the haze
> (Save where some slender patches of grey maize
> Are to be overleaped) that boy has crost
> The whole hill-side of dew and powder-frost
> Matting the balm and mountain camomile:
> Up and up goes he, singing all the while

Some unintelligible words to beat
The lark, God's poet, swooning at his feet
So worsted is he at the few fine locks
Stained like pale honey oozed from topmost rocks
Sun-blanched the livelong summer. – All that's left
Of the Goito lay! And thus bereft,
Sleep and forget, Sordello.

(VI, 849–66)

'Elys' is Sordello's signature tune, his monument which bereaves him of itself.

'Inapprehensiveness'

Ruskin appears in Browning's poetry for the last time in an apocalyptic poem called 'Inapprehensiveness' (1889).[15] The poem describes the tension between a man and a woman as they look at the view but not at each other. If they really looked at each other it would be explosive, the end of the world. Ruskin's name is invoked alongside the image of a ruined Italian tower near Asolo at sunset. The location appears in *Sordello,* Book VI, but the couple in this poem are very different from the little boy crossing the hillside at dawn in *Sordello.* Self-conscious, evasive and unable to forget, they are dominated by the past. 'How it towers / Yonder, the ruin o'er this vale of ours! / The West's faint flare behind it so relieves / Its rugged outline'. The phrase 'rugged outline' suggests Ruskin's descriptive prose, and recalls Browning's 'touches and bits and outlines which *succeed* if they bear the conception from me to you'. But as the title suggests the poem is about the failure of conception to move between a 'me' and a 'you'. Observation of the tower covers a dangerously strong passion which one character in the poem does not wish to apprehend in her companion.

To apprehend is to seize or lay hold of a person, object, opportunity or idea: it carries a sense of anticipation and fear as well as understanding. In *Sordello* the little boy and the bee at Goito were carefree, 'unfrighted' and indifferent to their surroundings. The Asolo landscape haunts and shadows the couple in 'Inapprehensiveness':

'. . . – sight perhaps deceives
Or I could almost fancy that I see
A branch wave plain – belike some wind-sown tree
Chance-rooted where a missing turret was.

> What would I give for the perspective glass
> At home, to make out if 'tis really so!
> Has Ruskin noticed here at Asolo
> That certain weed-growths on the ravaged wall
> Seem' ... something that I could not say at all ...

The weed-growths recall *Pippa Passes*, and the evening scene between Luigi and his mother, set 'Inside the Turret on the Hill above Asolo'. Luigi, who is debating whether to become a political assassin for the cause of Italian unification, has an apprehensive idea of what the weed-growths above him higher up the tower might be. He shouts to make an echo, and anxiously describes the sound as:

> The very ghost of a voice
> Whose body is caught and kept by ... what are those?
> Mere withered wallflowers, waving overhead?
> They seem an elvish group with thin bleached hair
> That lean out of their topmost fortress ...
>   (III, ll. 6–10)

These 'mountain men' have the power to apprehend, to catch and keep, living voices. For all the blitheness of *Sordello*'s running, singing boy and of Pippa herself, there is something eerily retentive or haunted about the Asolo landscape in both poems. 'Inapprehensiveness' also suggests something in the landscape that will not pass.

The man in 'Inapprehensiveness' takes on the characteristics of the tower as he silently 'stands, and may/So stand unnoticed until Judgement Day' beside the woman. The embrace of this couple would not be the 'good minute' described in 'Two in the Campagna', it would be apocalyptic, startling, bursting, ruinous. The look in this poem is withheld for similar reasons to those that underpin the ban on uttering God's name for the Hebrew in 'The Names', which was written about the same time: 'if from lips it fell,/Echo, back thundered by earth, heaven and hell,/Would own "Thou didst create us!"' The echo does not simply repeat. It marks a crossing from life to afterlife, it is apocalyptic and is connected with names and works of precursors.

Sordello links these themes most explicitly to Browning's own creativity in the passage where the narrator expels Shelley who has come down from his cloudy place to 'scare me ... with that pure face'. Like the elvish group imagined by Luigi, Shelley would somehow steal the body of other poetry (here the work of warrior poets Aeschylus and Philip Sidney) and leave only echo, martial noise as the ghost of a voice:

> The thunder-phrase of the Athenian, grown
> Up out of memories of Marathon,
> Would echo like his own sword's griding screech
> Braying a Persian shield, – the silver speech
> Of Sidney's self, the starry paladin,
> Turn intense as a trumpet sounding in
> The knights to tilt, – wert thou to hear!
>
> (I, ll. 65–71)

The threatened reduction of Aeschylus's language takes the form of a regression: poetry would become transitory noise from the remembered battle out of which the poet's voice had 'grown / Up'. Sidney's speech would become mere literal trumpeting. The movement from speech to chivalric blast reverses Shelley's wish to give voice to voiceless blowing at the end of 'Ode to the West Wind' (1820): 'Be through my lips to unawakened earth // The trumpet of a prophecy!' In *Sordello* Percy Shelley's listening presence must be banished, his name melted down to make the 'Persian shield' screechingly struck by Aeschylus's sword. Otherwise, it seems, Browning's poetry also may become a blend of echo and autobiographical material.

Shelley's Ode finds its most convincing response in Browning's 'Childe Roland to the Dark Tower Came' where Roland faces his lost precursors and 'Dauntless' sets the slug-horn to his lips and blows. Bloom points out that 'we do not know the content of this prophecy ... Roland is not performing his own poem, in direct contrast to Shelley at the close of the "Ode to the West Wind," where the words to be scattered among mankind are the text of the "Ode."'[16] The triumph is achieved by Roland. Browning never presents a pure face to confront the pure face or pure white light of lyric that he associates with Shelley and his incarnation Elizabeth Barrett. 'Inapprehensiveness' is still concerned with the alternatives to looking death in the face. The woman's 'inapprehensive stare' at the landscape and the sunset holds back impending destruction. Her tourist's attentiveness takes the place of the acknowledging 'look' which would unveil, not only passion, but a vengeful excess of life too immense for the eye to bear:

'One who, if once aware that your regard
Claimed what his heart holds, – woke as from its sward
The flower, the dormant passion, so to speak –
Then what a rush of life would startling wreak
Revenge on your inapprehensive stare
While, from the ruin and the West's faint flare,
You let your eyes meet mine, touch what you term
Quietude – that's an universe in germ –
The dormant passion needing but a look
To burst into immense life!'

The dark tower in this late poem is the apparent quietude of old age that hides the germ of an impossible flowering. There is no second Spring, no return to the imagination of 15-year-old Luigi and his echoic elves. Ruskin and Vernon Lee, aesthetic critics and writers on Italian landscape, come into the poem to sustain the deception, and hold off the meeting of eyes: '"No, the book / Which noticed how the wall-growths wave" said she / "Was not by Ruskin," / I said "Vernon Lee?"' The half-forgotten, half-remembered book was *Pippa Passes* by Robert Browning.

The engagements between Ruskin and Browning show the limits of a perceptual vocabulary for the interpretation of Browning poems. Monuments are not only the actual stone tombs that Ruskin studies, they can appear in language. To study poetic monuments it is necessary to abandon Ruskin's literalism and explore his responses to Browning without adopting his reading methods. The monuments in Browning poems are movements that emerge through reading, rather than separate objects. They take on memorial significance in relation to other poetic texts. In the context of poetic textuality, monuments and names cease to be fixtures, and take on a disturbing linguistic fluidity, like a wall that grows and waves, or the echoing ghost of a voice.

6
Arnold and Translation: *The Ring and the Book*

> *Behold, the people is one, and they have all one language: and this*
> *they begin to do: and now nothing will be restrained from them,*
> *which they have imagined to do. Go to, let us go down, and there*
> *confound their language, that they may not understand one*
> *another's speech. So the Lord scattered them abroad from thence,*
> *upon the face of all the earth: and they left off to build the city . . .*
> (Genesis XI: 6–7)

The poet and cultural critic Matthew Arnold's desire for aesthetic clarity, objectivity and perfection of form countered his anxious sense of the complexity and fragmentation of a world after Babel. As a young poet he found Browning's 'confused multitudinousness' lamentable and the older Arnold's prose describes modern cultural and social life itself in very similar terms: 'the confusion of the present times is great, the multitude of voices counselling different things bewildering' (Arnold, Letters I, p. 128; Poems, p. 599). His great cultural resource in the quest for wholeness and intelligibility was classical Greece, a resource that his contemporary Browning interprets and uses very differently.

Both writers were theorists and practitioners of translation; both worked in a tradition where learning, for schoolboys and for poets, was inseparable from translation from the 'dead' languages Latin and Greek. My epigraph from Genesis brings in another poetic and pedagogical tradition, the one associated with the Bible, Arnold's 'Hebraism' and English Protestant reading. The story of Babel tells that confusion began at the same moment as translation, when mankind is scattered by God before it can complete the imagined tower of Babel. God makes it impossible for a people or a language to be decidedly unified, 'one', as Arnold often wishes. Babel informs Browning's poetics as well as his ideas about translation. The story of Babel has a particular resonance with Browning's poetics of the imperfect.[1] It is a story of primordial imperfection that is the beginning of all attempts to translate; it presents as narrative the beginning of the rich and troubling relation between imagination and disunified language.

Browning's translation of *The Ring and the Book* (1868–9) from the Italian and lawyers' Latin of the Old Yellow Book introduces a number of projects which, in the 1870s, concentrate on translation from ancient Greek. The highly popular *Balaustion's Adventure* includes a 'transcription' of Euripides' *Alcestis* (1871) and the sequel to *Balaustion*, *Aristophanes' Apology*, contains a translation from Euripedes' horrifying tragedy *Heracles* (1875). Browning's translation phase culminates in his 'transcription' of Aeschylus's *Agamemnon* (1877), a version which was received with some perplexity for its literalness: Browning wanted to make English behave like Greek, while still remaining English. In each of these cases, Browning does not model his practice on classical precedent. He is interested in the foreignness of his material as such; the *Agamemnon* 'transcription' manifests this foreignness at the level of syntax and word order, where the difference between English and Greek is dramatized or performed. He is also interested in this particularly deformed, confused and mutilated original, I suspect, for its otherness in relation to itself, what Maurice Blanchot's essay 'Translating' identifies as the original's 'possibilities of being different from itself and foreign to itself'.[2] Blanchot adds further comment on the case of so-called 'dead' languages:

> As for classical works of art, which belong to a language that is not spoken, they demand to be translated all the more because they are, henceforth, the sole depositories of the life of a dead language and the only ones responsible for the future of a language that has no future. Only translated are these works alive; moreover, in the original language itself they are always as if retranslated and redirected toward what is most specific to them: toward their foreignness of origin.

It was the centrality of classical literature to Victorian literary and educational culture, the safeness of classical writing as a repository of human values, that Arnold liked. For Browning the very *deadness* of classical language provides an opening for the immense life bursting out of his poetry. In translation, and nowhere else, lies the chance of these ancient works. The classical translations of Browning provide a space for continued work on the poetics of futurity that Herbert Tucker has so powerfully described in terms of Browning's relation with Shelley. Shelley appears in Browning's work like a ghost, not like a guest star. He does not wait to be introduced, and, as a phantom, Shelley comes across as different from himself and other than himself. He has the foreignness of an original that asks to be translated. This foreignness is inherent in Shelley's work also, this is its appeal for Browning. Younger Browning could figure this in terms of the obscurity and lack of fame of the Sun-treader, who needed championing. Shelley was little read in the 1830s but by the late 1850s this was no longer so, thanks to other 'translators' than Browning. In 1858 Trelawny's *Records of Shelley* and Hogg's roguish *Life of Percy Bysshe Shelley* were published, along with Charles Middleton's *Shelley and His Writings*. Lady Jane Shelley responded to Hogg in 1859 with the more sedate *Shelley Memorials* in 1859: the 'Shelley Myth' was becoming public.[3] Browning had to find new ways of recovering the dangerous otherness that made Shelley such an appealing 'original' for the translations of his imaginative life. Blanchot describes literature in terms of a movement that affirms language's relation to something other than the present. A literary work that demands to be translated, articulates through this demand its own relation to the future: 'The original is never immobile, and all that a language contains of the future at a particular moment, all that there is in the language that points to or summons a state that is other, sometimes dangerously other, is affirmed in the solemn drift of literary works.' I will shortly discuss 'Thamuris Marching', a sublime confusion of the poetry of Browning and Shelley, in which the dangerous otherness of Shelley's poetic language undergoes translation, or in the poem's own word 'transport', and erupts as laughter. 'Thamuris Marching' shows that laughter is not incompatible with the dignity and solemnity of literature, its association with death and monumental values. Indeed, laughter transports these qualities towards the future.

Browning's translation poems of the period 1868–75 mix genres and literary modes. *The Ring and the Book*, which is discussed in the latter part of this chapter, can lay claim to being an epic, a tragedy, a history and a translation. *Balaustion's Adventure* consists of an adapted version of the tragicomedy *Alcestis*, repeated by a 'lyric girl' who thereby saves herself and a group of her fellow Kaunians in time of war (l. 186). In *Aristophanes' Apology* the comic dramatist defends his art to Balaustion and her husband, who are reading *Herakles* (as Browning's unconventional spelling has it) in tribute to the recently dead Euripedes. Comedy and tragedy contend, and in addition to the 'transcript' of *Herakles* the poem contains Aristophanes' performance of a song by Sophocles, 'Thamuris Marching' (ll. 5188–265). This poem is Browning's own, not a classical translation, and it translates Shelley's poetic language under the cover of translating a dead language.

Thamuris laughing

'Thamuris Laughing' might work as an alternative title, for this poem within a poem echoes with exuberant laughter from the poet-warrior Thamuris as he goes to his unequal, impossible singing contest with the Muses.[4] Laughter also emanates from the landscape he passes through: 'Was there a ravaged tree? it laughed compact / With gold'; 'Say not the beast's mirth bounded! that was flight'. This laughter is not simply identified with humour or levity or defiance, it also becomes serious by its closeness to the tragic; for according to Book II of Homer's *Iliad* the Muses behave badly towards Thamyris. Rather like the Old Testament God who determines to put a stop to the building of Babel, they are overcome with envy and ruin Thamyris's memory, without which he cannot be a poet. 'Thamuris Marching' starts before that moment, at the time of 'earth's community of purpose' and the 'ease of earth's fulfilled imaginings', when it also seems for Thamuris and his band that, in the words of Genesis, 'nothing can be restrained from them that they have imagined to do'. The laughter in 'Thamuris Marching' is the lifting of imaginative restraint, a 'fiery transport' that suspends the familiar limitations of being:

> So did the near and far appear to touch
> I' the moment's transport, – that an interchange
> Of function, far with near, seemed scarce too much;
>
> And had the rooted plant aspired to range
> With the snake's license, while the insect yearned
> To glow fixed as the flower, it were not strange –

This passage provides an extraordinary account of translation as an occurence already at work within nature, 'an interchange / Of function, far with near'. One of translation's aims is to abolish the distance, if not the difference, between languages. Elsewhere, Browning's 'Abt

Vogler' (1864) associates this mingling of opposites with the transport of musical improvisation in which earthly passion strikes a chord in nature and in heaven, so that:

> Novel splendours burst forth, grew familiar and dwelt with mine,
> Not a point nor peak but found and fixed its wandering star;
> Meteor-moons, balls of blaze: and they did not pale nor pine,
> For earth had attained to heaven, there was no more near nor far.

Abt Vogler ends by resigning himself and his music to the earth, but Thamuris, like Childe Roland, sustains his daring to the last. His song does not conclude, instead its performance fragments into laughter: Thamuris announces: '"Here I await the end of this ado:/Which wins – Earth's poet or the Heavenly Muse." ... //But song broke up in laughter'. It is not possible to know exactly who or what is laughing: Aristophanes is the next to speak, but for a moment there is just 'laughter' without a subject, without a voice. Laughter would thus be a breaking of form, a kind of confusion operating within the song's regular and powerful terza rima, making it impossible to close or classify it. As often in Browning, one thinks of Shelley's saying: 'I always go on until I am stopped, and I never am stopped', but here the 'I' loses itself in laughter.[5] Arnold's sober, anxious poetry and cultural theory give ancient Greece a special status: comparing his rather idealizing approach to translation and to the classical original with Browning's robust curiosity about the foreignness of his originals will further illuminate Browning's conception of literary language.

Arnold's 'Empedocles'

Two poems of the 1850s, Arnold's 'Empedocles on Etna' (1852) and Browning's 'Cleon' (1855), open the comparison. Arnold's dramatic poem is set on the slopes of Mount Etna in Sicily in the pre-Socratic period two to three thousand years ago, and describes the mental events leading up to the philosopher Empedocles's suicide. The poem steadily narrows its focus from an initial dramatic counterpoint between the lyric hopefulness of Empedocles's young follower Callicles and the moody philosopher's unsparing insight, to become the dialogue of 'a naked, eternally restless mind' with itself. As the poem gathers towards a climax at the volcano mouth, Empedocles utters his last cry: 'Receive me, save me!' and leaps into the fiery crater of Etna before 'the mists/Of despondency and gloom' can envelop his soul (ll. 414–16). Arnold's own commentary explains that Empedocles 'sees things as they are' and the sight is a 'severe and mind-tasking one: to know the mysteries which are communicated to others by fragments, in parables' (Arnold, *Poems*, p. 148). The opposition between genuine knowing and fragmentary or figurative communication informs much of Arnold's thinking about poetry and translation. Mist, confusion and linguistic or psychic fracture are to be avoided.

Belated in history and his own life, Empedocles has lived on 'into a time when the habits of Greek thought and feeling had begun fast to change, character to dwindle, the influence of the Sophists to prevail' (p. 591). The 1853 Preface claims Empedocles is modern, his fragmentary writings indicate the disappearance of earlier Greek characteristics ('calm cheerfulness, ... disinterested objectivity') and the beginning of 'the mind's dialogue with itself'. There was a time in Empedocles's youth when he and his friends 'received the shock of mighty thoughts / On simple minds with a pure natural joy' (ll. 242–3). Before he kills himself he looks back on these lost days when it seemed bearable to think without becoming prey to doubt and discouragement. After his death, Callicles, who does not know what has just happened, shifts the topos of the poem from Etna to Mount Helicon and restores calm with a vision of Apollo and the changeless song of the muses. He has learned nothing from the stern wisdom of his master. Callicles's untroubled closing hymn does not mourn Empedocles and struggles with no sense of discontinuity or fracture, no intimation of his own death or the end of divine order.

Arnold's hero dies to avoid a gloomy mist that would compromise the unambiguous clarity of his intellectual vision which has in its certainty induced the gloom. The situation appears tragic in its combination of unbearableness and inevitability, but 'Empedocles' was left out of the 1853 *Poems* because Arnold felt it was not a proper tragedy. He defended his decision to exclude 'Empedocles' by quoting Schiller's claim that 'All art is dedicated to Joy'. The hero's predicament is painful but fails to produce joy in the reader: 'suffering finds no vent in action' and 'mental distress is unrelieved by incident, hope, or resistance' (p. 592). Arnold's emphasis on the pleasurable effects of tragedy evades the profound uncertainty that tragedy induces in those who read or watch it.[6] According to Sidney's *Apology for Poetry* (1595), for example, tragedy 'teacheth the uncertainty of this world'.[7] It can also be argued that action, incident, hope and resistance are not in themselves essential to tragedy, as Arnold claims they are. Where these features are present, as they are in the plays

Arnold refers to as exemplary modern tragedies, *Hamlet* and Goethe's *Faust*, they do not produce simple joy, but increase the sense of uncertainty by enhancing suspense and emotional conflict for the reader or audience. Unlike Hamlet and Faust, Empedocles dies in order to avoid uncertainty: 'only death / Can cut his oscillations short, and so / Bring him to poise' (ll. 233–5). Callicles, the young poet who loves him, never learns of his death and to his last word remains confident in the gods. The old friend and disciple Pausanias has disappeared at the end of Act I to seek help for Empedocles in the city. Arnold's poem has no choric figure, no Horatio to articulate the sympathetic continuation of Empedocles's suffering after he has ended his own speech. As the poem ends there is no pity and no terror, no being torn apart by the two. Kenneth Allott points out that Arnold found the shock of poetic creation psychically shattering. He wrote in 1858 of the poet's temptation 'to transfer your operations to a region where form is everything. Perfection of a certain kind may there be attained or at least approached without knocking yourself to pieces'.[8] His adoption of Schiller's aesthetic theory, like the formalism of his tragedy *Merope*, seeks to avoid the arbitrariness of fragmentation and ruin that characterize the tragic. The contrast with Browning is extreme: the letters and poetry repeatedly suggest that the creative mind consists of sympathy for fragments. Inspiration and composition require a self that is temporally disjunct, radically imperfect and, as *Sordello* puts it, broken in its very relation to 'so pure a work of thought / As language'.

'Cleon': slaves and angels

The action of 'Cleon' happens in the Sporades in the 'latter days' when Greek pantheism overlapped with very early Christianity, about AD 52. The poem takes the form of a letter from the poet to his distant patron Protus, answering Protus's questions about the extraordinary range of Cleon's acheivements as poet, sculptor, painter, philosopher and musician. Bloom identifies the character Cleon as himself a translation: 'a kind of version of Matthew Arnold' in which the belatedness lamented by Arnold's Empedocles 'becomes a curious kind of inauthentic overconfidence in Cleon's self-defense'.[9] Cleon acknowledges that he is no Homer, Terpander or Phidias, but asks 'Say, is it nothing that I know them all?'

Protus has begun to build a tower, a symbol of aspiring aesthetic consciousness. Cleon imagines Protus hoping for the moment when, 'all the tumult of the building hushed, / Thou first of men mightst look

out to the East:/The vulgar saw thy tower, thou sawest the sun'.
He agrees with Protus that consciousness, 'the pleasure-house, / Watch-
tower and treasure-fortress of the soul ... A tower that crowns a
country', does not increase the human capacity for joy. You climb up,
see a world of possible pleasures, but can 'Take no jot more/Than ere
thou clombst the tower to look abroad'. There is no recuperation to be
found in art; the artist's expansive range of sympathies does not save
him from loss of the capacity to enjoy the limited life of his own
senses. The 'Essay on Shelley', written about the same time, puts it
succinctly: 'The man passes, the work remains.' Cleon vividly describes
to Protus how the survival of works of art does not compensate for the
fact of death, but mocks the fact of dying:

> The horror quickening still from year to year,
> The consummation coming past escape
> When I shall know most, and yet least enjoy –
> When all my works wherein I prove my worth,
> Being present still to mock me in men's mouths,
> Alive still, in the praise of such as thou,
> I, I the feeling, thinking, acting man,
> The man who loved his life so over-much
> Sleep in my urn.

So far Cleon is faithfully Arnoldian, but without Arnold's flinching
from extremes. Cleon is very much Browning's creation when he
articulates disparity and non-correspondence without despair. The
poem takes on the acute sense of joy and quickening horror, the
mockery of works that remain present and alive, beside the horrible
fact of one's own death. Cleon goes on to do something Arnold does
not allow Empedocles to do: he imagines something he knows is
impossible. He does not see things only as they are but as he knows
they cannot be: 'It is so horrible,/I dare at times imagine to my
need/Some future state revealed to us by Zeus,/Unlimited in capa-
bility/For joy, as this is in desire for joy.' This imagination is not
unfettered; Cleon's sense of what is possible is conditioned by his
Greek pantheism. He cannot quite translate into that idiom the
'future state' which might actually answer to his imaginative need.
The phrase is Shelley's, from the title of his prose work on death 'On
a Future State' (1840); this might make us hesitate to identify
completely with a messianic interpretation of the end of the poem.
Despite the unshaken faith of Browning the man, Christian afterlife

is not Cleon's answer to the conflict between desire and death. This conflict is left open: the early Christians Cleon knows are only slaves and their 'doctrine could be held by no sane man'.

While the last lines of the poem allude to Christ, Paul and the beginnings of Christianity, Cleon's sustained sense of imaginative conflict does not allow the poem to develop into a narrative of conversion or liberation from the beliefs that shore up that conflict. By contrast Arnold's Empedocles represents his wrath and gloom as forms of slavery and frees himself by dying: 'it hath been granted me / Not to die wholly, not to be all enslaved.' There are actual slaves in 'Cleon' and biographical facts would make it hard for Browning to ignore this aspect of Greek culture. His father's mother's family had owned a sugar plantation on St Kitts in the West Indies, and as a young man Robert Browning Senior had gone out to work there. He quickly left in disgust at the brutality of slaveholding, outraging his grandfather. In the 1850s plantation slavery still flourished in the southern states of the US. Much of Elizabeth Barrett's family money had come from Jamaican sugar plantations worked by slaves, and she was on the whole glad when litigation over the ownership of the plantations and slaves went against her branch of the family in 1824, although this meant the Moulton-Barretts had to live in considerably reduced circumstances. She was the author of 'The Runaway Slave at Pilgrim's Point' (published in the American abolitionist journal *The Liberty Bell* in 1848) and 'A Nation's Curse' (an anti-slavery poem published in her collection on Italian unification *Poems Before Congress* in 1860).

'Cleon' is not a work of anti-slavery propaganda, but it touches on the issues of race that were entangled with British colonial slavery. Cleon cheerfully compares the slaves unloaded from the boat with Protus's other gifts to decorative flooring: 'the group dispersed / Of black and white slaves (like the chequer-work / Pavement ...)'. Later the pavement recurs as an image of the 'perfect separate forms' that, according to Cleon, combine to make mankind. The fact of slavery in the poem makes one question the possibility of such a harmonics of race, and also question Cleon's presentation of himself. This questioning operates mainly through the figure of one of the slaves, a 'lyric woman' who is associated by Browning's language with Elizabeth Barrett and Shelley.

A 'white she-slave' has been sent to Cleon as a cupbearer. He promises Protus that he will use her as a mouthpiece, a monument; he will make 'this slave narrate thy fortunes, speak / Thy great words, and describe thy royal face' in ritual gratitude. Cleon imagines her as pure illiterate being, a poem in herself: 'I can write love-odes; thy fair slave's an ode.' Cleon does not let her share the status of 'the thinking, feeling, acting man' who must inevitably sleep the sleep of death in his urn: he describes her as a fruit of cultural progress like orchard plums or farmed honey, that 'young and tender crescent-moon, thy slave, / Sleeping above her robe as buoyed by clouds / Refines upon the women of my youth'. The slave's poignantly dispossessed sleep lies beyond Cleon's sympathy. She may have 'her robe' but her youth is not her own. The picturesque stillness of her body conveniently provides Cleon with an image to illustrate the theme of the refinement of his own sympathetic powers.

This figure of the lyric woman as a gift and as a poem in 'Cleon' recalls *The Ring and the Book*'s address to a 'lyric Love' who, like the slave, is a gift: 'God ... best taught song by gift of thee' (I, l. 404). Commentaries identify the passage as a loving tribute to the late Elizabeth Barrett Browning, but 'lyric' immediately also suggests Shelley. The lyric Love 'half-angel and half-bird' combines the blithe spirit of Shelley's skylark with ideas of Christian incarnation, along the lines of the 'Essay on Shelley' and *Pauline*. The 'posy' to Browning's ring summons a muse or messiah who is also a glorified slave, still able to be called, even out of death:

> When the first summons of the darkling earth
> Reached thee amid thy chambers, ...
>   ... – to drop down,
> To toil for man, to suffer or to die, –
> This is the same voice: can thy soul know change?
>   (I, ll. 1397–401)

The Ring and the Book calls its lyric Love with the 'same voice' which in *Pauline* '[d]rew down a god' and humbled him, or boasted of a craving after knowledge that 'lies in me a chained thing – still ready / To serve me, if I loose its slightest bond – / I cannot but be proud of my bright slave' (*Pauline* ll. 114, 631–3). The narrator of *Pauline* is also himself enslaved by his 'star', Shelley, the poet who combines hopes for mankind with seductive melodies. This Christ-like figure calls for a work of translation oriented towards the future. He

> Caught me, and set me, as to a sweet task,
> To gather every breathing of his songs.
> And woven with them there were words, which seemed
> A key to a new world; the muttering
> Of angels, of some thing unguessed by man.
>   (ll. 411–15)

In Browning's poetry angels can appear to be slaves, they bear messages from anywhere to anywhere, and there is no void across which they cannot journey, no place from which they cannot be called back.[10] This begins in *Pauline*, which describes the hero's imagination 'which/Has been an angel to me – coming not/In fitful visions, but beside me ever,/And never failing me' (ll. 284–7). Yet, like actual slaves, Browning's angels do escape. In *Sordello*, for example, angels are associated with the fantasy of absolute poetic mastery. The young Sordello, inwardly undecided whether to become a minstrel or a ruler, imagines combining the powers of both. He is Kaiser Friedrich, but he persuades his subjects with poetry:

> that arm indeed
> Has thunder for its slave; but where's the need
> Of thunder if the stricken multitude
> Hearkens, arrested in its angriest mood,
> While songs go up exulting, then dispread,
> Dispart, disperse, lingering overhead
> Like an escape of angels?
>
> (I, ll. 877–83)

Sordello's fantasy proves unworkable, the escapes or apparitions of language do not make the multitude hearken to him, any more than the British public hearkened to Browning. If the constant angel of imagination can spring up to save the *Pauline* poet from 'utter death', it is also in the nature of angels to 'dispread/Dispart, disperse' like the aftersparks of a firework display. Poetry works by dispersal, its messages have the character of apparitions, and they do not obey the law of the author's imperious 'right hand'. In Book Two of *Sordello*, an escaping angel represents the 'whole dream' that Sordello's carefully wrought armour of poetic language fails to hold: 'A few adhering rivets loosed, upsprings/The angel, sparkles off his mail, which rings/Whirled from each delicatest limb it warps' (II, ll. 603, 611–13).

The first escaped angel was Lucifer, and the Satan of *Paradise Lost* is the forerunner of the fallen angels in Browning who turn up and silently interfere with messages, scattering and scrambling them. Milton's Satan, like Cleon and the builders of Babel, dares to imagine. Cleon reveals himself as something of a bad angel when he fails to supply a line of communication between Protus and St Paul, pantheist Greece and Christianity: 'I cannot tell thy messenger aright/Where to deliver what he bears of thine/To one called Paulus'. Messages in

Browning often get scattered, overshoot, break up before they reach the intended receiver. I suspect that in Browning's reading of 'Empedocles' the philosopher who posts himself into the safety of the crater does not find Arnoldean 'deliverance' but Browningesque 'escape' as ashes and sparks ejaculate randomly and beautifully into the fragrant Sicilian night.

Towers of Babel: Arnold and Browning on translation

The fallen angel Satan also embodies another great figure of Browning's, the tower. In a passage identified by Burke as an example of the sublime, Milton in *Paradise Lost* describes Satan among his troops: 'he above the rest / In shape and gesture proudly eminent / Stood like a tower' (l, ll. 589–91).[11] Towers and other monuments are no security against divine authority; the tower built in 'Cleon' cannot defeat the externally imposed limitations of life. The Biblical prototype for Satan's towering defiance of God is in Genesis, the story of the tower of Babel. This story informs the many incomplete towers or ruined cities in Browning's writing (see Chapter 5, note 15). According to Genesis Babel was an ambitious attempt to make a name ('Go to, let us build us a city, and a tower, whose top may reach unto heaven, and let us make us a name, lest we be scattered abroad upon the face of the whole earth'). The name Babel monumentalizes the ruin or confounding of the attempt by a jealous and belated God, who looked on and said:

> Behold, the people is one, and they have all one language: and this they begin to do: and now nothing will be restrained from them, which they have imagined to do. Go to, let us go down, and there confound their language, that they may not understand one another's speech. So the Lord scattered them abroad from thence, upon the face of all the earth: and they left off to build the city: Therefore is the name of it called Babel [Confusion], because the Lord did there confound the language of all the earth: and from thence did the Lord scatter them abroad upon the face of all the earth.   (Genesis XI: 6–9)

The ruined tower speaks about the need to translate and the impossibility of translation. Browning was a scholar in several languages, a translator from classical Greek into English, cosmopolitan and well-travelled. He uses Greek, Latin, French and

Italian in his poems and letters; he knew Spanish, and as a poet he produced dramatic poems that articulate the various idioms of characters that are not his own. He could, and did, translate. Yet this did not diminish his sense of an internal foreignness in the languages and works he knew, and even in himself. A letter to Elizabeth Barrett describes his sense that he could not translate the real object of his mind into writing on any particular occasion because his mind is somewhere else, ahead of his 'scrawling':

> The little I *have* written, has been an inconscious scrawling with the mind fixed somewhere else: the subject of the scrawl may have previously been the real object of my mind on some similar occasion, – the very thing which *then* to miss, (finding in its place *such another* result of a still prior fancy-fit) – which then to see escape, or find escaped, was the vexation of the time! One cannot, (or *I* cannot) *finish up* the work in one's mind …[12]

Here, in a passage to put beside *Pauline*'s insistence on the imagination's angelic faithfulness, Browning describes a fitful and untimely relation between the mind and writing. Sometimes the result of this confusion is a bizarre poetic language which can read like a word-by-word translation from an unknown tongue. We might oppose to this poetics of displaced fixity, ruin and scattering Matthew Arnold's far more decorous, proper and faithful theories of translation. Arnold admired Browning's intellect and intentions but felt he failed in poetic achievement. The preface to *Poems* (1853) attacks difficulty and 'over-curiousness of expression' in general, and argues the superiority of 'one moral impression left by a great action treated as a whole' (Arnold, *Poems*, pp. 602–3). Arnold seems unlikely to have been comfortable with Browning's peculiar language and poetry of incidents and moments. The two men became personally friendly in 1862; Arnold enjoyed Browning's conversation and called him a 'man of genius with a reach of mind compared to which Tennyson's reach of mind is petty'.[13] In 1867 Arnold reinstated 'Empedocles' in his *New Poems*: 'Browning's desire that I should reprint "Empedocles" was really the cause of the volume appearing at all.'[14] Browning and Arnold shared a preparedness to write on classical subjects and perhaps Arnold was simply flattered by the charismatic older poet's praise of 'Empedocles'. In any case from 1867 onwards Arnold turned away from poetry and increasingly devoted himself to social and religious writing, much of which work identifies culture with political and moral safety. Browning did not care to be safe in his work: creativity, like belief, comes in 'fits'. According to Bishop Blougram, just 'when we are safest, there's a sunset-touch, / A fancy from a flower-bell, some one's death, / A chorus-ending from Euripides' and all certainty is lost (ll. 182–4).

Disagreement between Arnold and Browning erupts most explicitly in Browning's 1877 preface to his 'transcription' of Aeschylus's *Agamemnon*. Arnold had been developing his ideas on the value of ancient Greek culture for decades. His 1853 preface sees classical culture as potential deliverance from the post-Babelian chaos of modern life:

> The confusion of the present times is great, the multitude of voices counselling different things bewildering, the number of existing works capable of attracting a young writer's attention and of becoming his models, immense. What he wants is a hand to guide him through the confusion, a voice to prescribe to him the aim he should keep in view, and to explain to him that the value of the literary works that offer themselves to his attention is relative to their power of helping him forward on his road towards this aim. Such a guide the English writer at the present day will nowhere find.
>
> (Arnold, *Poems*, p. 599)

From the ancients the young writer may learn three crucial precepts: 'the all-importance of the choice of a subject; the necessity of accurate construction; and the subordinate character of expression' (p. 603). Browning, Blougram suggests, associates ancient Greek literature with unsettledness of feeling and language.

Arnold's lectures 'On Translating Homer' (1862) compare translations and judge which is the best vehicle of the author's thought and feeling. Arnold prefers not to dwell on the effects of linguistic diversity and linguistic difference that make his comparisons possible. His ideal is the transmission of ideas from one culture to another. The lectures focus on F. W. Newman's (brother of the cardinal-to-be) version of the Odyssey. Arnold quarrels with Newman in theory and practice: 'Mr. Newman ... declares that he "aims ... to retain every peculiarity of the original, so far as he is able, *with the greater care the more foreign it may happen to be;*" so that it may "never be forgotten that he is imitating, and imitating in a different material"' (Arnold I, p. 97). Newman's approach is rather like that which Browning outlines in his preface to the *Agamemnon* translation. Arnold, however, wants to leave nothing to chance by making sure that a translation has the same effect as the original. He argues, with unreserved respect for academia, that the translator's work should be assessed by eminent scholars such as the Provost of Eton, or Professor Thompson at Cambridge, or Professor Jowett 'here in Oxford':

> No one can tell [the translator] how Homer affected the Greeks; but there are those who can tell him how Homer affects *them*. These are scholars; who possess, at the same time with knowledge of Greek, adequate poetical taste and feeling. No translation will appear to them of much worth compared with the original; but they alone can say whether the translation produces more or less the same effect upon them as the original.   (pp. 98–9)

The 'strange language' of a poet provides Arnold with an analogy for the ideal translation. The poet is Coleridge, not the uncanny Coleridge of 'Frost at Midnight' or the visionary of 'Kubla Khan', but the anxious theorist, who shares Arnold's desire to use literary criticism to fasten poetry ever more closely to religion. If Browning seeks to 'save the soul' by linguistic indirection (save it not from a bad end, but from any end at all), Arnold's and Coleridge's identification of translation with religious experience depicts a salvation in the absence of difference between languages, that is, in the absence of language:

> Coleridge says, in his strange language, speaking of the union of the human soul with the divine essence, that this takes place 'Whene'er the mist, which stands 'twixt God and thee, / Defecates to a pure transparency;' [from 'Reason' (1830)] and so, too, it may be said of that union of the translator with his original, which alone can produce a good translation, that it takes place when the mist that stands between them – the mist of alien modes of thinking, speaking, and feeling on the translator's part – 'defecates to a pure transparency,' and disappears.   (p.103)

Arnold dislikes division and mist and likes unity and transparency: he generalizes from Newman's translation to a literary quality to be found abundantly in Browning: 'The eccentricity, ... the arbitrariness, of which Mr. Newman's conception of Homer offers so signal an example, are not a peculiar failing of Mr. Newman's own; in varying degrees they are the great defect of English intellect, the great blemish of English literature' (p. 140). Yet admiration for Browning's 'Artemis

Prologuizes' made him ask a friend to whom he was sending his tragedy *Merope* in the late 1850s: 'Make Browning look at it, if he is at Florence; one of the very best antique fragments I know is a fragment of a Hippolytus by him.'[15]

Merope comes with a substantial preface which speaks of classical culture as an alluring scene that distantly yet intimately inhabits the modern mind: 'Greek art – the antique – classical beauty – a nameless hope and interest attaches, I can often see, to these words, even in the minds of those who have been brought up among the productions of the romantic school' (Arnold, *Poems*, p. 38). Whole nations remain 'haunted with an indefinable interest in its name, with an inexplicable curiosity as to its nature', and Arnold wishes to put that name and nature into a 'living and familiar language'. Translation helps the modern reader get close to what might otherwise repulse them, for 'it may be doubted whether even those, whose enthusiasm shrinks from no toil, can ever so thoroughly press into the intimate feeling of works composed in a dead language as their enthusiasm would desire' (p. 39). Arnold wants translation to familiarize and revive a dead language that haunts modern consciousness. His thinking moves away from the indefinable and the inexplicable. Browning, however goes on being curious about the dead and is robustly interested in encounters with powerful ghosts in their unfamiliarity. This contrast extends to the poets' choice of subject-matter; Arnold is anxious to be original, Browning is happy to be influenced. Why the relatively obscure Merope? Why not Agamemnon or Alcestis? Arnold justifies the choice of Merope over one of the great works of Aeschylus or Sophocles in terms that suggest that what concerns him is a writer's unmediated relation to his subject. Euripedes' account of Merope survives only through hearsay (Aristotle and Plutarch) and modern versions in French, Italian and English: 'No man can do his best with a subject that does not penetrate him: no man can be penetrated by a subject which he does not conceive independently' (pp. 39–40).

Browning did not conceive of his major translation project himself. Allingham recounts Carlyle saying:

> I did often enough tell him he might do a most excellent book, by far the best he had ever done, by translating the Greek dramatists, but O dear! he's a very foolish fellow. He picks you out the English for the Greek word by word, and now and again sticks two or three words together with hyphens; then again he snips up the sense and jingles it into rhyme!
>
> (Diary, p. 258)

Browning's preface to his *Agamemnon* translation commends the closest possible contact between Greek and English. And far from fearing, like Arnold, that a great work might 'chill emulation by [its] grandeur', Browning cheerfully gives the 'immense fame' of the original as the reason for a wish to read a translation of it. He cultivates no Arnoldean mysteries of 'inexplicable curiosity' about the classical tradition. As a reader Browning 'should require [a translator] to be literal at every cost save that of absolute violence to our language' (1889 *Works* XIII, p. 261).

Browning offers much licence that Arnold would refuse. He would permit archaism of constructions which, unlike Arnold, he finds 'appropriate to archaic workmanship'. More, he would 'be tolerant for once ... of even a clumsy attempt to furnish me with the very turn of each phrase in as Greek a fashion as the English may bear'. Browning tolerates archaism or clumsiness of construction, and the living language furnishing every turn of phrase in the fashion of the dead. He also sanctions the recurrence of an 'old word ... with its congeners ... four times in three lines' (1889 *Works* XIII, p. 262). He is echoing Wordsworth's note to 'The Thorn' (1800): 'There is a numerous class of readers who imagine that the same words cannot be repeated without tautology: this is a great error; virtual tautology is oftener produced by using different words when the meaning is exactly the same'. According to Wordsworth 'repetition and tautology are frequently beauties of the highest kind'. Among the chief reasons for this 'is the interest which the mind attaches to words, not only as symbols of passion, but as *things*, active and efficient, which are of themselves part of the passion'. I suspect that this passage influences Browning's description of his own translation as a 'version of thing by thing, or at least word pregnant with thing'.

Wordsworth allows that words are passionate, and Browning eroticizes words and languages: English bears Greek, Greek impregnates English, English should translate Greek 'stroke by stroke'. The translator engages with beauty as an integral quality of the strokes of the original, and Browning puts himself in the position of a reader who knows no Greek. He says he would be satisfied with

> a mere strict bald version of thing by thing, or at least word pregnant with thing, I should hardly look for the reputed magniloquence and sonority of the Greek; and this with the less regret, inasmuch as there is abundant musicality elsewhere, but nowhere else than in his poem the ideas of the poet.
>
> (1889 *Works* XIII, p. 262)

These words have a proper passion for each other, they don't waste time seducing the reader with their music. Like the Poet in *Pauline* reading the work of Sun-treader, the translator's primary task is to 'disentangle, gather sense from song'. Magniloquence, sonority and musicality are not the main issues. Browning's lack of regret about this counters Arnold's admonitions on the 'grand style' and his concern that the translator should 'reproduce ... the *general effect* of Homer' upon the intelligent scholar.

Browning does not identify learning a language with acquiring sense: 'Learning Greek teaches Greek, and nothing else: certainly not common sense, if that have failed to precede the teaching.' This contradicts Arnold's argument in *On the Modern Element in Literature* (1869), where Thucydides is acclaimed for his '*modern* language' that brings thoughtfulness with it:

> It is the language of a thoughtful philosophic man of our own days; it is the language of Burke or Niebuhr assigning the true aim of history. And yet Thucydides is no mere literary man; no isolated thinker speaking far over the heads of his hearers to a future age – no: ... he represents the general intelligence of his age and nation.
>
> (Arnold I, p. 26)

A modern spirit demands and pursues 'intellectual deliverance' and according to Arnold 'the literature of ancient Greece is, even for modern times, a mighty agent of intellectual deliverance' (pp. 19–20).

For Arnold, intellectual deliverance is deliverance from the kind of excessive openness he finds in Browning. There are too many facts: all Arnold wants is some laws to manage and organize them. The need for deliverance 'arises, because the present age exhibits to the individual man who contemplates it the spectacle of a vast multitude of facts awaiting and inviting his comprehension'. Deliverance itself

> consists in man's comprehension of this present and past. It begins when our mind begins to enter into possession of the general ideas which are the law of this vast multitude of facts. It is perfect when we have acquired that harmonious acquiescence of mind which we feel in contemplating a grand spectacle that is intelligible to us; when we have lost that impatient irritation of mind which we feel in presence of an immense, moving, confused spectacle which, while it perpetually excites our curiosity, perpetually baffles our comprehension.
>
> (Arnold I, p. 20).

Arnold has little patience with 'impatient irritability of mind'; he seeks what is intelligible because he does not like the space between curiosity and comprehension. Browning may not have shared Keats's conviction that 'with a great poet the sense of Beauty overcomes every other consideration, or rather obliterates all consideration' yet he too desires a kind of *'Negative Capability'* in his readers.[16] Browning's poetry excites his readers' curiosity and calls upon their patience. At the end of *The Ring and the Book* he tries to divest the British Public of its faith in human speech, testimony and estimation so that they may understand that 'Art remains the one way possible / Of speaking truth' (XII, ll. 839–40). Only, as Browning goes on to explain, this truth is achieved by lies and omissions: 'Art may tell a truth / Obliquely, do the thing shall breed the thought, / Nor wrong the thought, missing the mediate word' (XII, ll. 855–7).

Arnold's 'impatient irritation of mind' is Coleridgean, for according to Keats Coleridge also was 'incapable of remaining content with half knowledge'. Arnold wrote to Clough in 1848, playfully acknowledging his own dislike of intellectual agitation and directly associating Browning with Keats:

> What a brute you were to tell me to read Keats' Letters. However it is over now: and reflexion resumes her power over agitation.
>   What harm he has done in English Poetry. As Browning is a man with a moderate gift passionately desiring movement & fulness, and obtaining nothing but a confused multitudinousness, so Keats with a very high gift, is yet also consumed by this desire: and cannot produce the truly living and moving, as his conscience keeps telling him. They will not be patient – neither understand that they must begin with an Idea of the world in order not to be prevailed over by the world's multitudinousness: or if they cannot get that, at least with isolated ideas: & all other things shall (perhaps) be added unto them.[17]

'They will not be patient' accuses Arnold, but Keats and Browning are stalwart enough to begin with multitudinousness rather than attempt to transcend language with a primary Idea. The reading of Keats is peculiar: of course he is not concerned with life and motion at the opening of *Hyperion*, in 'La Belle Dame sans Merci' or the 'Ode to Autumn'; he is the poet of a loitering patient stillness. His poem on translation, 'On First Looking into Chapman's Homer' (1816), links reading with going abroad and going out of oneself, perhaps never to return, but ends on a dramatic contemplative pause. The reader of Chapman's translation of Homer feels like the explorer Cortez as he 'stared at the Pacific, and all his men / Looked at each other with a wild surmise, / Silent'. Something unique, specific and unshared is happening to Cortez alone. Is he reading the sea? We cannot tell because the poem stops at the overwhelming moment of wild surmise and silence. Is this a lack of patience? *On Translating Homer* stolidly objects to the poem: 'but Keats could not read the original, and therefore could not really judge the translation' (Arnold I, p. 112).[18] Arnold's poetry gives a far more persuasive account of Keatsian moonlit nature in 'Dover Beach' (1867): 'The sea is calm tonight ...'

Browning's notion of poetic language demands that the reader accept 'less mediates' than Arnold's Homeric ideal. His Negative Capability as a requirement for the reader promotes thought rather than Keats's 'sense of Beauty': 'Art may ... / ... do the thing shall breed the thought, / Nor wrong the thought, missing the mediate word.' Arnold admires Homer as 'a poet most plain and direct in his style, .. most plain and direct in his ideas' (Arnold I, p. 119). Browning chooses Aeschylus: '"not easy to understand" in the opinion of his stoutest advocate among the ancients' (1889 Works XIII, p. 262). In addition to the inherent difficulty of thought in the Aeschylean thing, 'the text is sadly corrupt, probably interpolated, and certainly mutilated' (p. 263). As Yopie Prins notices, the poet's view of scholarship's concern to eliminate textual difficulty is suggestive to his readers: 'no unlearned person enjoys the scholar's privilege of trying his fancy on each obstacle whenever he comes to a stoppage, and effectually clearing the way by suppressing what seems to lie in it' (1889 Works XIII, p. 263).[19] Here, as in Arnold, the scholar is one whom learning has deprived of the Negative Capability which is necessary to read. Browning then proceeds to quote Arnold against himself by a sort of perverse translation that leaves words unchanged but alters their meaning. Yopie Prins describes how he

> ironically turns Arnold's argument against excessive literalism into a defence of literalism by quoting Arnold's 1853 Preface deliberately out of context. For example, Arnold's admiration of Greek as a language 'so simple and so well subordinated' actually serves to emphasise Browning's point about the unique difficulty of Aeschylean language, which is neither simple nor well subordinated. Similarly Arnold's observation about Greek ('not a word

wasted, not a sentiment capriciously thrown in, stroke on stroke!')
is reinterpreted by Browning as an injunction to translate word by
word (or 'stroke by stroke').   (p. 160)

Prins recognizes that Browning's translation has an inevitably violent,
murderous relation to the original. Furthermore, Browning finds the
original already 'mutilated' and beset by 'artistic confusion of tenses,
moods and persons' (1889 Works XIII, pp. 263–4). There never was a
whole living original for Browning's translation to murder.[20] The
description of the Old Yellow Book as a 'little, left / By the roadside'
acknowledges that the poet of *The Ring and the Book* also begins with
remains (I, ll. 672–3).

Arnold values Greece not for its ruins but for the perfection of its
cultural development. *Culture and Anarchy* (1869), born out of lectures
and periodical articles delivered between 1866 and 1868, insists that
culture does not belong in ruins but develops 'the sheer desire to see
things as they are' into '*a study of perfection*' (Arnold V, p. 91). This
notion of perfection Arnold chiefly associates with Hellenic Greece:
'true grace and serenity is that of which Greece and Greek art suggests
the admirable ideals of perfection, – a serenity which comes from
having made order among ideas and harmonised them' (p.125).
Hellenism shares the same aim as the value that Arnold opposes to it,
Hebraism: both seek human perfection. But whereas Hebraism, like its
inheritor Protestantism, is concerned with darkness, sin and obstacles
to perfection, Arnold's Hellenic ideal invests life with 'a kind of aerial
ease, clearness and radiancy; ... full of what we call sweetness and
light' (p. 167). Arnold believed that the time had come for a new
balance between these cultural values in a modern British life threat-
ened by despondency and violence. Arnold's version of Greek culture
provides a model of authoritative vision and spontaneous objectivity
but *Culture and Anarchy* idealizes Hellenism in two ways. Firstly, it
ignores the patent darknessess of Greece: slavery, the Maenadic strain
that inspired Carlyle's vision of the French Revolution, the profound
domestic horror and violence of Greek tragedy. Secondly, *Culture and
Anarchy* disregards the particular acts of translation which are essential
for the introduction of one culture into another. His work on trans-
lating Homer, earlier in the decade, entrusts translation to the care of
academic experts and authorities.

After his brief stay at London University between 1828 and 1829,
Browning was an autodidact. For him learning is a repetitious
process full of fresh starts: the 'Essay on Shelley' remarks that 'the

world is not to be learned and thrown aside but reverted to and relearned'. This seems to have been true of Browning's thinking about poetry and language: he must start again and again knowing that 'Just when I seemed about to learn' is the moment when knowledge escapes ('Two in the Campagna', 1855). Browning did not succeed Arnold as Professor of Poetry at Oxford, despite a move to make him eligible by hastening the award of an honorary MA, and a rash of Oxford dinners in the company of Arnold, who thought he should be his successor. Browning did take up a Fellowship at Balliol and made friends with Jowett, partly with his son Pen's advancement in mind, but his critical thought is far less involved in, and respectful of, academic institutions than Arnold's.[21] Arnold was pleased by the readiness with which the watchwords of *Culture and Anarchy* were assimilated: the terms 'Philistine', 'Hebraism and Hellenism', 'sweetness and light' were at once taken up by the newspapers. *On Translating Homer* and *Culture and Anarchy* support the notion of national academies instituted to determine correct usage, although Arnold emphasizes that English people would rebel against such centralization.

The Ring and the Book

In 1867 Sir Francis Doyle, according to Arnold 'very pleasant, but too much a man of the past for the poetry chair at Oxford', was duly elected.[22] Browning was working on *The Ring and the Book*, a poem that takes fragmentation as a structural principle. Twelve books voicing eleven points of view; Rome divided into two halves and a shadowy third, 'Tertium Quid'; a source book consisting of 18 documents in different hands; at the centre of the plot a marriage begun in deception, continued in violence and ended by murder. The poem vigorously elaborates various discourses on the 'pure crude fact' discovered in the 'square old yellow book' Browning came across in Florence in 1860 (I, ll. 35, 33).

The Old Yellow Book provided Browning with the makings of his 'Roman murder story'. As well as being a source of information about the case of Guido, Pompilia and Caponsacchi, the collection of trial documents and letters takes on a challenging and troubling status in Browning's poem. For although Browning offered his discovery to Tennyson and Trollope before embarking on the poem, *The Ring and the Book* occasions intensely Browningesque anxieties about composition and fragmentation, the life and death of texts. Book I narrates the discovery in Florence of the legal documents that inspire Browning's poem and constitute its factual source. It also tells and retells the story leading up to the trial of Guido Franceschini for the murder of his wife Pompilia and her parents Pietro and Violante Comparini, and recounts the aftermath which includes the composition of the poem.

The beginning of the poem describes the discovery and imitation of an object that has been buried alive. The forging of the Ring uses 'imitative craft' to copy the design of ancient gold 'found alive / Spark-like 'mid unearthed slope-side figtree roots / That roof old tombs' (I, ll. 4–5). This unearthed spark is not human, in contrast to the 'mystery of this heart which beats / So wild, so deep in us' described in Arnold's poem 'The Buried Life' (1852). Where Arnold's poem laments the rarity of moments in which the 'genuine self' can be known, Browning doesn't give a fig for the genuine self: he explores knowing as symbol and allegory through his book and his ring. Reading *The Ring and the Book* involves us in the life of narrative detail, the Florence market-stall, the poet picking his way through straw hats, ironmongery and airing laundry still reading his book, the special knife used to kill the Comparini, the lawyer Hyacinthus de Archangelis rubbing life into his cold fingers while he prepares his deposition, the bowl of milk tasted by Pompilia on her journey, the tapestry pictures that inspire Pompilia and Tisbe to play their child-hood games. Yet the poem articulates questions about itself that spoil the reader's sense of the simple completeness of this life of the story. Book I presents the poet's initial encounter with his source in terms that also apply to the reader's encounter with Browning's poem: 'Still read I on', '[b]etter translate' – and '[w]ord for word', too – the Latin title-page, and the discovery through cramp Latin and 'Italian streaks' that reading and translating are not secondary activities of belated newsgathering but the opening of an event: 'the trial / Itself, to all intents, being then as now / Here in the book and nowise out of it' (I, ll. 110, 121, 131, 138, 152–4). The effect resembles Blanchot's exploration of opposed tendencies of literary language during his discussion of Kafka's *The Castle*:[23]

> Where is the symbol? Where it appears, where it hides? Where there are only calm, firm appearances, where appearances grate and are torn apart? Where things are present with their natural obscurity, where behind things the emptiness emerges, behind the story the absence of story, behind the profundity of symbol the impossibility that erodes the work and forbids its accomplishment?[24]

In short Blanchot concludes that the condition of the symbol is to be 'buried alive'. Browning's ring that is 'found alive ... unearthed' at once reburies itself in words, and symbolizes a work of words. The ring is a thing that is reflexively literary and mimetic.

By calling a translation a 'version of thing by thing' the *Agamemnon* preface suggests that translation and reading engage with something other than language. But what is a 'thing'? This question makes us pause over the title of *The Ring and the Book*. A thing can be handled and seen: the narrator/translator says of the Old Yellow Book 'Give it me back! The thing's restorative / I' the touch and sight' (I, ll. 89–90). The ring, as the opening of the poem also tells us, is the book's symbol, a 'thing's sign' (I, l. 32). The word 'ring' in the title, then, refers to a figure that means 'book': the ring translates as the book. But the ring is also a sensory phenomenon: the poem asks 'Do you see this Ring?' and describes it as 'a ring-thing right to wear' (I, ll. 1, 17).

Browning had no great faith in the common reader and addresses the poem less to an audience of lovers than to the 'British Public, ye who like me not' (I, l. 410). The poem couches an introductory account of its genesis in terms of two talismanic objects. It is not the British Public who are to be safeguarded but the poet's project which needs protection against the fact that 'whoso runs may read' (I, l. 1381). The opening line is a somewhat ironic demonstration to someone who perhaps does not know how to read: 'Do you see this Ring?' The ring embossed with lilies is 'a figure, a symbol, say; / A thing's sign' (I, ll. 31–2) and it signifies the poem as a triumph of creativity. Browning explains this painstakingly. Making and working the ring requires craft, what the poem calls a 'trick' (I, l. 8). The poem offers the provisional figure of magic or miracle for the creative impulse that '[m]akes new beginnings, starts the dead alive' (I, l. 733). The ring symbolizes the effectiveness of a poet-mage's power to 'enter, spark-like, put old powers to play, / Push lines out to the limit, lead forth last / (By a moonrise through a ruin of a crypt) / What shall be mistily seen, murmuringly heard, / Mistakenly felt' (I, ll. 755–9). Browning's ambition is not satisfied with phantoms; he aspires to return the dead to life like Elisha, with the help of God. The ring's talismanic function relates to the reception of the poem and invokes the helping spirit of a 'lyric Love' – a composite figure incorporating Shelley and Elizabeth Barrett Browning (I, l. 1391; XII, l. 868). The ring is inscribed with a 'posy' addressed to this figure in a manoeuvre which insists that the Browning of *The Ring and the Book* should be considered a subjective poet, despite the removal of the alloy to leave the pristine ring without trace of anything of himself. The inscription promises never to begin any poem without summoning back the dead: 'some interchange/Of grace, some splendour once thy very thought,/Some benediction anciently thy smile' (I, ll. 1407–9). God and the dead are Browning's familiars, inevitable but also invited presences at the inception and conclusion of his work.

The Book is introduced as clearly as the Ring to a less than literate public: 'Do you see this square old yellow Book …?' (I, l. 33) – the invitation 'Examine it yourselves!' recalls the self-conscious mountebank-narrator at the beginning of *Sordello* with his '[m]otley on back and pointing pole in hand', introducing his characters (I, l. 30). The yellow book, gold in ingot-form "ere the ring was forged' is a talisman which takes profound effect on the poet's body (I, l. 141). It is 'restorative/I' the touch and sight!' and has 'medicinable leaves' (I, ll. 89–90, 773). Reading the book strangely animates him: 'A spirit laughs and leaps through every limb,/And lights my eye, and lifts me by the hair,/Letting me have my will again with these/– How title I the dead alive once more?' (I, ll 776–9). In contrast to his rather lumpen audience of viewers, the poet receives inspiration physically from the book. The spirit's laughter is uncannily ebullient, a harbinger of the purposeful laughter of Thamuris in the triumphant lyric which Browning loved to recite late in his life. Bloom demonstrates that in 'Thamuris Marching' the terza rima and the landscape are associated with Shelley: Browning's joyous quester is 'struggling *in* the visionary world of the precursor'. The account of handling and reading the Old Yellow Book demonstrates the delightful entry of the precursor's spirit into Browning. The relish and the energy with which this becoming one with the precursor is described differs sharply from the troubling, appalled or grotesque figurations of dead landscape or the returning dead in *Sordello* and many poems in *Men and Women*. In *The Ring and the Book* Browning 'sees' the book in figurative terms from the start and recognizes it as a vital oozing: 'book in shape but, really pure crude fact/Secreted from man's life when hearts beat hard,/And brains, high-blooded, ticked two centuries since./Give it me back!' (I, ll. 86–9). The British Public cannot be prevented from reading *The Ring and the Book* or the Old Yellow Book – Book XII even hopes that the British Public 'may like me yet' (l. 831) – but it is not Browning's ultimate readership and the question he most urgently returns to is not public popularity, but a more secretive influence.

The word 'thing' in Old English means something public, 'a meeting, assembly, *esp.* a deliberative or judicial assembly, a court, a council' and 'a matter brought before a court of law, a legal process; a charge brought, a suit or cause pleaded before a court' (OED). The 'Roman murder-case' is a thing, a legal process, but there is no assembly of people as in the Anglo-Saxon legal tradition, only an uncanny silence: 'wrangled, brangled, jangled they a month, / Only on paper, pleadings all in print, / Nor ever was, except i' the brains of men, / More noise by word of mouth than you hear now' (I, ll. 241–4). The poem stages a thing while insisting on the unfamiliarity of its way of existing. We have met to decide, but the poem strategically 'baffles . . . / Your sentence absolute for shine or shade' (I, ll. 1372–3). Upon whom would the verdict fall, and in whose name? Who presents the case and to whom? The title page tells us that it is too late to save Guido and his henchmen, or Pompilia their victim. Robert Browning also is on trial; he has 'fused my live soul' and the 'inert stuff' of the murder case: how will he be judged (I, l. 469)? The British Public are on trial: will it know how to read the poem? Everyone argues a case and defends their actions.

Can readers of the poem hope to fulfil Arnold's prescription for critics in 'On Translating Homer' and 'see the object as in itself it really is' (Arnold I, p. 140)? Visible evidence in the poem is dubious: its horrors and beauties are persuasive but cannot clinch any argument. Pompilia's defence lawyer, Doctor Johannes-Baptista Bottinius, argues by legal precedent but also seeks to make the law visually accessible. He regrets that current Roman law does not present any court scene for the lawyer to star in. He longs to abandon his papers: 'Far better say "Behold Pompilia!"' (IX, l. 162). However, he cannot abandon words and his appeal to the visual is supported by ancient verbal sources. The Greek courtesan Phryne proved her purity by taking her clothes off in court. Lucretia, raped by Tarquin's son, killed herself; when Tarquin claimed that she had consented Bottinius recounts that her 'corpse-clothes virginal, / Look'st the lie dead' (IX, ll. 179–80). In the appearance of each woman resides some wordless power to persuade the assembled court but she only appears through the lawyer's words. He hankers after what in this case will never be, a live court-room drama with all protagonists in attendance and the Pope presiding: 'Had I God's leave, how I would alter things! / If I might read instead of print my speech' (IX, ll. 1–2). How many other troubled Browning characters might share this desire to alter things in this way, and tip the balance towards their own interpretations of themselves and their world!

The Ring and the Book fragments and multiplies narratives, working from an original which is hardly 'straight' to start with. The poet's 'friend' asks in Book One:

> Do you tell the story, now, in off-hand style,
> Straight from the book? Or simply here and there
> (The while you vault it through the loose and large)
> Hang to a hint? Or is there book at all,
> And don't you deal in poetry, make-believe,
> And the white lies it sounds like?'
>   (I, ll. 441–2, 447–8, 451–7)

The poem's account of its narrative method revives the smithcraft metaphor for poetic creation from Book Two of *Sordello*. Sordello's chosen task as a young poet is to abandon imagining and 'try the stuff/That held the imaged thing ... his Language' (*Sordello* II, ll. 570–1, 573). This 'stuff' is worked like metal: Latin is melted, Latinate and modern dialect words are welded and the result is 'hammered out'. Characters and action come through a very different process – unmediated identification: 'he took/An action with its actors, quite forsook/Himself to live in each' (*Sordello* II, ll. 581–3). To achieve the work of thought that is language, to compose, Sordello has to tear these 'perceptions whole' into pieces, to 'diffuse/Destroy' in a way that leaves his audience with a painful job. They must tack the thoughts together in the attempt to get back to something other than thought, the whole perceptions or characters with whom they could identify. Where *Sordello* narrates failure and frustration as 'piece after piece that armour [of language] broke away' from his imaginings, the poet in *The Ring and the Book* puts the Old Yellow Book down and in a separate phase of creation 'fused my live soul and that inert stuff/*Before* attempting smithcraft' (I, ll. 469–70, my emphasis). Despite this appeal to fusion in fancy, fragmentation of earlier work is still crucial to the success of the later poem, which reinterprets the pieces that broke away in *Sordello* as starting-points. A 'piece' is a name for a play as well as a fragment; the poet in *The Ring and the Book* recounts how, after he reads the Old Yellow Book, as he imagines the actors and action to himself without taking up his pen 'Then and there/Acted itself over again once more/The tragic piece' (I, ll. 521–3).

Browning allows the Old Yellow Book to perform itself to him as a vision, but then immediately returns to pondering the book as a fragment that invites reconstruction. Characters and their deeds can be forgotten, monuments can scatter into grains of sand. *The Ring and the Book* compares the memory of the Franceschini affair to a pillar gradually ruined by time. The memory of 'the thing':

Which hitherto, however men supposed,
Had somehow plain and pillar-like prevailed
I' the midst of them, indisputably fact,
Granite, time's tooth should grate against, not graze, –
Why, this proved sandstone, friable, fast to fly
And give its grain away at wish o' the wind.

(I, ll. 661–8)

The pillar, strangely, diminishes into a fragment the size of a book, the elaborate architectural layers reduced to a square slab or abacus:

Ever and ever more diminutive,
Base gone, shaft lost, only entablature,
Dwindled into no bigger than a book,
Lay of the column; and that little, left
By the roadside 'mid the ordure, shards and weeds.
Until I haply, wandering that way,
Kicked it up, turned it over, and recognized,
For all the crumblement, this abacus,
This square old yellow book, – could calculate
By this the lost proportions of the style.

(I, ll. 669–78)

The words 'column' and 'style' suggest writing as well as classical architecture. The square Old Yellow Book is another of Browning's ruined towers, and he is as interested in and dependent upon what is 'gone' and 'lost' as what remains. Sordello fails to bring the body of his story together with the armour of his language and longs for a successful means of 'self-display' (*Sordello* II, l. 651). After the poet's vision of the whole drama in Book I of *The Ring and the Book*, we are told 'I disappeared; the book grew all in all' (I, l. 687). In his self-effacement the poet in *The Ring and the Book* is a cannier translator than Sordello was.

The Ring and the Book still has its uncanny moments. The first occurs when the poet describes how he has been taught to work with gold that comes in fragments: 'There's one trick / (Craftsmen instruct me)' that fits 'slivers of pure gold' to 'bear the file's tooth and the hammer's tap' (I, ll. 8–10, 14). Both the model for the ring, 'Etrurian circlets', and its raw material 'oozings from the mine' come from underground. To describe the unworked gold Browning mines his own work, recycling Sordello's fragment 'Elys' (itself based on a song by Eglamor) from thirty years before: '("Her head that's sharp and perfect like a pear, / So close and smooth are laid the few fine locks / Coloured like honey oozed from topmost rocks / Sun-blanched the livelong summer").' The fragment is again fragmented, slivered or melted into *The Ring and the Book*'s: 'mere oozings from the mine, / Virgin as oval tawny pendent tear / At beehive-edge when ripened combs o'erflow ...' (I, ll. 11–13). Here the tawny oozing, the adjectival 'virgin' which, capitalized, alludes to a person, the scattering of *Sordello*'s 'pear' into '*p*endent t*ear*', the similarity of shape as well as sound between a pear and a teardrop, the connection between 'combs' and women's hair, the downward flow of honey and late-summer ripeness: the passages appear to read one another more intimately and uncannily than any reader could – Elys, the name of a woman, the name of a song. (As 'Song' (1845) asks: 'Nay, but you, who do not love her, / Is she not pure gold, my mistress?') Sordello's verse that was Elys's fragmentary monument has continued to fragment or has melted in this oozing translation written in a language of 'wax' and 'honey' (I, ll. 18, 19). 'Elys' survives as 'the lilied loveliness' of a ring embossed with the fleur de lys.

Creative violence

The Ring and the Book is a poem of death and violence as well as benign craft, and a kind of ruthlessness comes into its devices. The facts of *The Ring and the Book* include damaged faces, ruined bodies, lies, forged letters and a perversely-used marriage. Further adulteration and damage goes on at the level of the explicit rhetorical elaborations of the lawyers and the manipulative self-defence of the protagonists. The craftsman works the thing into a ring, then '[j]ust a spirt / O' the proper fiery acid o'er its face, / And forth the alloy unfastened flies in fume' (I, ll. 23–5). 'Elys' has been unfastened from the ring with the 'alloy' that encrypts her name, her once 'sharp and perfect' head dissolves into the air. 'Elys' is surely also a cryptonym for Shelley: her face glimpsed in *The Ring and the Book* reprises the dangerous pure face of Shelley that almost halts Book One of *Sordello*. Browning emphasizes that 'Something of mine ... mixed up with the mass / Made it bear hammer and be firm to file' but when he describes his poem as raising the dead, he animates his material in another's name: the name of the prophet Elisha. I showed in Chapter 2 how Browning dismissed Shelley from *Sordello* in the manner of Marlowe's despairing Faustus, calling and rejecting him in the same gesture: 'come not'. *The Ring and the Book* finds a new way to commune with the dead: 'Oh Faust, why Faust? Was not Elisha once? – / Who bade them lay his staff on a corpse-face / ... 'Tis a credible feat / With the right man and way' (I, ll. 760–1, 771–2). Elisha, fleur de lys, lily, alloy, Elys and, from 'The Laboratory' and 'Cleon', Elise and she-slave: Browning has found what is foreign in the name Shelley, found what in the syllables of his name does not name Shelley himself, and trans- lated it into his poetry in a kind of secret alchemy that works across his oeuvre.[25] Byron called Shelley evocative names such as 'Shiloh' and 'Percy S.', Browning goes much further in nicknaming, making it a generative force in his poetry.

Swinburne wrote of the violent effect of reading *The Ring and the Book* in 1869: 'it simply kills all other matters of thought for the time.'[26] It remains, in terms of narrative content, a horrifying and heart-breaking poem. It is shocking to go from the playful setting-up of Book I, which can be read almost as a treatise on historical method, to the account of the murder of Pompilia and her parents Pietro and Violante Comparini by Guido in Book II. Rarely since *Sordello* has Browning written so spectacularly about the effects of violence:

> In trying to count stabs,
> People supposed Violante showed the most,
> Till somebody explained us the mistake;
> His wounds had been dealt out indifferent where,
> But she took all her stabbings in the face,
> Since punished thus solely for honour's sake ...
>   (II, ll. 23–8)

A bystander explains

>   how the dagger laid there at the feet,
> Caused the peculiar cuts; I mind its make,
> Triangular i' the blade, a Genoese,
> Armed with those little hook-teeth on the edge
> To open in the flesh nor shut again ...
>   (II, ll. 145–9)

The description of the making of a ring, or of the effects of erosion on stone present the poet as a craftsman/alchemist or as a restorer. The marks of metal on human faces and bodies produce nothing, they only open sympathetic wounds in the reader. In terms of Aristotle's tragic theory the injuries to Pietro and Violante inspire attentive pity in the reader. Yet Browning also remorselessly imagines a grotesque

attempt to kill thought, when Half-Rome imagines a punishment for
Pompilia and Caponsacchi. What if Guido and his brothers had

> Cloven each head, by some Rolando-stroke,
> In one clean cut from crown to clavicle,
> – Slain the priest-gallant, the wife-paramour,
> Sticking, for all defence, in each skull's cleft
> The rhyme and reason for each stroke thus dealt,
> To-wit, those letters and last evidence
> Of shame, each package in its proper place, –
> Bidding, who pitied, undistend the skulls ...
>   (II, ll. 1495–503)

The strokes of writing split heads: never did the acid spirit of creativity
look so criminal. '[L]etters and ... evidence' have moved from the
'square old yellow book' that was casually, happily found by the poet
in Book I to a 'proper place' jammed into two broken heads.
Caponsacchi says of himself and Pompilia: 'You see, we are / So very
pitiable, she and I, / Who had conceivably been otherwise' (VI, ll.
2069–71). It is in the area of pity, of sympathy, that I will close,
returning to Arnold and to the greatest Browning critic Henry James in
an attempt to describe the interplay or confusion of near and far in *The
Ring and the Book*.

   We have seen that for Browning both poetry and translation are
capable of a kind of transport in which there is no more near or far.
Arnold's thought upholds truth as what can bring a distant original
close to modern readers. He emphasizes the strangeness of Homer's
thought only to claim that a good modern translator can subsume that
strangeness into true feeling: 'Modern sentiment tries to make the
ancient not less than the modern world its own; but against modern
sentiment in its applications to Homer the translator, if he would feel
Homer truly – and unless he feels him truly, how can he render him
truly? – cannot be too much on his guard' (Arnold I, p. 101). For
Browning, thinking about truth in *The Ring and the Book* entails
thinking about the effects of forgetting and lying, feeling and loving.
He is more likely to engage us in a 'blunder incident to words' than in
critical effort as Arnold describes it, the endeavour 'to see the object as
in itself it really is' (IV, l. 512; Arnold I, p. 140). The rare and the
strange come at us and come so close that we confuse ourselves with
them and are transported. James's 'The Novel in *The Ring and the Book*'
puts it thus:

We move with [Browning] but in images and references and vast and far correspondences; we eat but of strange compounds and drink but of rare distillations; and very soon, after a course of this, we feel ourselves, however much or however little to our advantage we may on occasion pronounce it, in the world of Expression at any cost. That, essentially, *is* the world of poetry.[27]

Yet this world is not some remote realm. Browning often talked too loud and sometimes sat too close at evening parties in the last two decades of his life. James translates this bounciness into a metaphor for the effect of his writing:

Browning is 'upon' us, straighter upon us always, somehow, than anyone else of his race; and we thus recoil, we push our chair back, from the table he so tremendously spreads, just to see a little better what is on it. This makes a relation with him that is difficult to express; as if he came up against us, each time, on the same side of the street and not on the other side, across the way, where we mostly see the poets elegantly walk, and where we greet them without danger of concussion.

Browning is, James suggests, dangerously on '*our* side', mixed with us and at the same time magnificently alien.

7
Publishing, Copyright and Authorship

This chapter describes some of the 'ways and doings' of contemporary publishing as Browning knew it. He took an informed interest in the commercial aspects of modern authorship – reviews, the vagaries of the book market, the packaging of his work with sales in mind, and the law of copyright in England and the United States. Still, he wished to keep certain goods out of general circulation. He told Elizabeth Barrett, 'I don't quite lay open my resources to everybody'.[1] His relation to writing was a private economy that he distinguished from the business of the book trade. Another letter to Elizabeth Barrett confided that he did not enjoy reading or the act of writing:

> But you must read books in order to get words and forms for 'the public' if you *write*, and *that* you needs must do, if you fear God – I have no pleasure in writing myself – none, in the mere act, – tho' all pleasure in the sense of fulfilling a duty ... my heart sinks whenever I open this desk, and rises when I shut it.[2]

Writing is a primary duty to God: it is not done for the pleasure of the writer or to communicate with the world at large. 'Words and forms' and 'the public' are necessary evils in the production of a literary work.

Inspiration

Browning described inspiration as a pure unbroken light of mysterious origin, destined to be followed by a repetition that scatters it: '"Reflection" is exactly what it names itself – a *re*-presentation, in scattered rays from every angle of incidence, of what first of all became present in a great light, a whole one. So tell me how these lights are born, if you can!'[3] He associated the notion of primal light with the white radiance of Elizabeth Barrett's and Shelley's poetry. Fragmentation was an important phase in Browning's accounts of his own writing. John Woolford has outlined the initial phases of Browning's composition as conception, followed by a breaking-up of the original Idea into 'indirect reflexes'.[4] This phrase recalls Browning's description of inspiration and his image of a pure white light 'broken into prismatic hues' in his completed poetry.[5] The Idea or conception, what Browning calls '*the poem*', exists independently of the poem's appearance in script, its words and forms, or the 'accessories in the story'. Next in the process came condensed prose jottings, perhaps on tiny scraps of paper, and only then composition into verse. Browning used an amanuensis when he could, his sister Sarianna or, early in their marriage, Elizabeth. Then he would write out a fair copy for the printers.[6] He liked proofreading 'for, I cannot clearly see what is to be done, or undone, so long as it is through the medium of my own handwriting ... in print, or alien charactery, I *see* tolerably well'.[7] He was happy for textual variants of his poems to proliferate. According to Woolford, Browning's revisions were a kind of beginning again.

The market and literary value

If writing was an unpleasant but absolutely unavoidable duty, that duty was to God, and Browning always gave making poems absolute priority over selling what he had written. Yet he came to pride himself on his businesslike attitude to the commercial side of authorship. He told Elizabeth Barrett in 1846:

> Now the fact is, not having really cared about any thing except not losing too much money, I have taken very little care of my concerns in that way – not calling on Moxon [his publisher] for months together. But all will be different now – and I shall look into matters, and turn my experience to account, such as it is.[8]

Still, there is no evidence that he ever wrote a word for money or with sales or popularity in mind. He wanted acknowledgement, popular and critical, for his poetry, but he despised the notion of changing his work in the wake of poor reviews. He wrote to Elizabeth Barrett early in their correspondence: 'Tennyson reads "The Quarterly" and does as they bid him, with the most solemn face in the world – out goes this, in goes that, all is changed, and ranged .. Oh me!'[9] In the same letter Browning differentiates himself as writer, who writes in relation to God only, from the Browning known to contemporary literary London: 'I shall live always, – that is for *me*. I am living here this 1845, that is for London.' The letter compares his creativity, to a privately owned garden. In the economic terms of the day, the value of the garden has two aspects, use and exchange. Adam Smith opens his *Inquiry into the Nature and Causes of the Wealth of Nations* (1776) with a definition of these classic terms, which were taken up in the economic writings of John Stuart Mill and Karl Marx. Value 'sometimes expresses the utility of some particular object, and sometimes the power of purchasing other goods which the possession of that object conveys. The one may be called "value in use"; the other, "value in exchange"'.[10] The letter compares the literary market with the fruit and vegetable market at Covent Garden. Browning's garden, the site of his creativity, has potential exchange value: he could grow cabbages for sale. Yet if he can't sell these cabbages for cash, or exchange poems for good reviews, he can return to the use value of 'a garden full of rose-trees, and a soul full of comforts':

> The not being listened to by one human creature would, I hope, in nowise affect me. But of course I must, if for merely scientific purposes, know all about this 1845, its ways and doings, and something I do know, – as that for a dozen cabbages, if I pleased to grow them in the garden here, I might demand, say, a dozen pence at Covent Garden Market, – and that for a dozen scenes, of the average goodness, I may challenge as many plaudits at the theatre close by, – and a dozen pages of verse, brought to the Rialto where the verse-merchants most do congregate, ought to bring me a fair proportion of the Reviewers' gold-currency, seeing the other traders pouch their winnings, as I do see –: well, when they won't pay me for my cabbages, nor praise me for my poems, I may, if I please, say 'more's the shame,' and bid both parties 'decamp to the crows,' in Greek phrase, and YET go very light-hearted back to a garden-full of rose-trees, and a soul-full of comforts ...

Browning's economics are inseparable from his rhetoric. He characterizes the inalienable essence of his literary productivity in terms of its distance from buying and selling. The garden has a use value as a private, domestic, recreational space; it is a little Paradise in its seclusion. It belongs on the side of the poet's absolutely proper sense of himself when he writes 'I shall live always, – that is for *me*'. It would not be appropriate to grow cabbages as a cash-crop in such a place. Yet through Browning's use of rhetoric, a process of linguistic exchange, the garden loses its proper meaning in this letter. It moves from being his parent's actual plot 'the garden here', to being the site of production of imaginary cabbages intended for sale, to representing Browning's imaginative creativity, his refuge from the market in 'a garden full of rose-trees, and a soul-full of comforts'. If Browning's poetic labour resists being absorbed into the exchange of the literary market place, it never restricts itself to sniffing the flowers in an idealized bourgeois rose-garden. The letter is a good example of how a characteristic Browningesque slippage between proper and non-proper or metaphorical uses of language produces his work's peculiar value.

First steps in publication

Saunders & Otley, the publishers of *Pauline*, did not know who the poem's author was.[11] Browning characterized the firm to Fanny Haworth by telling her that 'they would print Montgomery's execrabilities'.[12] Poetry-readers were decreasing in number during the 1830s and at that time Saunders & Otley's most popular authors worked in prose. In poetry, they preferred self-funding new authors or safe bets like William Cowper (1731–1800), whose newly edited eight-volume *Life and Works* ran to four editions in 1835–6. The contemporary star Laetitia Landon's *Vow of the Peacock, and Other Poems* came out in 1835, in a volume that included the author's first published portrait. In 1838 the firm brought out Elizabeth Barrett's *The Seraphim and Other Poems*. Saunders & Otley also published the *Metropolitan Magazine: A Monthly Journal of Literature, Science and the Fine Arts*, which ran from 1832 to 1836 under the editorship of the popular novelist, Captain Marryat. *The Metropolitan Magazine* carried a rather cruel review of *Paracelsus*, which Saunders & Otley had rejected. It ends, 'Probably the moral intended to be contained in this mystical production, is that success and death are identical. There are many touches of beauty, almost Shakesperian, in the work; but its general tone is homely, and its contents crude. It is a poem ambitiously unpopular.'[13]

One reason for the decline in poetry sales was the rash of new journals that appeared between 1815 and 1832. Lee Erickson describes their detrimental effect: they 'offered a smorgasbord of short stories, essays, reviews and poetry' and 'directly undercut the sales of poetry'.[14] A remark to Allingham, when Browning was considering how to publish *The Ring and the Book*, suggests Browning's feelings about periodicals as a venue for his work: 'Magazine, you'll say: but no, I don't like the notion of being sandwiched between Politics and Deer-Stalking, say' (*Diary*, p. 181). Fox's *Monthly Repository* was the venue for five short early poems: the sonnet 'Eyes, calm beside thee' (1834), and after *Paracelsus*, 'The King' (1835), 'Porphyria', 'Johannes Agricola' and 'Lines ("Still ailing, wind?")' (1835).[15] Browning told Furnivall that 'Fox handed over the Editorship to others – for whom I did nothing'.[16] The comment confirms Browning's particular loyalty to Fox, and suggests that he felt he was conferring rather than receiving a benefit by publishing with the *Monthly Repository*. All appearances of his work in periodicals can be traced to Browning's particular literary community.

The Monthly Repository under Fox was not primarily a commercial project but a political and intellectual forum. *Hood's Magazine*, where Browning published a few poems in the mid-1840s, was very different. Thomas Hood was a poet, now remembered for the sentimental humanitarian 'Song of the Shirt'. He was also a professional journalist and in 1844 he needed large sales for his new publication. *Hood's* drew on the popular tradition of comic miscellany – the Prospectus clearly aims at entertainment: 'For the Sedate there will be papers of becoming gravity; and the lovers of Poetry will be supplied with numbers in each Number. As to politics, the Reader of *Hood's Magazine* will vainly search its pages for a Panacea for Agricultural Distress, or a Grand Catholicon for Irish Agitation.'[17] All began well with sales of 1500 for the first issue but in February 1844 the magazine fell into serious financial difficulty and could not afford to pay the printer. Hood, who was well-liked by many writers, called on his friends to help. Over the following year Browning's friend Richard Monckton Milnes contributed articles and Dickens promised a piece. Frederick Ward acted as unpaid editor in the winter of 1844–5 when Hood became ill, and poems were provided by Landor and by Browning. Browning admired Hood's gothicky poem 'The Haunted House', and 'The Bridge of Sighs', which describes the plight of a woman driven to infanticide and attempted suicide in contemporary London. When Ward asked him for something he immediately offered 'the best of whatever I can find in my desk likely to suit you', poems from the forthcoming *Bells and Pomegranates* series.[18] Thus 'The Laboratory' first appeared in June 1844 and 'The Tomb at St. Praxed's' (the original title of 'The Bishop Orders His Tomb at

St. Praxed's Church') and the first 215 lines of 'The Flight of the Duchess' appeared in the March and April 1845 issues of *Hood's*.

'So-called calamities of authors': the 'Essay on Chatterton'

Another friend of Browning's, John Forster, needed high quality contributions during his brief editorship of *The Foreign Quarterly Review* in 1841–3. He arrested the journal's decline by hard work and by getting distinguished friends to write articles. Contributors included Bulwer-Lytton, John Sterling, Landor, Trollope, G. H. Lewes, Carlyle and Browning, who provided an anonymous review of an American book on the Italian poet Tasso (1544–95), an article now known as his 'Essay on Chatterton'.[19] The piece uses Richard Wilde's approach to Tasso's poetry and biography to reassess the reputation of Thomas Chatterton (1752–70), whose works and life had also just been published. Chatterton was a charity-school boy, a lawyer's scrivener who began to forge medieval documents for Bristol patrons in 1767–8. He went on to invent a fifteenth-century monk who wrote poetry, called Thomas Rowley. He created, in Browning's words, 'a Man, a Time, a Language, all at once'. The Gothic novelist Horace Walpole briefly took up Rowley's work, but later withdrew his interest. Chatterton left Bristol for London in 1770 where he tried to make a living as a journalist; he killed himself a few months later. More broadly, the essay puts forth Browning's thinking on the themes of authorship, originality and publication. He takes the opportunity to reflect on the stakes of literary authorship in the conviction that the 'so-called calamities of authors ... have a common relationship'. Tasso was imprisoned and Chatterton driven to suicide. Browning argues that the work of both poets crossed and to some extent dissolved the border between reference to the world and reference to an invented, textual world. This got both poets into serious trouble: narrowly interpreted, their poetry became evidence against them. Tasso was locked up by the Duke of Ferrara and driven to real or feigned madness because of, in Richard Wilde's words, 'the accidental or treacherous disclosure of amatory poetry suspected to be addressed to the princess [Leonora of Ferrara]'. Chatterton's downfall was that the 'whole value' of his poetry to its first readers at Bristol 'consisted in its antiquity' rather than in its literary merit.

'The Essay on Chatterton' upholds the integrity of poets. Wilde's book supports Tasso's claim at the beginning of his *Rime*, 'True were the loves and transports which I sung', and Browning is determined to show that 'poor Chatterton's life was not the Lie it is so universally supposed to have been'. Chatterton's so-called forgeries were, Browning argues, legitimate literary imitations. Browning, as we have seen, described the first phase of his own 'Flight of the Duchess' as *'the poem'* which existed before it was written down and provided with narrative accessories. In the same way, Chatterton's poetry comes into being as a 'thing' that must have 'accompaniments' that are suitable to his poetic Idea. Chatterton, like all poets, must invent, articulate and authenticate his work at once. The presentation of 'Rowley's poetry with its fake fifteenth-century provenance is startling because of the originality and power of the thing to be presented:

> The startling nature of Chatterton's presentment, with all its strange and elaborately got up accompaniments, was in no more than strict keeping with that of the thing he presented. For one whose boy's essay was 'Rowley' (a Man, a Time, a Language, all at once) the simultaneous essay of inventing the details of the muniment-room treasures and yellow-roll discoveries, by no means exceeded in relative hardihood the mildest possible annexing – whatever the modern author's name may be – to the current poetry or prose of the time.

Chatterton's faking of a whole medieval archive and its accoutrements is no more a deception, Browning seems to be saying, than putting 'Richmond, October 22, 1832' at the end of his anonymous *Pauline*. Young poets tend to present their new work under another's name.

The deception is, Browning claims, an effect of reception that operates regardless of the writer's character. The young poet senses that his literary production 'will be resisted as a matter of course'. If at the level of the creative individual, writing obtains a 'free way for impulses that can find vent in no other channel', then other people, not being at liberty to write, tend not to accept that someone else has allowed himself to do so. This explains the popular mystique surrounding established poets and the popular hostility directed at powerful new ones. The presentation of a new work puts the poet and his audience 'in a new position with respect to each other'. In the loaded moment when the young poet reveals his work to a friend or family member, it becomes clear that he possesses a power denied to the other. By presenting his work in another's name, the young poet can continue to protect the freedom implied by his literary production. But still, as Chatterton found to his cost, the nature of the literary institution is such that, sooner or later, someone must be held accountable for the unaccountable liberty of literary production.

Browning's impassioned defence of Chatterton's reputation to readers of 1842, over seventy years after the young poet's suicide, is necessary because the first encounter with a work of literature, with the complex feelings that it evokes, can happen long after the death of the author. Literature is an institution founded on archives, places where its power to startle can be stored, waiting like a time bomb for the unwary reader. Archives also make the more sedate activities of scholarship possible. Browning's article and Richard Wilde's book on Tasso draw on archival sources to counter and mitigate the unaccountability of literature. The opening paragraphs of the 'Essay on Chatterton' refer to the future possibility of access to information on Tasso in 'Medicean Records . . . , . . . the Archive of Este . . . even . . . the Vatican' and lament the censorship of documents by the Duke of Modena's librarian. Wilde's researches make what are for Browning convincing links between phrases in Tasso's own poetry and passages in other documents. Browning's defence of Chatterton also depends on the location and interpretation of various written remains. Jacques Derrida contends in a recent essay that the systematic keeping of such remains is a prerequisite for the existence of literature as an institution. There must be an archive, 'over and above the traditional oral base'.[20] Derrida's second essential feature of the institution of literature is highly relevant to Chatterton:

> . . . the development of a positive law implying authors' rights, the identification of the signatory, of the corpus, names, titles, the distinction between the original and the copy, the original and the plagiarised version, and so forth. Literature is not reduced to this form of archivizing and this form of law, but it could not outlive them and still be called literature.

Browning's attempt to rescue Chatterton's reputation sheds light on the development of his own relation to the literary institution.

Browning uses archival scholarship and biography to mourn and monumentalize Chatterton and his name, even beyond the usual limits of authenticity:

> Surely, when such an Adventurer so perishes in the Desert, we do not limit his discoveries to the last authenticated spot of ground he pitched tent upon, dug intrenchments round, and wrote good

tidings home from – but rather give him the benefit of the very last heap of ashes we can trace him to have kindled, and call by his name the extreme point to which we can track his torn garments and abandoned treasures.

Literary biography attempts to work with remains by reclaiming even scattered ashes and rags in the author's name. This symbolic work of gathering 'treasures' in the wake of death defies the absolute desolation of abandonment that Browning's description also evokes.

Paracelsus: revelations

One reason that Forster had asked Browning for work was his *Paracelsus*, published by Effingham Wilson in 1835. *Paracelsus* attracted major positive reviews from Fox in *The Monthly Repository* and Forster in *The Examiner*. Forster wrote: 'It is some time since we read a work of more unequivocal power than this. We conclude that its author is a young man, as we do not recollect his having published before. If so, we may safely predict for him a brilliant career, if he continues true to the present promise of his genius.'[21] Six months later, having met the author at Macready's, he added Browning's name to the canon in *The New Monthly Magazine and Literary Journal*: 'Without the slightest hesitation we name Mr. Browning at once with Shelley, Coleridge, Wordsworth. He has entitled himself to a place among the acknowledged poets of the age.'[22] Leigh Hunt hailed *Paracelsus* with a significant review in the *London Journal*. Hunt was a figure from the literary world of Shelley's day: the acknowledgement of elder poets, also including Landor and Wordsworth, made real Forster's claim for Browning's place in the canon.

The poem's success made Browning 'safe' in the eyes of contemporaries like Horne, Forster and Ward. Browning was more open with family and friends about *Paracelsus* than he had been about *Pauline*. Robert Browning Senior underwrote the publisher's charges, as he continued to do until his son moved to Chapman & Hall in 1848. Wilson took the poem, which had been rejected by Moxon and Saunders & Otley, 'more, we understand on the ground of radical sympathies in Mr. Fox and the author than on that of its intrinsic worth' (Orr, *Life*, p. 71). Browning himself said of the poem 'the drift & scope are awfully radical'.[23] Surprisingly, in view of this, *Paracelsus* was dedicated to a young Royalist Frenchman called Amédée de Ripert-Monclar whom Browning had met in 1834. Monclar sent Browning a synopsis of the poem, which Browning annotated.[24] Yet, as we shall see, the politics of *Paracelsus* operate on a tiny scale and the poem's allegiances exist within groups of friends rather than political movements, cities or nations. The largest institution in *Paracelsus* is the university at which Paracelsus finds himself an alienated professor.

The preface to *Paracelsus* is more matter-of-fact than the Latin occultism at the beginning of *Pauline*, and in it Browning anticipates that his readers will have problems following the poem. He is clear about where the difficulties would come from: he intends 'to reverse the method usually adopted by writers whose aim it is to set forth any phenomenon of the mind or the passions, by the operation of events'. In the absence of the 'external machinery of events', *Paracelsus* will be a poem of effects and moods. The preface asks the reader to work from fragments. This task of reading is rather like the work of mourning that confronts the student of Chatterton's remains. In Browning's essay, ashes, torn clothing and abandoned treasures are to be symbolically gathered together in the name of the lost adventurer. In *Paracelsus*, it is meaning, rather than a person, which has wandered away and got lost. The poem's design is deliberately full of narrative gaps between the various scenes and correspondingly the end-product is an equivocal symbol: the reader's 'co-operating fancy ... supplying all chasms, shall connect the scattered lights into one constellation – a Lyre or a Crown'. These goals, symbols of creative and political power, are of course fictive. The lyre and crown are products of signification that don't exist in reality: nobody will know that better than the reader who has helped to produce them. To continue the analogy with the 'Essay on Chatterton', the work of mourning does not cancel loss. The preface introduces readers to the idea that literature produces and harbours its own referent, and that reading is part of that process of production. The preface's idea of success is a reading that connects the scattered lights to unveil something that has no existence outside the poem.

If this was tantalizing for some readers, it was more comprehensible than the secretiveness of Browning's previous poem, *Pauline*. Mill and others had read *Pauline* as a kind of private poetic effusion, and when Mill impatiently wondered what the promise that 'I shall be / Prepared' (ll. 974–5) referred to, Browning answered in the margin of the poem 'Why, "that's tellings," as schoolboys say'. After publication Browning even bought up all available copies of *Pauline* so that they could not circulate independently beyond his control.[25] With *Paracelsus*, an account of the inner life of a notorious sixteenth-century physician

and alchemist, Browning became less teasing. For the first time he put
his own name to his poem. He also firmly related his central character
to its historical original, by appending a long biographical note on
Paracelsus from the *Biographie Universelle*. He also annotated the
biographical material, disputing the *Biographie*'s judgements of
Paracelsus. The theme of knowledge is explicit in the poem and the
preface links the reader's work to the explorations of the central char-
acter: Paracelsus initially undertakes a systematic process of learning to
discover the secrets of nature. However, the acquisition of knowledge
is for him a disempowering and strange experience. Browning's note
on the poem emphasizes the unsteady, even apocalyptic way that
knowledge comes to his hero, through the 'sudden appearance' of the
poet Aprile, and through Aprile's immediate 'unveil[ing] to [Paracelsus
of] his own nature'. 'Then the truth flashes on Paracelsus, and he
attains a knowledge of his own error.' The Greek 'apokalupsis' means
the action of uncovering or disclosing.

Paracelsus's dangerous wish to know everything is countered by the
values of poetry and community, values the poem promulgates and
also enacts through its dramatic structure as a series of conversations.
Paracelsus became the foundation of Browning's corpus: subsequent
works until the late 1840s were marked on the title page 'by Robert
Browning, author of *Paracelsus*'. Browning's notes on the poem
describe genuine success as gradual and partial: '*success* should be
looked for as obtainable *degree by degree*, each perfect in itself, not in
one grand and conclusive attainment precluding further advance.'
Browning kept to this notion of 'success', yet he hands over responsi-
bility for it to readers, who must in turn surrender the idea that
Browning has merely hidden a grand conclusion in the work for them
to find. The preface to *Paracelsus* begs the 'indulgence' of its future
readers and ends with the request that the reader 'will not be preju-
diced against other productions which may follow in a more popular,
and perhaps less difficult form'. Browning openly challenges the
reader to grant him permission to be surprising, unconventional and
difficult. The chasms in his poem are the foundation of a community
of future readers who through sympathy and intelligence may come to
share a symbolic relation to what is not there.

The content and quasi-dramatic form of the poem, which has
historical scenes, several characters and a five-part structure echoing
that of a play, opens up political questions which are also central in
Sordello. Aspiration, difficulty and failure are presented as historical
and social phenomena: the character of Paracelsus does not stand

alone but has precedents, successors and, crucially, friends. He addresses his friends, the couple Festus and Michal, at the beginning of the poem, in lines that simultaneously address the poem's readership as a community:

> Come close to me, dear friends; still closer – thus;
> Close to the heart which, though long time roll by
> . . .
> At least henceforth your memories shall make
> Quiet and fragrant as befits their home.
> Nor shall my memory want a home in yours.
>
> (I, ll. 1–7)

The imperative 'come', which in this passage both calls together a community and signals a leave-taking, becomes an important motif in the poem. In Book Two 'come' is the key word in the lyric that announces the arrival of the poet Aprile, Paracelsus's alter ego, who exists not to know but to love and be loved. A 'voice within' calls to Paracelsus 'Lost, lost! yet come/With our wan troop make thy home:/Come, come!' (II, ll. 275–7). The summons invites Paracelsus to join a community of the lost, and to a home-coming on the other side of failure.

Paracelsus goes to pursue 'God's great commission', the discovery of a 'great secret' (I, ll. 144, 324). His passion to know alarms Festus and Michal but Paracelsus cites that desire as what authenticates his quest: 'What fairer seal/Shall I require to my authentic mission/Than this fierce energy?' (I, ll. 354–6). The seal, like the word 'come' refers to 'The Revelation of St. John the Divine', the last book of the Bible. The seven seals are unsealed by the angel of the Lord, releasing the catastrophically fierce energy of the Apocalypse, the end of the world. Revelation enjoins the reader 'Seal not the sayings of the prophecy of this book: for the time is at hand' (XXII: 10). Browning's understanding of publication was informed by an awareness that to read a poem is to set a seal to it, authenticating it, and at the same time to unseal its mission, laying it open to the future and to chance. The comings and goings of Paracelsus explore the idea of reading as an apocalyptic activity.

Shelley has a sonnet warning 'Lift not the painted veil which those who live/Call Life' (1824), a poem taken up by George Eliot's fantastic novella on the dangers of clairvoyance, *The Lifted Veil* (1859). Paracelsus aims to discover the secrets of life and disregards the link that Shelley and Eliot make between absolute knowledge and absolute danger. He abandons the traditional forms of scholarship, desiring that 'the earth shall yield her secrets up / And every object shall be charged to strike, / To teach, to gratify and to suggest' (I, ll. 385–7). By the beginning of Book Two, 14 years on, Paracelsus has begun to realize that he must live in time, must pause: '*Now!* I can go no farther: well or ill – / 'Tis done. I must desist and keep my chance; / I cannot keep at this' (II, ll. 53–5). As he reflects on the cost of his mission, the voice invites him to join the 'wan troop' of spirits: 'lost and last one, come! / How coulds't understand, alas, / What our pale ghosts strove to say' (II, ll. 294–6). Paracelsus does not accept the invitation, but the voice introduces the idea that he is, in fact, part of a succession of figures who shared his desire to know. At this point enters the poet Aprile, the last of a line of poets, who has failed in his ambition to re-create everything, say everything and then perfect his work by supplying 'all chasms with music' (II, l. 425).[26]

Paracelsus: epitaphs

Aprile laments his failure to create absolute plenitude in a lyrical passage that changes Paracelsus for ever. But before Paracelsus can learn how to love from him, Aprile dies. Paracelsus has found his other half only to lose it immediately. He spends Book Three explaining to Festus that he is not successful, as he appears to be at the University of Basil (Basle in Switzerland), but engaged in a stagnant corrupt mimicry of scholarship. He again rejects the teaching of his predecessors in medicine and alchemy and despairs of community, telling Festus 'I tell – you listen: I explain – perhaps / You understand: there our communion ends' (III, ll. 729–30). In Book Four he returns openly to his original quest for knowledge, but he has begun to learn a relation to partial knowledge. He sings to Festus the story of a group of men who misguidedly fixed their precious statues on a deserted island and could not be bothered to move them to an inhabited one. The story is an allegory of his own condition. He tells Festus that he read the story in

> tracings faint
> On rugged stones, strewn here and there, but piled
> In order once; then follows – mark what follows –
> '*The sad rhyme of the men who proudly clung*
> *To their first fault, and wither'd in their pride!*'
> *Festus*. Come back, then, Aureole; as you fear God, come!

> This is foul sin; come back: renounce the past,
> Forswear the future; look for joy no more,
> But wait for death ...
> *Paracelsus*. No way, no way ...
>
> (IV, ll. 495–506)

Here Browning quarrels with literary ghosts about posterity: Wordsworth wrote 'A Poet's Epitaph' (1800) and more than one 'Essay upon Epitaphs'. He is also the author of a poem written on 'rugged stones, strewn here and there, but piled / In order once', called 'Lines: Written with a Slate-Pencil upon a Stone, the Largest of a Heap Lying near a Deserted Quarry, upon one of the Islands at Rydale'. The words of the 'tracings faint' in *Paracelsus* echo Wordsworth's lines on Chatterton in 'Resolution and Independence' (1807): 'the marvellous boy / The sleepless soul who perish'd in his pride' (ll. 43–4). Browning's essay denies Wordsworth's verdict, claiming that 'Chatterton's life was not the lie it is so universally supposed to have been; nor did he "perish in the pride" of refusing to surrender Falsehood and enter on the ways of Truth'. The epitaph is too narrow for Chatterton or for Paracelsus. Beyond Wordsworth, Browning's scene of strewn stones 'but piled / In order once' recalls Milton's question in the 'Epitaph on Shakespeare': 'What needs my Shakespeare for his honoured bones / The labour of an age in piled stones.' Festus attempts to call Paracelsus back, momentarily forgetting that he cannot be judged by 'old rules' (IV, l. 610). In this Paracelsus resembles Shakespeare in Milton's poem, who 'in our wonder and astonishment / Hast built thyself a livelong monument'.

How long is livelong? Milton does not put his trust in stone, as Wordsworth is sometimes tempted to do, but in books. 'Livelong' means as long as Shakespeare's 'unvalued book' continues to produce a community of readers. The nature of this community is suggested by the movement of Milton's poem from the possessive composure of the phrase 'my Shakespeare' at the beginning, to the separateness of 'each [reading] heart' and the discomposure of 'our wonder and astonishment'. Shakespeare's tomb gets built by being scattered into 'us'. The tomb's completion is still to come: 'Then thou our fancy of itself bereaving, / Dost make us marble with too much conceiving / And so sepulchred in such pomp dost lie, / That kings for such a tomb would wish to die.'

The apocalypticism of *Paracelsus* is also subject to incompleteness. The poem invokes an impossible community and a posterity in fragments. Nearing death, Paracelsus calls Festus 'Stay, stay with me!' and Festus replies 'I will; I am come here to stay with you' (V, ll. 105–6). But Festus is alive at the end of the poem, and Paracelsus is dead. Paracelsus asks Aprile to 'Keep by me' but Aprile is now a fleeting apparition (V, l. 210). The 'voice within' that says 'Come' invites Paracelsus to join and complete a community of ghosts: 'Lost one, come! the last / Who, living, hast life o'erpast / And all together we / Will ask for us and ask for thee . . . Coulds't not sing one song for us?' (II, ll. 280–9). Yet then it will be too late, for there can be no communion between the living and the dead: 'How coulds't understand, alas, / What our pale ghosts strove to say, / As their shades did glance and pass / Before thee, night and day . . . / O come, come!' How would the next generation benefit from the lesson of the undoing of Paracelsus, if he were a ghost too: 'How shall we clothe, how arm the spirit / Who next shall thy post inherit – / How guard him from thy speedy ruin?' The voice that says 'come' is untimely: 'Anguish! ever and for ever; / Still beginning, ending never!'

Book Five is an extended communal death scene in which Festus stays with Paracelsus in his cell, 'a tomb-like place' (V, l.33). Voices and identities proliferate as Paracelsus deliriously addresses his predecessors, familiars and successors: 'I am young, old, happy, sad, / Hoping, desponding, acting, taking rest / And all at once' (V, ll. 469–70). He now sets revelation in the context of a community of those to whom death will come: 'I turn new knowledge upon old events, / And the effect is . . . But I must not tell; / It is not fair. Your own turn will arrive / Some day. Dear Festus you will die like me' (V, ll. 488–91). He dies 'hand in hand' with the living Festus and the dead Aprile, facing, not the unveiling of the light which he had sought but

> a dark tremendous sea of cloud,
> But 'tis but for a time; I press God's lamp
> Close to my breast – its splendour, soon or late,
> Will pierce the gloom: I shall emerge one day.
> You understand me? I have said enough?
> (V, ll. 886–90)

Has he said enough? Is there rapport? The unveiling of the final line of the poem 'And this was Paracelsus!' is spoken by Festus after the final disappearance of Paracelsus. The poetics of loss and revelation in *Paracelsus* are also political because they depend on communal acts of mourning and friendship. Paracelsus's rapport with Festus and Aprile defers the unveiling of absolute knowledge, through what he calls the '[a]mbiguous warfare' of conversation.

Strafford

Browning's next venture was a tragedy, the genre which has been since its origins in Greek theatre an experience both communal and alienating, binding together the people who see it on the basis of a tragic consciousness that transforms their vision to one of disunity, uncertainty and conflict. The great contemporary classicist Jean-Pierre Vernant has argued that in Greek tragedy

> the language becomes transparent and the message gets across to [the spectator] provided he makes the discovery that words, values, men themselves are ambiguous, that the universe is one of conflict, only if he relinquishes his earlier convictions, accepts a problematic vision of the world and, through the dramatic spectacle, himself acquires a tragic consciousness.[27]

The historical tragedy *Strafford*, published by Longman, Rees, Orme, Brown, Green & Longman in 1837, reached Browning's widest audience so far through the five nights of its performance and the 22 notices that appeared in various journals.[28] The play was dedicated to its star Macready, whose famous theatrical name appears on the dedication page in much larger letters than Browning's name on the title page. Many reviews refer to the large and satisfied houses to which the tragedy played. Yet Browning's preface to *Strafford* hints that his first play is a minor project, a diversion from the protracted composition of a poem to come (*Sordello*). There is a strong orientation towards the future, to the publication of Forster's biographies of Eliot and Strafford and the re-presentation of a revised version of *Strafford*:

> I had for some time been engaged in a Poem of a very different nature, when induced to make the present attempt; and am not without apprehension that my eagerness to freshen a jaded mind by diverting it into the healthy natures of a grand epoch, may have operated unfavourably on the represented play, which is one of Action in Character rather than Character in Action. To remedy this, in some degree, considerable curtailment will be necessary, and, in a few instances, the supplying details not required, I suppose, by the mere reader. While a trifling success would much gratify, failure will not wholly discourage me from another effort: experience is to come, and earnest endeavour may yet remove many disadvantages.

Strafford is strangely effaced, rather than prefaced, by the emphasis on the 'Poem of a very different nature', by the modest and apprehensive estimate of the play as it stood and the faithfulness of the play's historical representations. Browning cross-refers to contemporary popular history: 'The portraits are, I think, faithful; and I am exceedingly fortunate in being able, in proof of this, to refer to the subtle and eloquent exposition of the characters of Eliot and Strafford, in the Lives of Eminent British Statesmen now in the course of publication in Lardner's Cyclopaedia, by a writer whom I am proud to call my friend.' (Browning does not mention that he helped Forster to write the life of Strafford, partly creating his own guarantee of fidelity.) Forster continued his warm support of Browning with a review of a performance of *Strafford* in 1837, reiterating his faith in Browning's future: 'This is the work of a writer who is capable of achieving the highest objects and triumphs of dramatic literature. They are not achieved here, but here they lie, "in the rough".'[29]

Authorship and transgression

The historical concerns that Forster and Browning shared are related to the poet's Dissenting family background and to his radical political sympathies, which in turn play an important part in Browning's sense of authorship. Further back lies the immensely potent poetic and political figure of Milton.[30] The figures Browning and Forster wrote about in their works on the English Civil War were contemporaries of Milton. John Lilburne (1614?–47), an extreme Puritan, political activist and pamphleteer during the Civil War period, provided Browning with a vivid example of authorship and publishing as self-enfranchising transgression. Lilburne was tried and punished in 1637–8 for printing and circulating unlicensed books, under the repressive legislation that Milton attacked in 'Areopagitica' (1644). Lilburne did not so much defend himself against the charges as dispute the legitimacy of the legal system under which he was charged. Sentenced regardless, Lilburne denounced the Bishops from the pillory, 'threw some . . . tracts among the crowd, and, as he refused to be silent, was finally gagged' (*DNB*). Browning refers to these events in a letter to Domett: 'consider these scratches but as so many energetic "kickings of the feet" (such as those by which John Lilburne "signified his meaning" when they gagged his jaws at the pillory.)'[31] Browning's reference to 'scratches' (elsewhere he calls his poetry 'inconscious scrawling') suggests that writing is an irrepressible act of resistance. But resistance to what? Perhaps Browning's political and historical interest in the English Civil War did not lie in the 'healthy natures of a grand Epoch'. No one in *Strafford*, least of all the physically and morally wrecked central character, could be justly described as possessing a healthy nature. Lilburne shares with Browning's Strafford a gloriously perverse response to a predicament that strikes onlookers as defeat but the protagonist as a chance to triumph. Responsibility cannot in Browning's work be extricated from a sense of tragedy somewhere, although as his work evolves it develops a capacity for all shades of the tragicomic.

According to Michel Foucault's classic essay 'What is an Author?' there is an intrinsic relationship between authorial responsibility and transgression: 'texts, books, and discourses really began to have authors ... to the extent that authors became subject to punishment, that is, to the extent that discourses could be transgressive'.[32] Authorship originates, Foucault continues, as 'an act placed in the bipolar field of the sacred and the profane, the licit and the illicit, the religious and the blasphemous. Historically, it was a gesture fraught with risks before becoming goods caught up in a circuit of ownership'. It was so for Tasso, Lilburne and Chatterton. Browning's poetry incorporates a sense of writing as an irrevocable act and a personal risk through, for example, the confession of unspecified transgression in *Pauline*, through a variety of strangely irresponsible admissions of responsibility in, for instance, 'Porphyria', 'The Laboratory', 'Fra Lippo Lippi' and 'Mr. Sludge, the "Medium"', to the violent crimes and contestation of responsibility for them in *The Ring and the Book* and *The Inn-Album*. Author's notes, prefaces and the like could be seen as attempts to mitigate or mediate the absolute risk of entrusting one's intentions to scratches, kickings and scrawlings, or what Browning dismissively calls 'words and forms for "the Public"' in the letter that opens this chapter. *Pauline* and *Paracelsus* have defensive explanatory prefaces and lengthy footnotes. *Sordello* incorporates a long internal note in Book Three ...

The essays on Chatterton and Shelley attempt to salvage the name and memory of beloved poets by a symbolic work of language, including archival research: Chatterton was to be proved not a liar, Shelley not an atheist. Browning tries to establish the genuine drift of his subjects' lives by other means than the testimony of witnesses. His essays acknowledge the dissolution of the boundaries between the life and the work, which would make it impossible finally to prove his case. From the 1860s *poetic* prologues and epilogues began to appear, for example the 'Epilogue' to *Dramatis Personae* (1864). *Fifine at the Fair* (1872),

Pacchiarotto and How He Worked in Distemper (1875), *Ferishtah's Fancies* (1884), the *Parleyings* (1887) and *Asolando* (1889) all have a 'Prologue' and 'Epilogue', and short untitled poems preface *La Saisiaz* and *Two Poets of Croisic* (both 1878). Poetry itself already bears traces of criticism and interpretation, it resists itself, and Harold Bloom suggests that resistance against Browning's powerful self-interpretations may be the poet's great gift to his readers.[33]

The gift is also a curse, for transgression and danger remain part of the relation between Browning and his readers. His poetry dictates that we receive it in the dead silence with which God and murdered Porphyria receive the words of 'Porphyria's Lover'. We also inherit from it the inclination, despite gagged jaws, to dispute, annotate, interpret, registering what cannot or has not yet been received. In a recent work on annotation, Derrida articulates a familiar experience for readers of Browning's poetry . An original work says:

> 'Be quiet, all has been said, you have nothing to say, obey in silence,' while at the same time it implores, it cries out, it says, 'Read me and respond: if you want to read me and hear me, you must understand me, know me, interpret me, translate me, and hence, in responding to me and speaking to me, you must begin to speak in my place, to enter into rivalry with me.'[34]

And of course, this is also what Browning's precursors say to him. The self-resistance that Bloom identifies in Browning's poetry can also be read as a response to the double and contradictory injunction which his strong poetry passes on to us. Mill, Macready, Carlyle, Ruskin, Arnold and a host of reviewers felt that Browning transgressed all the time. Where Lilburne's writing and publishing activities led to charges of blasphemy and seditious libel, Browning was accused of not being a poet by Mill, of being Shelley (writing posthumously and under another name), of being out of his mind by Macready, of not doing what he could by Carlyle, of leaving ellipses for his reader to tumble into by Ruskin, of producing confused multitudinousness by Arnold, and of not being a poet again by Alfred Austin.

Copyright: 'their thoughts become our thoughts'

Despite, or perhaps because of, his contested critical status, Browning engaged in legal and social struggle over authors' rights. Copyright was of passionate interest to authors of the day in verse and prose, especially Wordsworth, Dickens and Carlyle. Browning signed Talfourd's petitions for the extension of copyright, along with writers Harriet Martineau, Leigh Hunt, Mary Russell Mitford, Samuel Rogers and Joanna Baillie. Talfourd addressed Parliament in 1837, demanding 'that the term of property in all works of learning, genius, and art, to be produced hereafter, or in which the statutable copyright now subsists, shall be extended to sixty years, to be computed from the death of the author'.[35] Susan Eilenberg outlines the state of affairs he addressed in 1837, and again in 1838 and 1839:

> Copyright was never the property a writer had in his intellectual productions; it had, in its origins, everything to do with booksellers and nothing to do with authors, involving manufacturing and selling rights rather than the ownership of particular texts as texts. Until 1709 it was available only to printers and publishers, who regarded their copyrights as perpetual investments. The 1709 Statute of Anne first made it legal for anyone – even a writer – to own a copyright, but only for fourteen years (or twenty-eight if the author survived the first fourteen).[36]

George Curtis describes the extensions of this basic law, giving 'authors of dramatic compositions the sole right of representing their plays or causing them to be represented in the British dominions' and in 1838 allowing copyright to foreign authors under reciprocal government agreement, but the 28-year limit was the chief restriction in domestic copyright which concerned Talfourd (p. 68). By the 1830s authors had a real stake in copyright reform:

> [It was] no longer, as it had been in the 1770s, absurd to speak of an author's legal and financial interests in his writings; authors might now profit for as long as the copyrights to their works lasted. Booksellers, meanwhile, many of whom now specialized in works whose copyrights had lapsed, had a sometimes considerable stake in their expiration.   (Eilenberg, p. 203)

The financial aspects of copyright were entangled with its symbolic value for authors in relation to posterity. It was all very well for Browning to write in 1845 'I shall live always' and to assure Elizabeth Barrett in 1846 'As to my copyrights, I never meant to sell them – it would be foolish',[37] but in law at that date he could not pass on the copyright of his published writings to his legatees for more than seven years. Eilenberg notes that Moxon, Wordsworth's publisher, and from 1840 to 1849 Browning's also, was 'unusual in siding with the authors against his fellow publishers in this matter' (p. 266n.). Perhaps this was because he was also a poet and a friend of poets in an age that was preoccupied with the relation of writing to the past and the future.

Wordsworth saw copyright as a form of posterity and copyright reform as a proper tribute to dead poets. He took an apocalyptic view in which 'copyright is not just a market mechanism but a means of judgement in which life and death – eternal life, eternal death – are at stake' (p. 205). His preoccupation with copyright is connected with a sense of the possibility of an absolute catastrophe that would destroy, not 'living presence' but the literary archive, books:

> A thought is with me sometimes, and I say,
> 'Should earth by inward throes be wrenched throughout,
> Or fire be sent from far to wither all
> Her pleasant habitations, and dry up
> Old Ocean in his bed, left singed and bare,
> Yet would the living presence still subsist
> Victorious; and composure would ensue,
> And kindlings like the morning – presage, sure,
> Though slow perhaps, of a returning day.'
> But all the meditations of mankind,
> Yea, all the adamantine holds of truth
> By reason built, or passion (which itself
> Is highest reason in a soul sublime),
> The consecrated works of bard and sage
> Sensuous or intellectual, wrought by men,
> Twin labourers and heirs of the same hopes –
> Where would they be? Oh, why hath not the mind
> Some element to stamp her image on
> In nature somewhat nearer to her own?
> Why, gifted with such powers to send abroad
> Her spirit, must it lodge in shrines so frail?
>   (*Prelude*, 1805: V, ll. 28–48)

Talfourd was influenced by Wordsworth's thinking on the subject and his address to Parliament takes Wordsworth as prime example of a contemporary author who deserved to profit by a change to the law. He argues in terms of authors' inheritance and the period of survival of 'works of truth and beauty' which, a reference to Milton suggests, is conceivably 'a duration coequal with [Milton's] language'. He reiterates the breadth of this general principle of survival in his delineation of the 'liberality of genius'. Literary genius is antipathetic to the notion of property, and therefore needs the protection of the laws of property all the more. Talfourd suggests an anti-monumental theory of literary posterity, referring to the 'profuseness', 'boundless research' and 'scattered ... seeds' of literary work:

> The late Mr Coleridge gave an example not merely of [genius's] liberality but its profuseness; while he sought not even to appropriate to his fame the vast intellectual treasures which he had derived from boundless research, and colored by a glorious imagination; while he scattered abroad the seeds of beauty and wisdom to take root in congenial minds, and was content to witness their fruits in the productions of those who heard him.
>
> (Curtis, p. 70n.)

Talfourd argues that the very influence of genius contributes to the assimilation of its contribution 'because their thoughts become our thoughts, and their phrases unconsciously enrich our daily language' (p. 71n.). Works also generate laws: 'harmonious by the laws of their own nature, [works of genius] suggest to us the rules of composition by which their imitators should be guided'. Because literary works tend to survive, to separate themselves from their authors, readers become proprietorial about them: 'we cannot fancy them apart from ourselves, or admit that they have any property except in our praise' and we allow the laws of the works to be broken, the authors' 'fame to be frittered away in abridgements, and polluted by base intermixtures'. Talfourd did not succeed in changing the law: Parliament was eventually persuaded by Macaulay in 1842 to give copyright for a date of 42 years from the date of publication, or until seven years after the author's death, whichever was the longer. This remained unchanged until 1911.

Moxon, Chapman & Hall and Smith, Elder

The phenomena of reception that Talfourd describes can be negotiated by law and politics, but as the terms of his speech suggest they should also be understood in terms of literariness and its relation to the author. The politics and poetics of authorship are the chief subjects of *Sordello*. To publish it Browning chose Edward Moxon, the most literary publisher and the most supportive of copyright reform. So bad was the critical reception, so poor the sales, that with a lesser publisher the relationship might have ended there. Yet in 1841 came a great innovation, the cheap series called *Bells and Pomegranates* that began with *Pippa Passes*.[38] Moxon was the first publisher with whom Browning appears to have had a close relationship, sharing professional advice, gossip and news. He was also a poetry specialist.[39] At the back of *Sordello*'s first edition there are 14 pages of advertisements for literature: Shakespeare, Jonson, Massinger and Ford, literary anthologies by Isaac D'Israeli, a translation of Cicero, numbers of works by Wordsworth, Rogers, Thomas Campbell, Shelley and Lamb.[40] The rest of Moxon's list in the 1840s was devoted to history, literary history, history of art, ancient history, poems by various authors including Richard Chevenix Trench and John Sterling, drama by Talfourd and James Sheridan Knowles. (One title seems out of place: *Hints on Horsemanship* by an Officer of the Household Brigade of Cavalry.) Finally a page details 'Cheap Editions' of Campbell, Rogers, Lamb, Sheridan and Barry Cornwall, and the whole catalogue ends with 'In the Press' – Beaumont and Fletcher, Restoration drama and Edmund Spenser. If earlier Browning works had appeared isolated in their wrappings of dedications to friends, anxious prefaces and explanatory notes, here was plenty of the grandest possible literary company for *Sordello* from a publisher who was devoted to past and present literary culture. There is a happy resemblance to the audience of living friends and dead poets addressed at the beginning of *Sordello*.

Moxon's shop was a popular haunt for writers: Leigh Hunt said he was more of a 'secreter' than a publisher of books. He had close friendly relations with Wordsworth and Tennyson. Browning evidently chatted with him about other authors: 'Moxon ... tells me that [Tennyson] is miserably thin-skinned, sensitive to criticism (foolish criticism), wishes to see no notices that contain the least possible depreciatory expressions – poor fellow!'[41] Browning's pitying tone masks the fact that Tennyson was considerably better received than *he* was. A general economic depression, which affected buying patterns, was a significant commercial obstacle to Browning's wish to reach a larger audience in the 1830s and 1840s. A book was liable to be withdrawn from sale if it did not go quickly and in large numbers. It was a less spectacular form of the wholesale destruction of the 'works of bard and sage' feared by Wordsworth. The English book trade worked to a short-term system: often an edition that was not immediately successful would quickly be auctioned or sold off cheaply, or stacked in a back room at the publisher's. Moxon kept the unsold copies of *Sordello*; in 1855 he still had more than 250 on his shelves. By the time *Sordello* was printed, not only *Pauline* but also *Paracelsus* and *Strafford* may well have disappeared from the market.

Moxon's typical commercial practice was to pay publication and advertising costs, recoup them and then share profits with the author, but this was not the case for Browning. Usually new poets paid costs themselves. Browning described the fate of a rare exception to this rule, Coventry Patmore's *Poems*. Browning describes publishing in terms of backing racehorses: 'Moxon was told by the knowing ones of the literary turf that Patmore was "safe to win"; so Moxon relented from his stern purpose of publishing no verse on his own account.'[42] The knowing ones then failed to provide supportive reviews, leaving Patmore 'in a manner, planté là [stuck there] – only, of course, in the detestable trade sense of the word, for "Lilian" could never be anything other than a great and – for a man of twenty – wonderful success under any circumstances'. Poor notices powerfully affected even a publisher who, like Moxon, had reason to trust his own judgement. When Patmore's book was the subject of 'a brutal paper in Blackwood' it had 'the old almost-fabulous effect – the poor fellow despairs, and the sale of his book stops short, whereat Moxon smiles grimly with a super-Ossianic joy of grief, and says calmly, "I published that one book at my own risk – when I publish another ..."'[43] Things improved for Patmore, whose sequence of poems *The Angel in the House* (1854–63) later became a best-seller.

Browning took Moxon's advice about when and how to sell his work material, but he grew impatient with his slowness and caution. When Browning married he promised Elizabeth Barrett to promote his work more assiduously and this led to a change of publisher in 1848. (Browning remained on good terms with Moxon and in 1851 Moxon chose Browning to write an introduction for a new volume of Shelley's letters which he had bought at Sotheby's. In 1865 a selection of Browning poems was published in Moxon's Miniature Poets series.) Browning approached George Smith of Smith, Elder from Italy, but Smith was in serious financial difficulties and declined to take Browning on. The Brownings moved to Chapman & Hall where Forster acted as literary adviser. Forster was a solid, influential admirer of Browning, but the fact that Browning brought with him his far more popular wife must have been reassuring for the somewhat cautious Chapman. Elizabeth Barrett Browning contributed *Poems: New Edition* (1850), *Casa Guidi Windows* (1851), *Aurora Leigh* (1857), *Poems before*

Congress (1860), *Last Poems* (1862) and the posthumous five-volume *Elizabeth Barrett Browning's Poetical Works* (1866).

During the 1830s Chapman & Hall were a less specialized business than Moxon, concentrating on a popular entertainment and education.[44] After Forster's arrival in the late 1830s Chapman & Hall developed a significant 'respectable' strand to balance their popular output: in 1843 Forster brought Carlyle in, and in 1848 the Brownings. Chapman agreed to pay for the printing and publishing of Browning's works himself. Yet the nine years with Chapman were commercially more tantalizing than satisfactory and Browning left just as he was becoming popular. The relationship began with the publication of Browning's first collected *Poems* (1849). The exclusion of *Pauline* and the difficult, derided *Sordello* suggests that this was intended to consolidate Browning's reputation as a relatively accessible poet. However, sales were unspectacular and *The Eclectic Review* compared Browning unfavourably to Tennyson. The review's denial that Browning was *always* obscure might have cheered Chapman: 'There are passages and whole poems, of which the meaning and beauty may be transparent to any, and at once.'[45] A new work, *Christmas-Eve and Easter Day* received more attention the following year, including a respectful review from William Rossetti in the pre-Raphaelite journal, *The Germ*. The next publication was *Men and Women*, which Browning wanted to be popular.[46] It is now thought of as his best collection and was strongly admired by Ruskin and Carlyle, but it did not sell well. There was a stark contrast with Barrett Browning's *Aurora Leigh* (1856), also brought out by Chapman to big sales, repeat editions and much extravagant praise.

Between *Men and Women* and the early 1860s Browning published nothing. When Chapman brought out the three-volume *Poetical Works* of 1863, he printed only a thousand copies.[47] He did not bother to use stereotyping, an innovation that made it possible to reprint from moulds that could be easily stored, and redistributed the original type for re-use.[48] The 1863 *Works* included *Sordello*, which Browning had begun to revise before the publication of *Men and Women*. Browning introduced the poem with a dedication to his friend Milsand and an eye to a future when the poem might be better understood. He claimed to have abandoned revision of the poem: 'after all, I imagined another thing at first, and therefore leave as I find it' (Longman I, p. 353n.). In fact there are considerable small differences from the 1840 text. In the event the 1863 *Poetical Works*, dedicated to Forster, sold well, as did Chapman & Hall's volume of Browning selections chosen by Forster and Proctor. *Dramatis Personae* (1864) was the first Browning volume to go to a second edition.[49] In 1866 Browning left Chapman, whom he had found inefficient, slow to promote his work and rather ungenerous. He moved to Smith, Elder & Company, whom he had first approached in the late 1840s.[50] Smith, Elder brought out a six-volume *Poetical Works* in 1868 and paid him five times as much as Chapman.[51] The new *Works* included *Pauline*, in order to forestall unauthorized editions. Browning had told R. H. Shepherd in 1867 that he could only publish extracts approved by himself, and must associate *Pauline* with later dramatic work such as *Men and Women*. Shepherd's project did not come to fruition but Browning's instructions are echoed in his headnote to *Pauline* in the 1868 *Poetical Works* where he quotes the 'Advertisement' to *Dramatic Lyrics*: 'This thing was my earliest attempt at "poetry always dramatic in principle, and so many utterances of so many imaginary persons, not mine".' Browning wanted *Pauline* to be read in the context of the dramatic poetry that came after it.

The Ring and the Book: 'the whole / By parts'

The Ring and the Book came out in 1868–9 in four monthly instalments, three books at a time. Linda K. Hughes and Michael Lund point out that this gave Browning a particular opportunity to influence how his poem would be read: 'If serialization was on one hand a device to prevent readers from skipping over certain monologues …, serialization was on the other hand an implicit validation of linear time and sequence.'[52] Browning spoke to Allingham of wanting to give people 'time to read and digest it, part by part, but not to forget what has gone before' (*Diary*, p.181). The reference to taking poetry by parts is a further instance of *Sordello* providing a resource for *The Ring and the Book*. Browning had found a way to avoid *Sordello's* difficulties with his contemporary public. In Book II Sordello is having trouble getting the Mantuans to listen to his poetry, which at that time consists of prefabricated characters coated with a separately made language. Because these characters exist as dream-creations into which Sordello directly projects himself, they and their covering of language do not belong together, and accordingly they come apart. The narrator comments that thought is incompatible with perception: 'Being its mere presentment – of the Whole / By Parts, the Simultaneous and the Sole / By the Successive and the Many' (II, pp. 593–5). This incompatibility leads Sordello into alienation from his audience, who interpret his work with no regard to his intention to project himself in and through it. The linguistic predicament also divides Sordello from himself. The Man longs for recognition *through* poetry; the Poet cannot bring this about. In *The Ring and the Book* Browning does something different with this rather severe antithesis between poetic language on the one hand, and being (identified with dreams, 'perceptions whole', simultaneity and oneness) on the other. The title of the later poem promises unity through symbols, a ring and a book, not through character. 'Sordello' names both a living being and a poet, part of language. The ring and the book are things *and* words and provide a space for the enactment of the conflict between being and language, and the dissolution of distinctions between being and language, without this becoming a definitive psychic conflict or a final psychic dissolution. The ring and the book are precious because they are at once lively and inert. In the earlier poem Sordello's breakdown, 'each spectral part at strife / With each', arises from language's a-human indifference to the being that depends upon it (II, ll. 657–8). Sordello finds that a poet's office is to 'diffuse / Destroy' not only 'perceptions whole', but also *oneself* conceived of as whole, simultaneous and sole. Readers who commit themselves to the poetry of *Sordello* risk being caught up, through their sympathy, in diffusion and destruction. Yet the opening of the poem promises that 'Who believes me shall behold / The man' (I, ll. 2–3). Daniel Karlin identifies the phrase 'behold the man', cunningly disguised by the line break, as the Authorized Version translation of 'Ecce homo', Pilate's words representing Jesus to the people (John XIX:5). The coming that the poem announces is associated with beliefs about poetry and reading that Sordello's story denies. The closing line, 'Who would has heard Sordello's story told', qualifies the poem's revelation. Which of its readers could say, in the words of John of Patmos, 'And I ... saw these things, and heard them' (Revelation XXI:8)? A story has been told, but in such a way that it remains sealed: 'And I saw a strong angel, proclaiming with a loud voice; "Who is worthy to open the book, and to loose the seals thereof?"' (Revelation V:2).

The later poem is clearer, more masterful and less disturbing because it articulates this predicament in terms of the reader's and the narrator's relation to symbolic objects and not a central poet-hero. The perception-hungry Mantuans tacked Sordello's thoughts together to make whole recognizable characters. They did not put the discomposed Sordello together again. Browning offers his contemporary Mantuans, the British Public invoked in *The Ring and the Book*, a different way of approaching the incompatibility between perception and the pure work of thought that is language. When he asks 'Do you see this ring?' he does not ask people to see a self in a poem, as Sordello longs for the Mantuans to do, and as the narrator of *Sordello* encourages the reader to distinguish Sordello.

Sordello is a 'mere singer' in an oral culture; he comes into literature only as the precursor of the literary author Dante, the undercurrent which Browning's poem must 'disentwine .../ From its fierce mate in the majestic mass / Leavened as the sea was mixt with glass / In John's transcendent vision' (*Sordello* I, ll. 361–5). Browning's plan to 'launch once more' the separate lustre of Sordello's name, by distinguishing him from Dante, makes the terminal meltdown of apocalypse into a beginning rather than an end. Browning has modern technological resources through which to make war on his readers' desire to grasp his work all at once. He used serialization to promote his readers' work of thought through the extended repetitious complexities of his poem. There was of course no guarantee of success, and remarks in *The Spectator* show how persistently critical thought resists the notion that reading and writing might be primarily acts of fragmentation rather than synthesis:

> As Mr. Browning issues his new poem in instalments, we may well suppose that he wishes it to be read, and studied and conceived in instalments; indeed that, with the help his prologue gives us, each of the subsequent parts ... will form a whole in itself, organically complete, though suited, like each of the parts of the old Greek trilogies, to constitute, in conjunction with the other poetic facets or developments of the same story, a still more impressive and various whole.[53]

This return to the 'same' and the 'whole' is just what Browning wants to hold off.

Alfred Austin: 'he is not a poet'

Greater popularity and wider acknowledgement did not exempt Browning from an infuriating attack by the minor poet and journalist Alfred Austin in 1869. His nasty article on Browning was ostentatiously not a review of *The Ring and the Book*, although it came out in the *Temple Bar* shortly after the poem's serial publication. Matthew Arnold privately commended Austin's article and its companion pieces on Tennyson and Swinburne for their 'ability', independence of judgement and 'clearly conceived demands' upon the poets of the day.[54] Austin refers to Browning's 'so-called poetical works' and quotes *Paracelsus* with the comment: 'Not only do we think it not poetry, but we think it detestable gibberish, even if we look at it as prose.' He repeats: 'He is not a poet, and yet he would fain write poetry.'[55] Browning took the occasion to return to the old theme of how (not) to read. *Pacchiarotto and How He Worked in Distemper* (1876) is a collection about criticism. In the title poem Browning takes on Alfred Austin's verse forms and satiric stance, stealing his voice to animate Browning's own reformer of painting Pacchiarotto. He also directly abuses the diminutive critic as 'Quilp-Hop-o'-my-thumb' and 'Banjo-Byron', and rounds on critics in general:

> Was it 'grammar' wherein you would 'coach' me –
> You, – pacing in even that paddock
> Of language allotted you *ad hoc*,
> With a clog at your fetlocks, – you – scorners
> Of me free of all its four corners?
> Was it 'clearness of words which convey thought'?
> Ay, if words never needed enswathe aught
> But ignorance, impudence, envy
> And malice – what word-swathe would then vie
> With yours for a clearness crystalline?
>
> (ll. 554–63)

If this response suggests a falling-off from Browning's earlier and later struggles with Wordsworth and Shelley, then the 'Epilogue' to *Pacchiarotto* puts out an explicit challenge to the non-reader of Shakespeare, Milton – and Browning. 'Pay me with deeds, not words!' insists the poet, and demands more reading:

> You hate your bard! A fig for your rage!
> Free him from cellarage!
>
> 'Tis said I brew stiff drink,
>   But the deuce of a flavour of grape is there.
> Hardly a May-go-down, 'tis just
> A sort of gruff Go-down-it-must –
> No Merry-go-down, no gracious gust
>   Commingles the racy with Springtide's rare!

> 'What wonder,' say you, 'that we cough, and blink
> At Autumn's heady drink?'

If *Sordello* remains the most powerfully *un*canny articulation of the outrage offered to sense by Browning's poetry and poetry in general, *Pacchiarotto* is the volume in which Browning most cannily shoulders responsibility before his contemporaries for the critical transgressions of his work. 'Autumn's heady drink' refers to Keats's 'Ode to Autumn', and the oozings that Autumn watches emerging from the cider-press 'hour by hour'. Browning advises a similar patience for would-be consumers of his output. A poetry of the future, Browning's work should be stowed away until 'the century's close' which will be the beginning of its sweetness. Still, the cough and blink suggest something in this work that is resistant to the process of digestion which Browning had hoped to promote by the serial release of *The Ring and the Book*.

Last years: 'as if I were dead and *begun* with'

The years with Smith, Elder were productive: Browning's poetry had begun to sell and to be recognized as enduring. By 1888–9 the new *Poetical Works* had swollen to 16 volumes. The popularity of the works of the early 1880s was perhaps stimulated by the foundation of a Browning Society by Frederick Furnivall and Emily Hickey in 1881. Within three years there were 22 Browning Societies in various countries, devoted to the discussion and dissemination of the poet's work. Browning was delighted: 'It makes me feel … as if I were dead and *begun* with, after half a century', he wrote to Mrs Thomas Fitzgerald.[56] He maintained the cyclical view of public opinion that he had put forward in the 'Essay on Shelley': 'The exaggerations probably come of the fifty years'-long charge of unintelligibility against my books: such reactions are possible, though I never looked for the beginning of one so soon.'[57] He added: 'That there is a grotesque side to the thing is certain.' Unintelligible, intelligible: Browning remained faithful to his poems' resistance to being done with. While he was preparing the 16-volume *Poetical Works* he wrote to George Smith:

> I have changed my mind about the *notes* I thought of adding to the poems in my own case. I am so out of sympathy with all this 'biographical matter' connected with works that ought to stand or fall by their own merits quite independently of the writer's life and

habits, that I prefer leaving my poems to speak for themselves as they best can – and to end as I began long ago.[58]

That long ago beginning, *Pauline*, was still not a closed case in 1888 when Browning saw the proofs of the first volume:

> On looking at that unlucky *Pauline*, which I have not touched for half a century, a sudden impulse came over me to take the opportunity of just correcting the most obvious faults of expression, versification and construction, letting the *thoughts* – such as they are – remain exactly as at first ... Not a line is displaced, none added, none taken away. I have just sent it to the printer's with an explanatory word.[59]

As he had written to Elizabeth Barrett forty-odd years earlier: 'One cannot, or *I* cannot) *finish up* the work in one's mind, put away the old projects and take up new ...'[60]

Chronology of Browning's Literary Life

1793	Birth of actor and theatre manager William Charles Macready.
1795	Birth of Thomas Carlyle.
1806	Birth of John Stuart Mill and EBB.
1809	Birth of Alfred Tennyson.
1812	RB born at Camberwell, South-East London.
1819	Birth of John Ruskin.
c. 1820	RB studies at Revd Thomas Ready's school, Peckham.
1822	Birth of Matthew Arnold. Death of Shelley.
1826	RB reads Shelley, *Miscellaneous Poems*. Puts together *Incondita*, unpublished volume of poems, later destroyed.
1828	Mill reads Wordsworth's miscellaneous poems in the two-volume edition of 1815, and emerges from a severe depression.
1828–9	RB attends London University. Tennyson's 'Timbuctoo' wins Chancellor's poetry prize at Cambridge.
c. 1830	RB belongs to 'the Set' or 'the Colloquials', informal literary and debating group and contributes to its journal, the *Trifler*.
1833	*Monthly Repository* publishes Mill's 'What is Poetry?' and 'The Two Kinds of Poetry'. EBB, *Prometheus Bound*. *Pauline* (publ. anonymously by Saunders & Otley): no sales and few reviews.
1834	RB journeys to St Petersburg with the Russian Consul-General. Meets Amédée de Ripert-Monclar.
1835	*Paracelsus*: some critical success. RB becomes friendly with John Forster, editor of the *Examiner,* and with William Macready.
1836	'Madhouse Cells' published under the name 'Z' in Fox's *Monthly Repository*. Meets Thomas Carlyle. Forster publishes a *Life of Strafford*, partly written by RB. Meets Walter Savage Landor. Macready requests a play.
1837	*Strafford* performed five times at Covent Garden: numerous reviews, several good. Reads Carlyle's *Sartor Resartus*. Carlyle, *The French Revolution*.
1838	RB's first trip to Italy: visits Venice, Treviso, Bassano, Vicenza, Padua and Asolo. EBB, *The Seraphim*.
1840	*Sordello*: bad notices. Attends Carlyle's lectures *On Heroes and Hero-Worship*.
1841	*Bells and Pomegranates*, a series of cheaply produced pamphlets (publ. Edward Moxon), begins with *Pippa Passes*.
1842	*Bells and Pomegranates* continues with a play *King Victor and King Charles*. Anonymous essay on Chatterton in the *Foreign Quarterly Review*. *Bells and Pomegranates* continues with *Dramatic Lyrics*.
1843	*Bells and Pomegranates* continues with two more plays, *The Return of the Druses* and *A Blot in the 'Scutcheon*. *A Blot* has three unsuccessful performances at Drury Lane. Arnold wins Newdigate Prize for 'Cromwell'. Carlyle, *Past and Present*. Ruskin, *Modern Painters* I.

1844	*Bells and Pomegranates* continues with *Colombe's Birthday*, RB's last stage play. Journey to Italy: visits Naples, Rome and Florence. EBB contributes to R. H. Horne's survey of contemporary literature and culture, *A New Spirit of the Age*. EBB, *Poems*.
1845	RB begins correspondence with EBB. First visits her on May 20. *Bells and Pomegranates* continues with *Dramatic Romances and Lyrics*. Carlyle, *Oliver Cromwell's Letters and Speeches*.
1846	*Bells and Pomegranates* ends with two closet dramas, *Luria* and *A Soul's Tragedy*. Marriage to EBB on 12 September; they depart for Italy, 19 September. Ruskin, *Modern Painters* II.
1847	RB and EBB settle in Florence at Casa Guidi. Dante Gabriel Rossetti reads *Pauline* 'with warm admiration' in the British Museum. He guesses RB is the author and writes to him.
1849	*Poems* in two volumes (publ. Chapman & Hall). *Sordello* among a number of works excluded. Son 'Pen' born. Death of Browning's mother. Unauthorized edition of *Poems* published in the US by Ticknor, Reed & Fields.
1850	*Christmas-Eve and Easter Day*. EBB, *Poems* including *Sonnets from the Portuguese*, love sonnets written during the courtship. Tennyson Poet Laureate.
1851	EBB, *Casa Guidi Windows*. Brownings travel to Paris and visit England. Ruskin, *Stones of Venice* I.
1852	*Essay on Shelley* introduces a collection of Shelley's letters (publ. Moxon). Letters turn out to be forged, book withdrawn. Meets Joseph Milsand. Trip to England. Meets Ruskin. Arnold, *Empedocles on Etna, and Other Poems*.
1853	Ruskin, *Stones of Venice* II and III.
1855	*Men and Women*: no great success.
1856	EBB, *Aurora Leigh*: a hit with critics and public. Bequest from John Kenyon leaves Brownings financially secure. Ruskin, *Modern Painters* III and IV.
1857	Arnold Professor of Poetry at Oxford, inaugural lecture 'On the Modern Element in Literature'. Ruskin, *Elements of Drawing* and *The Political Economy of Art*.
1858–65	Carlyle, *History of Frederick the Great*.
1860	EBB, *Poems Before Congress*. RB comes across the 'Old Yellow Book' on a market-stall in Florence. Ruskin, *Modern Painters* V.
1861	Death of EBB on 29 June. RB returns to live in London, taking regular summer trips abroad. Arnold, *On Translating Homer*.
1862	*Selections* from RB's poetry, chosen by Forster and B. W. Proctor (dated 1863). EBB, *Last Poems*. Arnold re-elected Professor of Poetry at Oxford.
1863	*Poetical Works* in three volumes, including *Sordello*. Meets Julia Wedgwood.
1864	*Dramatis Personae*; goes to a second edition. Beginning of RB's popularity.
1865	Revised *Poetical Works* (publ. Chapman & Hall). Selected poems (publ. Moxon's Miniature Poets). Julia Wedgwood breaks off friendship.

1866	Death of Robert Browning Senior.
1867	Academic honours, an MA from Oxford and a fellowship at Balliol. Sir Francis Doyle Professor of Poetry at Oxford.
1868	*Poetical Works* in six volumes, including *Pauline* (publ. Smith, Elder). Refuses rectorship of St Andrews University.
1868–9	Serial publication of *The Ring and the Book* (publ. Smith, Elder): enthusiastic critical reception. Arnold, *Culture and Anarchy*.
1869	Attacked by Alfred Austin in 'The Poetry of the Period' published in the *Temple Bar* (June). Meets Queen Victoria. Refuses to marry Louisa, Lady Ashburton.
1870	Second revised reissue of *Poetical Works*.
1871	*Balaustion's Adventure*: a popular success, several editions issued. *Prince Hohenstiel-Schwangau, Saviour of Society*.
1872	Second edition of *The Ring and the Book*. Also *Selections from the Poetical Works*, to be reissued many times. *Fifine at the Fair* poorly received and offends Dante Gabriel Rossetti, who believes it to be an attack on him along the lines of R. W. Buchanan's article, 'The Fleshly School of Poetry'.
1873	*Red Cotton Night-Cap Country*. Deaths of Mill and Macready.
1875	*Aristophanes' Apology*, *The Inn-Album* and a third revised reissue of the six-volume *Poetical Works*.
1876	*Pacchiarotto and How He Worked in Distemper: with Other Poems*.
1877	Translation: *The Agamemnon of Aeschylus*. Again refused Rectorship of St Andrews. Carlyle, *Characteristics*.
1878	*La Saisiaz* and *The Two Poets of Croisic*.
1879	*Dramatic Idyls*. Honorary LL D from Cambridge.
1880	*Selections from the Poetical Works, Second Series*, companion volume to the 1872 selection. *Dramatic Idyls, Second Series*.
1881	First meeting of Frederick Furnivall and Emily Hickey's Browning Society. Death of Carlyle.
1882	Honorary DCL from Oxford.
1883	*Jocoseria* successful, reaches several editions.
1884	Honorary LLD from Edinburgh University. *Ferishtah's Fancies* very popular, reaches several editions.
1885	Refuses Presidency of the new Shelley Society.
1887	*Parleyings with Certain People of Importance in Their Day*.
1888–9	*Poetical Works* in 16 volumes. Death of Arnold.
1889	*Asolando*. RB dies in Venice.
1891	Buried in Poets' Corner, Westminster Abbey.
1892	Death of Tennyson.
1900	Death of Ruskin.

Notes

Preface

1. The standard biographies of EBB are Gardner B. Taplin's *The Life of Elizabeth Barrett Browning* (London, 1957) and Margaret Forster's convincing demolition of the Andromeda myth, *Elizabeth Barrett Browning: a Biography* (London, 1988).
2. Stone's invaluable book is in the Macmillan Women Writers series. She outlines the contributions of Helen Cooper, Cora Kaplan, Angela Leighton, Dorothy Mermin and others. See also Andrew Stauffer, 'Elizabeth Barrett Browning's (Re)visions of Slavery', *English Language Notes*, 34.4 (1997) 29–48; Sarah Brophy, 'Elizabeth Barrett Browning's "The Runaway Slave at Pilgrim's Point" and the Politics of Interpretation', *Victorian Poetry*, 36.3 (1998) 273–88; David Reide, 'Elizabeth Barrett: The Poet as Angel', *Victorian Poetry*, 32.2 (1994) 121–39; Pauline Simonsen, 'Elizabeth Barrett Browning's Redundant Women', *Victorian Poetry*, 35.4 (1997) 509–32.
3. Pioneering work on the Brownings and gender includes Nina Auerbach, 'Robert Browning's Last Word', *Victorian Poetry*, 22.2 (1984) 161–73; Susan Brown, 'Pompilia: the Woman (in) Question', *Victorian Poetry*, 34.1 (1996) 15–37; Laura E. Haigwood, 'Gender-to-Gender Anxiety and Influence in Robert Browning's *Men and Women*', *Browning Institute Studies*, 14 (1986) 97–118; Marjorie Stone, 'Bile and the Brownings: A New Poem by RB, EBB's "My Heart and I," and New Questions about the Browning's Marriage', in *Robert Browning in Contexts*, ed. John Woolford (Winfield, KS, 1998) 213–31; John Woolford, 'Elizabeth Barrett and the Wordsworthian Sublime', *Essays in Criticism*, 45.1 (1995) 36–56.
4. EBB to Richard Hengist Horne, 1 May 1843: Kelley VII, p. 99. Long before EBB was in a position to directly affect Browning's composition, she praised the nobility and passion of his poetry but found it lacking in harmony: 'And the verse .. the lyrics .. *where is the ear?*'
5. RB to EBB, 13 July 1845: Kelley X, p. 306: 'I like so much to fancy that you see, and will see, what I do as *I* see it, while it is doing, as nobody else in the world should, certainly.'
6. 30 November 1846: Kelley XIV, p. 368.
7. Maisie Ward, *The Tragi-Comedy of Pen Browning* (London, 1972) p. 131.
8. movies.excite.com: *The Barretts of Wimpole Street* (1934) [database online – cited 24 February 2000]. Available at http://movies.excite.com.
9. Rudolf Besier, *The Barretts of Wimpole Street* (London, 1930) p. 57.
10. 23 February 1846: Kelley XII, p. 98.
11. EBB to Sarianna Browning [end of March 1861]: *Letters of Elizabeth Barrett Browning*, ed. Frederick Kenyon (London, 1897) II, p. 434.
12. Browning didn't believe in monarchs, spirits or long-haired boys. See Margaret Forster's *Biography*, pp. 263–5, 279–81 and 238–41 for an account of these marital disagreements.

Introduction: 'Browning in Westminster Abbey'

1. Litzinger and Smalley, p. 530.
2. Kelley III, pp. 340, 344.
3. See Henry Jones, *Browning as a Philosophical and Religious Teacher* (London, 1891).
4. See Oscar Wilde, 'The True Function and Value of Criticism' (1890): Litzinger and Smalley, pp. 524–6.
5. Horace, *Odes* III, 30, 1. The first words were a familiar tag in the nineteenth century; Browning wrote to Monclar, 5 December 1834 (Kelley III, p. 109): '*Paracelsus* is done! *exegi monumentum* – good or ill, it is done.'
6. 'George Chapman', in Swinburne XII, p. 146.
7. Letter to John Ruskin, 10 December 1855: Woolford and Karlin, p. 257.
8. *The Disappearance of God: Five Nineteenth-Century Writers* (Cambridge, MA, 1963) p. 118.
9. My translation from *Les fins de l'homme: a partir du travail de Jacques Derrida* (Paris, 1981) p. 229.

Chapter 1 *Pauline* and Mill

1. Sarah Flower to W. J. Fox, 31 May 1827: quoted Longman I, p. 3.
2. Letter to EBB, 3 August 1845: Kelley XI, p. 15. Browning was delighted to find that Elizabeth Barrett was attracted to chapel worship.
3. Letter to Amédée de Ripert-Monclar, 9 August 1837: Kelley III, p. 264.
4. These are collected in Penguin II, pp. 935–40 and Longman I, pp. 5–13.
5. Letter quoted Longman I, p. 4.
6. See also Marjorie Levinson, *The Romantic Fragment Poem: a Critique of a Form* (London, 1986).
7. John Maynard, *Browning's Youth* (Cambridge, MA, 1977) p. 139.
8. Letter to EBB, 11 February 1845: Kelley X, p. 69.
9. *The Foreign Quarterly Review* (July 1842): Longman II, p. 488.
10. Bloom and Munich, p. 2.
11. Longman I, p. 17. The notes are given in full in W. S. Peterson and F. L. Standley, 'The J. S. Mill Marginalia in Robert Browning's Pauline: A History and Transcription', *PBSA*, LXVI (1972) 135–70.
12. Browning critics Harold Bloom and Herbert Tucker do far more than identify Shelley as a source for certain Browningesque moments. These critics have provided an alternative to the prosaic task of filling in the gaps or translating the unknown into the known. Their readings enact or extend the movements of Browning's poetry, performing where explication alone would stifle its remarkable impulsion. Their work shares a symptomatic force with earlier hostile Browning criticism, and adds to that force a capacity for invaluable reflection on the critical process.
13. Notice of *Pauline*, August 1833: Kelley III, p. 346.
14. Letter to Amédée Ripert-Monclar, 9 August 1837: Kelley III, p. 265.
15. Letter to Euphrasia Fanny Haworth, I July 1837: Kelley III, p. 256.
16. Letter to Fox, 4 March 1833: Kelley III, p. 73.
17. Review of *Pauline*, *Monthly Repository*, April 1833: Kelley III, p. 341.

18. Letter to Fox, 16 April 1835: Kelley III, p. 134. Browning refers to Fox's review of *Pauline* in *The Monthly Repository*.
19. Notice of *Pauline*, 23 March 1833: Kelley III, p. 340.
20. Kelley III, p. 343.
21. Review of *Pauline*, 14 April 1833: Kelley III, p. 345.
22. 'The True Function and Value of Criticism', *The Nineteenth Century*, July 1890: Litzinger and Smalley, p. 526.
23. Marked at ll. 163–7, 173–80, 222–9. Other passages were 'very fine': ll. 429–31; 'finely painted': ll. 447–9; 'striking': ll. 574–6; 'deeply true': ll. 678–80; and 'good descriptive writing': ll. 767–77.
24. Allen Cunningham, review of *Pauline*, 6 April 1833: Kelley III, p. 345.
25. 'The Poets of the Day: Batch the Third', December 1833: Kelley III, p. 346.
26. Letter to Fox, 4 March 1833: Kelley III, p. 74.
27. Letter to Ruskin, 10 December 1855: Woolford and Karlin, p. 258.
28. 'George Chapman', Swinburne XII, p. 146.
29. Collected for publication in Mill's *Dissertations and Discussions*, 2nd edn (1867) under the title 'Thoughts on Poetry and Its Varieties'.
30. Trinity College, Dublin. Quoted in Maisie Ward, *Robert Browning and His World: Two Robert Brownings?* (London, 1969) p. 221.

Chapter 2 *Sordello* and the Reviewers

1. Letters to Amédée de Ripert-Monclar, 5 December 1834 and 9 August 1837: Kelley III, pp. 109, 265; to William Macready, 28 May 1836: Kelley III, p. 173; to Fanny Haworth, 1 July 1837 and 24 July 1838: Kelley III, pp. 256–7 and IV, pp. 67–8.
2. Letter to James T. Fields, 9 October 1855: Ian Jack, 'Browning on *Sordello* and *Men and Women*: Unpublished Letters to James T. Fields', *HLQ*, XLV (1982) 190.
3. *The Athenaeum*, 30 May 1840: Kelley IV, pp. 422, 424.
4. *The Monthly Chronicle*, May 1840: Kelley IV, p. 421.
5. *The Spectator*, 15 August 1846: Kelley IV, p. 416.
6. *The Church of England Quarterly*, October 1842: Kelley VI, p. 388.
7. EBB to RB, 9 September 1845: Kelley XI, p. 67.
8. Letter to James T. Fields, in Jack, op. cit., p. 196.
9. Letter to Ruskin, 10 December 1855: Woolford and Karlin, p. 257.
10. Joseph Milsand, 'La Poesie Expressive et Dramatique en Angleterre: M. Robert Browning', *Revue Contemporaine*, 15 September 1856, p. 523.
11. Sidney defends poets for their use of invented names, citing the use of fictitious names John-a-stiles and John-a-nokes by lawyers to describe the two parties in a legal action. See *Miscellaneous Prose of Sir Philip Sidney*, eds Katherine Duncan-Jones and Jan van Dorsten (Oxford, 1973) p.102.
12. Letter to Domett [23 March 1840]: Kelley IV, p. 261.
13. Letter to W. G. Kingsland, 27 November 1868: quoted Woolford and Karlin, p. 184. They also supply the Wordsworth quotation from 'A Poet's Epitaph': 'You must love him, ere to you / He will seem worthy of your love.'
14. Letter to John Gisborne, 22 October 1821: *The Letters of Percy Bysshe Shelley*, ed. F. L. Jones (Oxford, 1964) II, p. 363.

15. Letter to Fanny Haworth, [May, 1840]: Kelley IV, p. 269.
16. Letter to EBB, 13 January 1845: Kelley X, p. 22.

Chapter 3 Drama, Macready and Dramatic Poetry

1. Letter to Domett, 22 May 1842: Kelley V, p. 355.
2. This phrase occurs in the Advertisement to *Dramatic Lyrics* (1842) and is quoted by Browning in his preface to the reprinting of *Pauline* for his 1868 *Poetical Works*.
3. See Andrew Bennett and Nicholas Royle, *An Introduction to Literature, Criticism and Theory*, 2nd edn (London, 1999) pp. 103–4.
4. See Longman I, p. 23 for contemporary accounts.
5. Woolford and Karlin, p. 256.
6. Letter to Macready, [?late April 1841]: Kelley V, p. 37.
7. 27 February 1845: Kelley X, p. 101.
8. *The Novels and Tales of Henry James* (26 vols), reissued by Augustus M. Kelley (New York, 1971–6) XVII, pp. xii–xiii.
9. Letter to Domett 13 July 1846: Kelley XIII, p. 156.
10. *The Anxiety of Influence: A Theory of Poetry* (Oxford, 1973) p. 96. Bloom defines criticism as 'the art of knowing the hidden roads that go from poem to poem'.
11. 29 March 1846: Kelley XII, p. 187.
12. Letter to Domett, May 22, 1842: Kelley V, p. 356. George Darley's play was *Thomas à Becket: A Dramatic Chronicle* (1840). The 'Eastern play' *is The Return of the Druses* (1843), fourth in the *Bells and Pomegranates* series. The 'metaphysical play' is *A Soul's Tragedy* (1846), seventh of *Bells and Pomegranates*.
13. Letter to Domett, 15 May 1843: Kelley VII, p. 125.
14. The 'Alkestis' (Browning adopted unconventional spellings of many Greek names) is closely embedded in *Balaustion's Adventure*, whereas the 'Herakles' translation was separately composed and the MS of *Aristophanes' Apology* is physically divided around it.
15. *The Diaries of William Charles Macready 1833–1851*, 2 vols, ed. William Toynbee (London, 1912) I, p. 355.
16. Herbert Tucker, *Browning's Beginnings: the Art of Disclosure* (Minneapolis, 1980) p. 120.
17. 22 May 1842: Kelley V, p. 356.
18. 28 May 1836: Kelley III, p. 173.
19. 20 December 1835: Kelley III, p. 161. Browning's emphasis.
20. *Aristotle's Treatise on Poetry*, 2nd edn (2 vols), trans. Thomas Twining, (London, 1812) I, pp. 118–19.
21. Westland Marston, quoted in Richard Cave, 'Romantic Drama in Performance', *The Romantic Theatre: an International Symposium*, ed. Richard Cave (Gerrards Cross, Buckinghamshire, 1986) p. 96.
22. [9 August] 1840: Kelley IV, p. 294.
23. Bloom and Munich, p. 38.
24. Letter to EBB, 13 January 1845: Kelley X, p. 22.
25. EBB to RB, 21 July 1845: Kelley X, p. 315.

26. W. L. Phelps, *Robert Browning* (Hamden, CT, 1968 [*c*.1932]) p. 200.
27. 10 January 1845: Kelley X, p. 17.
28. Betty Miller, *Robert Browning: a Portrait* (London, 1952) p. 283.
29. *The Courtship of Robert Browning and Elizabeth Barrett* (Oxford, 1987) p. 182.
30. 27 February 1845: Kelley X, p. 103.
31. [10 September 1846]: Kelley XIII, p. 355.

Chapter 4 Browning's Now versus Carlyle's Today

1. *On Heroes, Hero-Worship, and the Heroic in History* [1841]: Carlyle V, p. 78.
2. *ABC of Reading* (London, 1961) p. 46.
3. 'Three Cantos: I', *Poetry* X, June 1917, p. 114.
4. See also Betty Flowers, *Browning and the Modern Tradition* (London, 1976). Herbert Tucker's 'Epiphany and Browning: Character Made Manifest', *PMLA*, 107 (1992) 1208–21 argues convincingly that Browning could still teach the modernists a thing or two about privileged moments.
5. Cornelia J. Pearsall reads the figuration of a female body in the stone of 'The Bishop Orders His Tomb': 'Browning and the Poetics of the Sepulchral Body', *Victorian Poetry*, 30.1 (Spring 1992) 43–61.
6. The importance of touch and its brushing against the intangible in the *Sordello* passage and in 'Two in the Campagna' recalls Browning's formulation of his poetic practice: 'by various artifices I try to make shift by touches and bits and outlines which succeed if they bear the conception from me to you' (Woolford and Karlin, p. 257). Perhaps these are in turn versions of Wordsworth's 'unimaginable touch of time'.
7. Paul de Man, 'Literary History and Literary Modernity', *Blindness and Insight: Essays in the Rhetoric of Contemporary Criticism*, 2nd edn (London, 1983) p. 161.
8. Letter to EBB, 26 February 1845: Kelley X, p. 98.
9. See also the 'ruined palace step / At Venice' where Browning muses during a pause in the writing of Sordello (III, ll. 676–7) and the stall where he found the Old Yellow Book 'precisely on that palace-step / Which, meant for lounging slaves o' the Medici, / Now serves re-venders to display their ware' (I, ll. 50–2). Both steps mark a crossing between the poem of life and the authored poem.
10. This was only Browning's ninth letter. His first had already said 'I do, as I say, love [your] Books with all my heart – and I love you too' (10 January 1845: Kelley X, p. 17). He overstepped the bounds in a letter (missing from the collection) of 21 or 22 May 1845, a day or two after the first meeting. Elizabeth Barrett told him to 'forget' so that his 'fancies' 'will die out between you & me alone, like a misprint between you & the printer' (23 May 1845: Kelley X, p. 232).
11. Letter to Domett, 23 February 1845: Kelley X, p. 89.
12. 'Cavalier Tunes' polemically introduces *Dramatic Lyrics* as a demonstration of the technique of dramatic sympathy. Browning's Cavalier persona was the antithesis of his own Republican position.
13. 21 August 1846: Kelley XIII, p. 276.
14. Letter to Fanny Haworth, [May 1840]: Kelley IV, p. 269.

15. Carlyle to Browning, 21 June 1841: *Collected Letters of Thomas and Jane Welsh Carlyle* XIII, p. 155.
16. *William Allingham: A Diary*, eds Helen Allingham and Dollie Radford (London, 1908) p. 310.
17. Charles Richard Sanders, 'The Carlyle–Browning Correspondence and Relationship', *Bulletin of the John Rylands Library*, LVII (1974–5) 452.
18. *Sartor Resartus* (1833) has Teufelsdrockh asking 'Who am I; what is this ME?' and deciding that 'The secret of Man's Being is still like the Sphinx's secret: a riddle that he cannot rede' (Carlyle I, pp. 41–2).
19. Elizabeth Barrett and Richard H. Horne, unsigned essay, *A New Spirit of the Age* (New York, 1844) pp. 333–48, in *Thomas Carlyle: the Critical Heritage*, ed. J. P. Seigel (1995) p. 242.
20. EBB to RB, 27 February 1845: Kelley X, p. 101.
21. Letter to EBB, [28 June 1846]: Kelley XIII, p. 90.
22. Elizabeth Barrett's *Aurora Leigh* (1857) takes the contrasting view that the most fitting subjects for poetry are to be found in contemporary settings and that a poet should not reject his own ties to seek inspiration from earlier civilizations.
23. EBB to RB, 17 February 1845: Kelley X, p. 81.
24. Letter to EBB, 26 February 1845: Kelley X, p. 98.
25. Margaret Fuller wrote to Emerson at about the same time: 'For the higher kinds of poetry [Carlyle] has no sense, and his talk on that subject is delightfully and gorgeously absurd' (Sanders, op. cit., p. 216).
26. Ibid., p. 230.
27. Letter to Domett, 31 [*sic*] September 1842: Kelley VI, p. 89.
28. EBB to RB, 16 May 1846: Kelley XII, p. 334.
29. The 'Essay on Shelley' refers to past poetry which has been assimilated into popular consciousness as 'the straw of last year's harvest'.
30. Letter to EBB, 17 May 1846: Kelley XII, p. 335.
31. *Letters of Thomas Carlyle: to John Stuart Mill, John Sterling and Robert Browning*, ed. Alexander Carlyle (London, 1923) p. 291.
32. Letter to Isa Blagden, 19 September 1872: *Dearest Isa: Letters of Robert Browning to Isabella Blagden*, ed. Edward McAleer (Austin, TX, 1951) p. 385.
33. *Athenaeum*, 30 May 1840: Kelley IV, p. 422. See also Richard D. Altick, 'Browning's Transcendentalism', *Journal of English and German Philology*, LVIII (January 1959) 24–8.
34. Browning was acquainted with New England transcendentalism through his American friends in Florence in the late 1840s and early 1850s. Elizabeth Barrett and Richard Horne's essay on Carlyle has an epigraph from Emerson, who founded the Transcendental Club with Frederick H. Hedge and others in 1836. His transcendentalism had, according to Cabot's 1887 biography of Emerson, 'no very direct connection with the transcendental philosophy of Germany, the philosophy of Kant and his successors'. Emerson instead wished to transcend conventional or traditional opinions.
35. Ann Wordsworth, 'Communication Different', *Browning Society Notes*, 13.1 (n. d.) 14.
36. Longman I, p. 665, note to ll. 116–224.
37. Letter to EBB, 19 December 1845: Kelley XI, p. 248.
38. I am indebted to Catherine Maxwell for this connection.

39. Carlyle to RB, 27 January 1856: Sanders, op. cit., p. 445.
40. Ibid., p. 456.
41. *Écrits: A Selection,* tr. Alan Sheridan (London, 1980) p. 34.

Chapter 5 Browning and Ruskin: Reading and Seeing

1. Letter to Joseph Milsand, 24 February 1853: N. Thomas, 'Deux lettres inédites de Robert Browning à Joseph Milsand', *Revue Germanique, 1921,* XII, 253.
2. Letter to EBB, 13 January 1845: Kelley X, p. 22.
3. Letter to EBB, 26 February 1845: Kelley X, p. 99.
4. Letter to EBB, 10 January 1845: Kelley X, p. 17.
5. Harold Bloom, 'Ruskin as Literary Critic', in *The Ringers in the Tower* (London, 1971) pp. 176–7.
6. Ruskin to Revd W. L. Brown, 28 September 1847: Ruskin, XXXVI, p. 80.
7. Annotation survives in, for example, the mock-epigraphs to 'The Heretic's Tragedy' and 'Holy Cross Day' (1855). Later on there are square-bracketed passages surrounding 'A Death in the Desert' and 'Caliban Upon Setebos' (1864).
8. Rossetti to William Allingham, [?] April 1856: *The Letters of Dante Gabriel Rossetti*, eds Oswald Doughty and John Robert Wahl (Oxford, 1965) I, pp. 299–300.
9. Scott, *The Talisman* (Oxford, 1912) p. 103.
10. Richard Rand, 'o'erbrimmed', *Difference in Translation*, ed. Joseph F. Graham (Ithaca, NY, 1985) pp. 81–101.
11. Woolford and Karlin, p. 252. They print both Ruskin's letter and Browning's reply in an appendix, pp. 252–9.
12. 4 January 1846: Kelley XI, pp. 277–8.
13. The 'font-tomb' in this context may not only refer to the characteristic togetherness of creation and death in Browning, but to the font of type ('the complete set or assortment of a particular sort of type', OED) that makes possible the inscription and dissolution of names.
14. See also Chapter 6. Longman mentions the Introduction to *Pippa Passes*, 'Italy in England' ('The Italian in England'), 'England in Italy' ('The Englishman in Italy'), 'Love Among the Ruins', 'By the Fire-Side', 'De Gustibus', 'Two in the Campagna', *The Ring and the Book* X, and *Prince Hohenstiel-Schwangau*. One might add *Sordello*, the 'Essay on Shelley', 'Childe Roland', 'Cleon,' 'Inapprehensiveness' and 'Bad Dreams'.
15. *The Inn-Album* (1875) uses Ruskin's name when the Young Man describes the ambitions abandoned under the worldly influence of the Elder Man. Ruskin devoted much thought to the best way to spend the fortune he inherited from his father. In 1859 he gave a lecture on the subject, *The Political Economy of Art* (Ruskin XVI, pp. 102–3). The young Man had once imagined a life blending Ruskinian and Shelleyan characteristics: philanthropy, isolation in a tower by the sea, chemistry, botany and star-gazing: 'Letting my cash accumulate the while / In England – to lay out in lump at last / As Ruskin should direct me!' (I, ll. 300–2). Ruskin wanted to regard poetry as a benign force; his letter to EBB in April 1855

makes writing into a form of philanthropy: 'you ought to consider with yourself, not merely how the poetry may be made absolutely as good as possible, but how also it may be put into a form which shall do as much good as possible' (Ruskin XXXVI, p. 196). This kind of advice is more appropriate to the politically ambitious author of 'The Runaway Slave at Pilgrim's Point', the boldly feminist *Aurora Leigh* and *Poems before Congress*, than for her husband who rarely wanted to do good in the world with his poetry.

16. Bloom and Munich, p. 11.

Chapter 6 Arnold and Translation: *The Ring and the Book*

1. With many others: see Hillis Miller, *The Disappearance of God: Five Nineteenth-Century Writers* (Cambridge, MA, 1963) p. 93, and Tucker: 'as a moralist Browning champions the imperfect as the definitive note of the human condition', *Browning's Beginnings: the Art of Disclosure* (Minneapolis, 1990) p. 4.

2. Maurice Blanchot, *Friendship*, trans. Catherine Mandel (Stanford, CA, 1997) p. 59.

3. Karsten Klejs Oldenberg, *The Making of the Shelley Myth: an Annotated Bibliography of Criticism of Percy Bysshe Shelley 1822–1860* (London, 1988).

4. The distinctively *poetic* joy of this song is described in an amazing commentary by Harold Bloom in *Poetry and Repression: Revisionism from Blake to Stevens* (New Haven, CT, 1976) pp. 201–4.

5. Edward Trelawny, *Records of Shelley, Byron and the Author* (London 1858) p. 67.

6. See Andrew Bennett and Nicholas Royle, *An Introduction to Literature, Criticism and Theory*, 2nd edn (London, 1999), pp. 99–109.

7. *Miscellaneous Prose of Philip Sidney*, eds Katherine Duncan-Jones and Jan van Dorsten (Oxford, 1973) p. 96.

8. Arnold to 'K' [Jane Martha Arnold Forster], 6 [September] 1858: Arnold, *Letters* I, p. 402.

9. *Poetry and Repression: Revisionism from Blake to Stevens* (New Haven, CT, 1976) p. 177.

10. For example, in the two poems that flank 'Cleon' in *Men and Women*, the hard-worked seraph in 'The Guardian-Angel' or the one who fabulously disguises itself as a beggar in 'The Twins'. John Schad associates the escape of Browning's angels with deconstruction in *Victorians in Theory: from Derrida to Browning* (Manchester, 1999) pp. 84–90. By contrast Arnold's reductive description of Shelley as 'a beautiful ineffectual angel, beating in the void his luminous wings in vain' lacks any sense of the power to call and be called by poetry – what you might call its catchiness (Arnold XI, p. 327).

11. This connection is conceived and developed in Catherine Maxwell's fascinating *Bearing Blindness: the Female Sublime from Milton to Swinburne* (Manchester, forthcoming) chapter 3.

12. Letter to EBB, 29 March 1846: Kelley XII, p. 187.

13. Park Honan, *Matthew Arnold: A Life* (London, 1981) p. 315.

220 *Notes*

14. Arnold to Edward Arnold, 23 July 1867: Arnold, *Letters* III, p. 162.
15. Arnold to Fanny du Quaire, 9 February 1858: *Letters* I, p. 383.
16. 'Negative Capability, that is when man is capable of being in uncertainties, Mysteries, doubts, without any irritable reaching after fact & reason' – Keats to George and Tom Keats, 21, 27 (?) December 1817: Keats, *The Letters of John Keats 1814–1821*, ed. Hyder E. Robbins (Cambridge, 1958) I, pp. 193–4.
17. Arnold to Arthur Hugh Clough, [?early December] 1848: Arnold, *Letters* I, p. 128.
18. Arnold also criticizes Chapman for his un-Homeric use of language as a 'medium': 'the Elizabethan poet fails to render Homer because he cannot forbear to interpose a play of thought between his object and his expression ... Homer, on the other hand, sees his object and conveys it to us immediately' (Arnold I, p. 116).
19. Yopie Prins was first to recognize the preface to Browning's translation as a polemic against Arnold in: '"Violence Bridling Speech": Browning's Translation of Aeschylus' Agamemnon', *Victorian Poetry*, 27.3–4 (Autumn–Winter 1989) 151–70.
20. This thought is also explored in the account of translation in 'Development' (1889).
21. In 1879 Cambridge awarded him an honorary LL D, Oxford gave him an honorary Doctorate of Civil Law in 1882 and Edinburgh University made him an honorary LL D in 1884.
22. Arnold to Mary Penrose Arnold, 22 February 1867: Arnold, *Letters* III, p. 116. Doyle (1810–88) wrote the memorable recitation piece 'The Private of the Buffs' (*Senilia*, London, 1888).
23. Borges and Bloom claim Browning as a precursor of Kafka. Richard Burgin, *Conversations with Jorge Luis Borges* (New York, 1970) p. 73; Bloom and Munich, p. 4.
24. *The Work of Fire,* trans. Elizabeth Rottenberg (Stanford, CA, 1995) p. 84.
25. For the significance of alchemy see Adam Roberts, '*The Ring and the Book*: the Mage, the Alchemist and the Poet', *Victorian Poetry*, 36.1 (Spring 1998) 37–46 .
26. Swinburne to Lord Houghton [Richard Monckton Milnes] [1869]: *The Letters of Algernon Charles Swinburne,* 2 vols eds Edmund Gosse and Thomas J. Wise (London, 1918) I, p. 77.
27. *The Quarterly Review*, July 1912, reprinted in Henry James, *The Critical Muse: Selected Literary Criticism*, ed. Roger Gard (Harmondsworth, 1987) p. 580.

Chapter 7 Publishing, Copyright and Authorship

1. 11 February 1845: Kelley X, p. 71.
2. 11 March 1845: Kelley X, p. 121. See also 15 April 1845: Kelley X, p. 166, on the value of travel: 'you get, too, a little .. perhaps a considerable, good in finding the world's accepted moulds every where, into which you may run and fix your own fused metal, – but not a grain Troy-weight do you get of new gold, silver or brass. After this you go boldly on your own resources, and are justified to yourself, that's all.'

3. Letter to EBB, 14 June 1845: Kelley X, p. 265.

4. Woolford and Karlin, pp. 1–37. John Woolford quotes the letter to EBB, 25 July 1845: Kelley XI, p. 3.

5. Letter to EBB, 13 January 1845: Kelley X, p. 22.

6. Few early Browning manuscripts survived being used as a printer's copy. Manuscripts were commonly thrown away after the proof sheets were printed. Older Browning retrieved and kept his manuscripts from *Dramatis Personae* to *Asolando* (1864–89).

7. Letter to Julia Wedgwood, 1 February 1868: in R. Curle (ed.), *Robert Browning and Julia Wedgwood: a Broken Friendship as Revealed in their Letters* (London, 1937) p. 175.

8. 28 August 1846: Kelley XIII, p. 308.

9. See also RB to Domett, 11 July 1842: Kelley VI, pp. 32–3: 'I send with this Tennyson's new vol [the first volume of Tennyson's *Poems of 1842*] – &, alas, the old with it .. that is, what he calls old .. you will see, and groan! The alterations are insane. WhatEVER is touched is spoiled ... But how good when good he is – that noble Locksley Hall, for instance, & the St. Simeon Stylites – which I think perfect – ... To think that he had omitted the musical "Forget-me-not" song, & "the Hesperides" – & the Deserted House – & "every thing that is his" – as distinguished from what is every-bodys!'

10. Adam Smith, *An Inquiry into the Nature and Causes of the Wealth of Nations* (1776) (Oxford, 1976) p. 44. See also Mill, *Principles of Political Economy* (1848) and Marx, *A Contribution to the Critique of Political Economy* (1859).

11. Saunders & Otley set up in 1826. Their popular authors in the 1830s were Bulwer-Lytton, Anna Jameson, Harriet Martineau (who gave Browning his copy of Carlyle's *Sartor Resartus* in 1837) and Captain Marryat. See Elizabeth Sanders Arbuckle, 'Saunders and Otley', *DLB,* 106, pp. 271–4.

12. [May 1842]: Kelley V, p. 328. James Montgomery's 'The Wanderer of Switzerland' (1806) was successful; he was also known as author of the religious epic *The World Before the Flood* (1813). Saunders & Otley brought out his last, poorly received volume, *The Pelican Island*, in 1827.

13. October 1835: Kelley III, p. 352.

14. *The Economy of Literary Form: English Literature and the Industrialization of Publishing 1800–1850* (London, 1996) p. 28.

15. 'The King' becomes Pippa's third song in *Pippa Passes* (1841) and 'Porphyria' and 'Johannes Agricola' reappear in *Dramatic Lyrics* (1842) as 'Porphyria's Lover' and 'Johannes Agricola in Meditation'. 'Lines' appears in 'James Lee's Wife' (*Dramatic Personae*, 1864).

16. William S. Peterson, *Browning's Trumpeter: The Correspondence of Robert Browning and Frederick J. Furnivall 1872–1889* (Washington, 1979) p. 32.

17. J. C. Reid, *Thomas Hood* (London, 1963) p. 210.

18. Letter to Frederick Oldfield Ward, 22 May 1844: Kelley VII, p. 318.

19. The essay is reprinted as an appendix in Longman II, pp. 478–503.

20. Jacques Derrida, 'No Apocalypse, Not Now', *Diacritics* (Summer 1984) 26.

21. 6 September 1835: Kelley III, p. 352.

22. March 1836: Kelley III, p. 373.

23. Letter to Fox, 16 April 1835: Kelley III, p. 134.

24. Monclar and Browning's other French friend Joseph Milsand were

exceptional for their interest in English poetry; there was no French edition of Browning's poems in his lifetime. Monclar's note and Browning's addenda are reprinted as an appendix in Kelley III, pp. 416–24.

25. Browning wrote to Elizabeth Barrett of *Pauline*: 'When you speak of the "Bookseller" – I smile, in glorious security – having a whole bale of sheets at the house-top: he never knew my name even! – and I withdrew these after a very little time' – 15 January 1846: Kelley XI, p. 317. He gave Mill's annotated copy to Forster.

26. Herbert Tucker describes the complex temporality of the relation between Aprile and Paracelsus, *Browning's Beginnings the Act of Disclosure* (Minneapolis, 1980), pp. 54–8.

27. Jean-Pierre Vernant and Pierre Vidal-Nacquet, *Myth and Tragedy in Ancient Greece*, trans. Janet Lloyd (New York, 1988) p. 43.

28. Rees & Longman (founded 1806) published plays performed at Covent Garden, Drury Lane and the Haymarket, printed from the prompt books.

29. *The Examiner*, 7 May 1837: Kelley III, p. 400.

30. Browning appealed to Milton's example when Mill criticized the diction of *Pauline*. See also 'The Lost Leader', *Pacchiarotto* and the Parleying 'With Christopher Smart'.

31. 31 July 1844: Kelley IX, p. 69.

32. In *Textual Strategies: Perspectives in Post-Structuralist Criticism*, ed. Josue V. Harari (Ithaca, NY, 1979) p. 148.

33. Bloom and Munich, p. 2.

34. Jacques Derrida, 'This is not an Oral Footnote', in *Annotation and Its Texts*, ed. Stephen A. Barney (Oxford, 1991) p. 202.

35. George Ticknor Curtis, *A Treatise on the Law of Copyright* (London, 1847) p. 69n.

36. Susan Eilenberg, *Strange Power of Speech: Wordsworth, Coleridge and Literary Possession* (Oxford, 1992) p. 202.

37. 28 August 1846: Kelley XIII, p. 308.

38. *Bells and Pomegranates* did not sell well in England, but it helped Browning find an important new public in the US. Some volumes reached Ralph Waldo Emerson and Margaret Fuller, who admired them. An unauthorized edition of Chapman & Hall's 1849 *Poems* was published in the US by Ticknor, Reed & Fields. To Browning's delight, Ticknor offered him sixty pounds for the right to print *Men and Women*.

39. Moxon's expertise in poetry let him remain upmarket. He popularized poetry through the introduction of cheaper one-volume collections. A journal, the *Englishman's Magazine*, ran from April to October 1831 and published Tennyson, Arthur Hallam, Leigh Hunt, John Clare, Charles Cowden Clarke and Forster. In 1844 Moxon published a two-volume edition of Elizabeth Barrett's *Poems*. Richard Hengist Horne, who wrote an important review praising *Sordello* and with whom Elizabeth Barrett collaborated on the *New Spirit of the Age* (1842), also brought out two dramas with Moxon. See Hans Ostrum, 'Moxon', *DLB*, 106, pp. 213–17.

40. One of the Shelley volumes contained an uncut version of 'Queen Mab' and in 1841 Moxon was tried for 'blasphemous libel'. Historically this kind of charge was used to silence anti-government protest and was the law used against John Lilburne. Moxon was eloquently defended by Talfourd, and

found guilty but not punished. He printed Shelley without the offending passages after that, but the case marked a shift in the handling of blasphemous libel in the courts and by the late 1840s the charge no longer posed a real risk to authors and publishers.

41. Letter to Domett, 13 July 1842: Kelley VI, p. 32.
42. Letter to Domett, 31 July 1844: Kelley IX, p. 69, 1844.
43. Letter to Domett, 23 February 1845: Kelley X, p. 89.
44. In 1836 Chapman & Hall published *Sketches by Boz*; they worked with Dickens until 1844. Other literary authors with Chapman at this time included Arthur Hugh Clough, Sir Henry Taylor, Bulwer-Lytton and the popular poet Philip Bailey, author of *Festus* as well as Browning's friend, Bryan Waller Proctor and William Allingham who later knew the poet well.
45. August 1849: Litzinger and Smalley, p. 136.
46. Browning wrote to James Fields of Ticknor & Fields to arrange for the simultaneous American publication of *Men and Women* and also offered him *Strafford* and a corrected version of *Sordello*, volunteering to destroy the remaining 250 copies. The plan to change nothing in *Sordello* save by 'writing in the unwritten every-other-line' never came to fruition.
47. Known as *Poetical Works* (Third Edition): because the original editions of the poems were first editions, *Poems* of 1849 was called the second, hence 1863 was the third and 1865 the fourth.
48. The Fourth Edition of the *Works* (1865) was designed to look like that of 1863, but Browning used the opportunity of a completely new setting, requiring a printer's copy prepared and checked by him, to make hundreds of small changes.
49. There is a so-called 'second edition' of *A Blot in the 'Scutcheon* but it is not an edition in the proper sense, merely a reissue for the *Bells and Pomegranates* series, rushed into print for the day of the play's performance in 1843, on account of the unauthorized changes made to the acting script by Macready. A new typesetting was needed for the second edition of *Dramatis Personae*, which gave Browning the chance to make revisions.
50. Smith later recalled: 'He trusted me absolutely. I was deeply touched when his son related that, on his death-bed, his father told him that if he was ever in any difficulty he was to go to me and act exactly on my advice; and that all matters of business in regard to his works were to be left absolutely in my hands.' Leonard Huxley, *The House of Smith, Elder* (London, 1923) p. 156.
51. The 1868 typesetting was not preserved in stereotype, which would have guaranteed the possibility of reprints without the drawback of storing bulky set type that might be needed for other purposes. Thus Browning had another chance to revise. He did so over a period of about six months in 1870.
52. Linda K. Hughes and Michael Lund, *The Victorian Serial* (Charlottesville, VA, 1996) p. 90. Their discussion of *The Ring and the Book* as a serial points out the similarities of effect between a trial and a serial publication (pp. 91–3, 97).
53. 12 December 1868: Litzinger and Smalley, p. 288.
54. Arnold to Mary Penrose Arnold, 5 June 1869: Arnold, *Letters* III, p. 347.
55. *The Temple Bar* (June 1876): Litzinger and Smalley, pp. 341–2, 347.

56. Letter to Eliza Fitzgerald, 6 September 1881: *Learned Lady: Letters from Robert Browning to Mrs. Thomas Fitzgerald*, ed. Edward C. McAleer (Cambridge, MA, 1966) p. 125.

57. Letter to Mr Yates, *c.* 1882: *Letters of Robert Browning Collected by Thomas J. Wise*, ed. Thurman L. Hood (London, 1933) p. 212.

58. Letter to George Smith, 12 November 1887: William S. Peterson, *Browning's Trumpeter: the Correspondence of Robert Browning and Frederick J. Furnivall, 1872–1889* (Washington, 1979) p. 198n.

59. Letter to George Smith, 27 February 1888: Philip Kelley and William S. Peterson, 'Browning's Final Revisions', *Browning Institute Studies*, 1 (1973) p. 92.

60. Letter to EBB, 29 March 1846: Kelley XII, p. 187.

Index